ESSAYS ON
FAITH AND MORALS

ESSAYS ON
FAITH AND MORALS

WILLIAM JAMES

Selected by Ralph Barton Perry

A MERIDIAN BOOK
NEW AMERICAN LIBRARY
TIMES MIRROR

WILLIAM JAMES

William James, son of Henry James, Sr., and brother of the novelist, was born in New York City in 1842 and died in 1910. From 1872 to 1907 he taught at Harvard, moving from physiology to psychology and finally to philosophy. Jamesian pragmatism and radical empiricism became dominant influences in American thought during his lifetime. Among James's major works are *The Principles of Psychology*, *The Varieties of Religious Experience*, *The Meaning of Truth*, *Pragmatism* (Meridian Books, M16), and *The Will to Believe and Other Essays*, from which six of the essays in this book are reprinted.

Library of Congress Catalog Card Number: 62-10170
ISBN 0-529-01895-0

 MERIDIAN TRADEMARK REG. PAT. U.S. OFF. AND FOREIGN COUNTRIES
REGISTERED TRADEMARK—MARCA REGISTRADA
HECHO EN WESTFORD, MASS., U.S.A.

SIGNET, SIGNET CLASSICS, MENTOR, PLUME, MERIDIAN AND NAL BOOKS *are published by The New American Library, Inc.*, *1633 Broadway, New York, New York 10019*

FIRST PRINTING/WORLD PUBLISHING COMPANY, 1962
FIRST PRINTING/NEW AMERICAN LIBRARY, MARCH 1974

2 3 4 5 6 7 8 9 10

PRINTED IN THE UNITED STATES OF AMERICA

EDITOR'S PREFACE

IT so happens that James's utterances on ethics were occasional, and that in their scattered published form they failed to convey an adequate sense of the author's constant preoccupation with moral questions, or of the consistency of his thought in that field. His only systematic discussion of the problems of ethical theory is contained in the essay entitled "The Moral Philosopher and the Moral Life," while the most forceful statements of his own moral attitude are contained in essays entitled "Is Life Worth Living?" and "On a Certain Blindness in Human Beings." Of the last he said that it "is really the perception on which my whole individualistic philosophy is based," and "I care very much for the truth which it so inadequately tries to express." * The first two of these essays appeared in the volume published in 1898 under the title of *The Will to Believe and other Essays in Popular Philosophy*, where they were combined with miscellaneous essays dealing largely with man's right to hold beliefs in excess of theoretical proof, provided they reinforce his moral will. The third of the above essays was published obscurely in the last part of a volume entitled *Talks to Teachers on Psychology: and to Students on Some of Life's Ideals* (1899). In 1910 James published in pamphlet form the famous essay

* R. B. Perry, *The Thought and Character of William James*, vol. II, pp. 265-266.

on "The Moral Equivalent of War" which has recently inspired the William James Camp at Tun-
bridge, Vermont, and other groups of American youth
who have sought to combine physical labor with
public service.   This essay was published posthumously
in 1911 in a volume entitled *Memories and Studies.*

It has seemed best, therefore, to republish these four
essays with others taken from the same volumes, and
dealing with the closely associated themes of faith and
morals. The grouping of these essays together will
not only promote a better understanding of this important portion of James's thought, but make available
to American and English readers an impressive statement of the cause for which they are now fighting.
James believed in a difference between right and
wrong, and he believed that men should *believe* — to
the extent of staking their lives on the truth of their
beliefs. Detesting war, he nevertheless felt that in its
absence men must still find some way — some humane
way — by which they can draw upon their latent energies, run risks, and act together, for an object of faith.

The three essays from *Talks to Teachers, etc.,* are
included in this volume with the courteous consent of
Messrs. Henry Holt and Company.

RALPH BARTON PERRY

CAMBRIDGE, MASSACHUSETTS
September 1, 1942

CONTENTS*

* Essays I–VI are reprinted from *The Will to Believe and Other
Essays* (originally dedicated to C. S. Peirce); essays VIII–X from
Talks to Teachers and to Students on Some of Life's Ideals; VII, XI from
Memories and Studies.

Contents   ix

IS LIFE WORTH LIVING? *

WHEN Mr. Mallock's book with this title appeared some fifteen years ago, the jocose answer that " it depends on the *liver* " had great cur-
rency in the newspapers. The answer which I propose
to give to-night cannot be jocose. In the words of
one of Shakespeare's prologues, —

" I come no more to make you laugh; things now,
That bear a weighty and a serious brow,
Sad, high, and working, full of state and woe," —

must be my theme. In the deepest heart of all of us
there is a corner in which the ultimate mystery of
things works sadly; and I know not what such an
association as yours intends, nor what you ask of
those whom you invite to address you, unless it be to
lead you from the surface-glamour of existence, and
for an hour at least to make you heedless to the
buzzing and jigging and vibration of small interests
and excitements that form the tissue of our ordinary
consciousness. Without further explanation or apol-
ogy, then, I ask you to join me in turning an attention, commonly too unwilling, to the profounder bass-
note of life. Let us search the lonely depths for an
hour together, and see what answers in the last folds
and recesses of things our question may find.

* An Address to the Harvard Young Men's Christian Association.
Published in the International Journal of Ethics for October, 1895,
and as a pocket volume by S. B. Weston, Philadelphia, 1896.

I

WITH many men the question of life's worth is answered by a temperamental optimism which makes them incapable of believing that anything seriously evil can exist. Our dear old Walt Whitman's works are the standing text-book of this kind of optimism. The mere joy of living is so immense in Walt Whitman's veins that it abolishes the possibility of any other kind of feeling: —

"To breathe the air, how delicious!
To speak, to walk, to seize something by the hand! . . .
To be this incredible God I am! . . .
O amazement of things, even the least particle!
O spirituality of things!
I too carol the Sun, usher'd or at noon, or as now,
‸ setting;
I too throb to the brain and beauty of the earth and of all the growths of the earth. . . .

I sing to the last the equalities, modern or old,
I sing the endless finales of things,
I say Nature continues — glory continues.
I praise with electric voice,
For I do not see one imperfection in the universe,
And I do not see one cause or result lamentable at last."

So Rousseau, writing of the nine years he spent at Annecy, with nothing but his happiness to tell: —

" How tell what was neither said nor done nor even thought, but tasted only and felt, with no object of my felicity but the emotion of felicity itself! I rose with the sun, and I was happy; I went to walk, and I was happy; I saw 'Maman,' and I was happy; I left her, and I was happy. I rambled through the woods and over the vine-slopes, I wandered in the valleys, I read, I lounged, I worked in the garden, I gathered the fruits, I helped at the indoor work, and happiness followed me everywhere. It was in no one assignable thing; it was all within myself; it could not leave me for a single instant."

If moods like this could be made permanent, and constitutions like these universal, there would never be any occasion for such discourses as the present one. No philosopher would seek to prove articulately that life is worth living, for the fact that it absolutely is so would vouch for itself, and the problem disappear in the vanishing of the question rather than in the coming of anything like a reply. But we are not magicians to make the optimistic temperament universal; and alongside of the deliverances of temperamental optimism concerning life, those of temperamental pessimism always exist, and oppose to them a standing refutation. In what is called 'circular insanity,' phases of melancholy succeed phases of mania, with no outward cause that we can discover; and often enough to one and the same well person life will present incarnate radiance to-day and incarnate dreariness to-morrow, according to the fluctuations of what the older medical books used to call " the concoction of the humors." In the words of the newspaper joke, " it depends on the liver." Rousseau's ill-balanced constitution undergoes a change, and behold him in his latter evil days a prey to melancholy and black delusions of suspicion and fear. Some men seem launched upon the world even from their birth with souls as incapable of happiness as Walt Whitman's

was of gloom, and they have left us their messages
in even more lasting verse than his, — the exquisite
Leopardi, for example; or our own contemporary,
James Thomson, in that pathetic book, The City of
Dreadful Night, which I think is less well-known
than it should be for its literary beauty, simply because men are afraid to quote its words, — they are
so gloomy, and at the same time so sincere. In one
place the poet describes a congregation gathered to
listen to a preacher in a great unillumined cathedral
at night. The sermon is too long to quote, but it
ends thus: —

  "'O Brothers of sad lives! they are so brief;
    A few short years must bring us all relief:
      Can we not bear these years of laboring breath.
    But if you would not this poor life fulfil,
    Lo, you are free to end it when you will,
      Without the fear of waking after death.' —

  "The organ-like vibrations of his voice
    Thrilled through the vaulted aisles and died
      away;
    The yearning of the tones which bade rejoice
    Was sad and tender as a requiem lay:
    Our shadowy congregation rested still,
    As brooding on that 'End it when you will.'
   .   .   .   .

  "Our shadowy congregation rested still,
    As musing on that message we had heard,
    And brooding on that 'End it when you will,'
    Perchance awaiting yet some other word;
    When keen as lightning through a muffled sky
    Sprang forth a shrill and lamentable cry: —

  "'The man speaks sooth, alas! the man speaks sooth;
    We have no personal life beyond the grave;

There is no God; Fate knows nor wrath nor ruth:
    Can I find here the comfort which I crave?

" ' In all eternity I had one chance,
    One few years' term of gracious human life, —
The splendors of the intellect's advance,
    The sweetness of the home with babes and wife;

" ' The social pleasures with their genial wit;
    The fascination of the worlds of art;
The glories of the worlds of Nature lit
    By large imagination's glowing heart;

" ' The rapture of mere being, full of health;
    The careless childhood and the ardent youth;
The strenuous manhood winning various wealth,
    The reverend age serene with life's long truth:

" ' All the sublime prerogatives of Man;
    The storied memories of the times of old,
The patient tracking of the world's great plan
    Through sequences and changes myriadfold.

" ' This chance was never offered me before;
    For me the infinite past is blank and dumb;
This chance recurreth never, nevermore;
    Blank, blank for me the infinite To-come.

" ' And this sole chance was frustrate from my birth,
    A mockery, a delusion; and my breath
Of noble human life upon this earth
    So racks me that I sigh for senseless death.

" ' My wine of life is poison mixed with gall,
    My noonday passes in a nightmare dream,
I worse than lose the years which are my all:
    What can console me for the loss supreme?

" ' Speak not of comfort where no comfort is,
    Speak not at all: can words make foul things fair?

Our life's a cheat, our death a black abyss:
Hush, and be mute, envisaging despair.'

" This vehement voice came from the northern aisle,
Rapid and shrill to its abrupt harsh close;
And none gave answer for a certain while,
For words must shrink from these most wordless
woes;
At last the pulpit speaker simply said,
With humid eyes and thoughtful, drooping head, —

" ' My brother, my poor Brothers, it is thus:
This life holds nothing good for us,
But it ends soon and nevermore can be;
And we knew nothing of it ere our birth,
And shall know nothing when consigned to earth:
I ponder these thoughts, and they comfort me.' "

" It ends soon, and never more can be," " Lo, you
are free to end it when you will," — these verses flow
truthfully from the melancholy Thomson's pen, and
are in truth a consolation for all to whom, as to him,
the world is far more like a steady den of fear than a
continual fountain of delight. That life is *not* worth
living the whole army of suicides declare, — an army
whose roll-call, like the famous evening gun of the
British army, follows the sun round the world and
never terminates. We, too, as we sit here in our comfort, must ' ponder these things ' also, for we are of
one substance with these suicides, and their life is the
life we share. The plainest intellectual integrity, —
nay, more, the simplest manliness and honor, forbid
us to forget their case.

" If suddenly," says Mr. Ruskin, " in the midst of
the enjoyments of the palate and lightnesses of heart
of a London dinner-party, the walls of the chamber

were parted, and through their gap the nearest human beings who were famishing and in misery were borne into the midst of the company feasting and fancy free; if, pale from death, horrible in destitution, broken by despair, body by body they were laid upon the soft carpet, one beside the chair of every guest, — would only the crumbs of the dainties be cast to them; would only a passing glance, a passing thought, be vouchsafed to them? Yet the actual facts, the real relation of each Dives and Lazarus, are not altered by the intervention of the house-wall between the table and the sick-bed, — by the few feet of ground (how few!) which are, indeed, all that separate the merriment from the misery."

II

To COME immediately to the heart of my theme, then, what I propose is to imagine ourselves reasoning with a fellow-mortal who is on such terms with life that the only comfort left him is to brood on the assurance, "You may end it when you will." What reasons can we plead that may render such a brother (or sister) willing to take up the burden again? Ordinary Christians, reasoning with would-be suicides, have little to offer them beyond the usual negative, "Thou shalt not." God alone is master of life and death, they say, and it is a blasphemous act to anticipate his absolving hand. But can *we* find nothing richer or more positive than this, no reflections to urge whereby the suicide may actually see, and in all sad seriousness feel, that in spite of adverse appearances even for him life is still worth living? There are suicides and suicides (in the United States about three thousand of them every year), and I must frankly confess that with perhaps the majority

of these my suggestions are impotent to deal. Where
suicide is the result of insanity or sudden frenzied
impulse, reflection is impotent to arrest its headway;
and cases like these belong to the ultimate mystery
of evil, concerning which I can only offer considerations tending toward religious patience at the end of
this hour. My task, let me say now, is practically
narrow, and my words are to deal only with that
metaphysical *tedium vitæ* which is peculiar to reflecting men. Most of you are devoted, for good or ill,
to the reflective life. Many of you are students of
philosophy, and have already felt in your own persons the scepticism and unreality that too much
grubbing in the abstract roots of things will breed.
This is, indeed, one of the regular fruits of the over-
studious career. Too much questioning and too
little active responsibility lead, almost as often as
too much sensualism does, to the edge of the slope,
at the bottom of which lie pessimism and the nightmare or suicidal view of life. But to the diseases
which reflection breeds, still further reflection can oppose effective remedies; and it is of the melancholy
and *Weltschmerz* bred of reflection that I now proceed
to speak.

Let me say, immediately, that my final appeal is to
nothing more recondite than religious faith. So far
as my argument is to be destructive, it will consist in
nothing more than the sweeping away of certain views
that often keep the springs of religious faith com-
pressed; and so far as it is to be constructive, it will
consist in holding up to the light of day certain considerations calculated to let loose these springs in a
normal, natural way. Pessimism is essentially a religious disease. In the form of it to which you are

most liable, it consists in nothing but a religious demand to which there comes no normal religious reply.

Now, there are two stages of recovery from this disease, two different levels upon which one may emerge from the midnight view to the daylight view of things, and I must treat of them in turn. The second stage is the more complete and joyous, and it corresponds to the freer exercise of religious trust and fancy. There are, as is well known, persons who are naturally very free in this regard, others who are not at all so. There are persons, for instance, whom we find indulging to their heart's content in prospects of immortality; and there are others who experience the greatest difficulty in making such a notion seem real to themselves at all. These latter persons are tied to their senses, restricted to their natural experience; and many of them, moreover, feel a sort of intellectual loyalty to what they call 'hard facts,' which is positively shocked by the easy excursions into the unseen that other people make at the bare call of sentiment. Minds of either class may, however, be intensely religious. They may equally desire atonement and reconciliation, and crave acquiescence and communion with the total soul of things. But the craving, when the mind is pent in to the hard facts, especially as science now reveals them, can breed pessimism, quite as easily as it breeds optimism when it inspires religious trust and fancy to wing their way to another and a better world.

That is why I call pessimism an essentially religious disease. The nightmare view of life has plenty of organic sources; but its great reflective source has at all times been the contradiction between the phe-

nomena of nature and the craving of the heart to
believe that behind nature there is a spirit whose
expression nature is. What philosophers call 'natural theology' has been one way of appeasing this
craving; that poetry of nature in which our English
literature is so rich has been another way. Now,
suppose a mind of the latter of our two classes, whose
imagination is pent in consequently, and who take its
facts 'hard'; suppose it, moreover, to feel strongly
the craving for communion, and yet to realize how
desperately difficult it is to construe the scientific
order of nature either theologically or poetically, —
and what result *can* there be but inner discord and
contradiction? Now, this inner discord (merely as
discord) can be relieved in either of two ways: The
longing to read the facts religiously may cease, and
leave the bare facts by themselves; or, supplementary
facts may be discovered or believed-in, which permit
the religious reading to go on. These two ways of
relief are the two stages of recovery, the two levels of
escape from pessimism, to which I made allusion a
moment ago, and which the sequel will, I trust, make
more clear.

III

STARTING then with nature, we naturally tend, if we
have the religious craving, to say with Marcus Aure-
lius, "O Universe! what thou wishest I wish." Our
sacred books and traditions tell us of one God who
made heaven and earth, and, looking on them, saw
that they were good. Yet, on more intimate acquaintance, the visible surfaces of heaven and earth refuse
to be brought by us into any intelligible unity at all.
Every phenomenon that we would praise there exists
cheek by jowl with some contrary phenomenon that

cancels all its religious effect upon the mind. Beauty and hideousness, love and cruelty, life and death keep house together in indissoluble partnership; and there gradually steals over us, instead of the old warm notion of a man-loving Deity, that of an awful power that neither hates nor loves, but rolls all things together meaninglessly to a common doom. This is an uncanny, a sinister, a nightmare view of life, and its peculiar *unheimlichkeit*, or poisonousness, lies expressly in our holding two things together which cannot possibly agree, — in our clinging, on the one hand, to the demand that there shall be a living spirit of the whole; and, on the other, to the belief that the course of nature must be such a spirit's adequate manifestation and expression. It is in the contradiction between the supposed being of a spirit that encompasses and owns us, and with which we ought to have some communion, and the character of such a spirit as revealed by the visible world's course, that this particular death-in-life paradox and this melancholy-breeding puzzle reside. Carlyle expresses the result in that chapter of his immortal 'Sartor Resartus' entitled 'The Everlasting No.' " I lived," writes poor Teufelsdröckh, " in a continual, indefinite, pining fear; tremulous, pusillanimous, apprehensive of I knew not what: it seemed as if all things in the heavens above and the earth beneath would hurt me; as if the heavens and the earth were but boundless jaws of a devouring monster, wherein I, palpitating, lay waiting to be devoured."

This is the first stage of speculative melancholy. No brute can have this sort of melancholy; no man who is irreligious can become its prey. It is the sick shudder of the frustrated religious demand, and not the mere necessary outcome of animal experience.

Teufelsdröckh himself could have made shift to face
the general chaos and bedevilment of this world's
experiences very well, were he not the victim of an
originally unlimited trust and affection towards them.
If he might meet them piecemeal, with no suspicion
of any whole expressing itself in them, shunning the
bitter parts and husbanding the sweet ones, as the
occasion served, and as the day was foul or fair, he
could have zigzagged toward an easy end, and felt
no obligation to make the air vocal with his lamen-
tations. The mood of levity, of ' I don't care,' is for
this world's ills a sovereign and practical anæsthetic.
But, no! something deep down in Teufelsdröckh and
in the rest of us tells us that there *is* a Spirit in things
to which we owe allegiance, and for whose sake we
must keep up the serious mood. And so the inner
fever and discord also are kept up; for nature taken
on her visible surface reveals no such Spirit, and beyond the facts of nature we are at the present stage
of our inquiry not supposing ourselves to look.

Now, I do not hesitate frankly and sincerely to confess to you that this real and genuine discord seems
to me to carry with it the inevitable bankruptcy of
natural religion naïvely and simply taken. There
were times when Leibnitzes with their heads buried
in monstrous wigs could compose Theodicies, and
when stall-fed officials of an established church could
prove by the valves in the heart and the round liga-
ment of the hip-joint the existence of a " Moral and
Intelligent Contriver of the World." But those times
are past; and we of the nineteenth century, with our
evolutionary theories and our mechanical philosophies, already know nature too impartially and too
well to worship unreservedly any God of whose character she can be an adequate expression. Truly, all

we know of good and duty proceeds from nature;
but none the less so all we know of evil. Visible
nature is all plasticity and indifference, — a moral
multiverse, as one might call it, and not a moral universe. To such a harlot we owe no allegiance; with
her as a whole we can establish no moral communion; and we are free in our dealings with her several
parts to obey or destroy, and to follow no law but
that of prudence in coming to terms with such of her
particular features as will help us to our private ends.
If there be a divine Spirit of the universe, nature,
such as we know her, cannot possibly be its *ultimate
word* to man. Either there is no Spirit revealed in
nature, or else it is inadequately revealed there; and
(as all the higher religions have assumed) what we
call visible nature, or *this* world, must be but a veil
and surface-show whose full meaning resides in a
supplementary unseen or *other* world.

I cannot help, therefore, accounting it on the whole
a gain (though it may seem for certain poetic constitutions a very sad loss) that the naturalistic superstition, the worship of the God of nature, simply taken
as such, should have begun to loosen its hold upon
the educated mind. In fact, if I am to express my
personal opinion unreservedly, I should say (in spite
of its sounding blasphemous at first to certain ears)
that the initial step towards getting into healthy ultimate relations with the universe is the act of rebellion
against the idea that such a God exists. Such rebellion essentially is that which in the chapter I have
quoted from Carlyle goes on to describe: —

" ' Wherefore, like a coward, dost thou forever pip
and whimper, and go cowering and trembling? Des-
picable biped! . . . Hast thou not a heart; canst

thou not suffer whatsoever it be; and, as a Child of
Freedom, though outcast, trample Tophet itself under
thy feet, while it consumes thee? Let it come, then; I
will meet it and defy it!' And as I so thought, there
rushed like a stream of fire over my whole soul; and I
shook base Fear away from me forever. . . .

"Thus had the Everlasting No pealed authoritatively through all the recesses of my being, of my Me;
and then was it that my whole Me stood up, in native
God-created majesty, and recorded its Protest. Such
a Protest, the most important transaction in life, may
that same Indignation and Defiance, in a psychological
point of view, be fitly called. The Everlasting No had
said: 'Behold, thou art fatherless, outcast, and the
Universe is mine;' to which my whole Me now made
answer: 'I am not thine, but Free, and forever hate
thee!' From that hour," Teufelsdröckh-Carlyle adds,
"I began to be a man."

And our poor friend, James Thomson, similarly
writes: —

"Who is most wretched in this dolorous place?
    I think myself; yet I would rather be
    My miserable self than He, than He
Who formed such creatures to his own disgrace.

The vilest thing must be less vile than Thou
    From whom it had its being, God and Lord!
    Creator of all woe and sin! abhorred,
Malignant and implacable! I vow

That not for all Thy power furled and unfurled,
    For all the temples to Thy glory built,
    Would I assume the ignominious guilt
Of having made such men in such a world."

We are familiar enough in this community with the spectacle of persons exulting in their emancipation from belief in the God of their ancestral Calvinism, — him who made the garden and the serpent, and pre-appointed the eternal fires of hell. Some of them have found humaner gods to worship, others are simply converts from all theology; but, both alike, they assure us that to have got rid of the sophistication of thinking they could feel any reverence or duty toward that impossible idol gave a tremendous happiness to their souls. Now, to make an idol of the spirit of nature, and worship it, also leads to sophistication; and in souls that are religious and would also be scientific the sophistication breeds a philosophical melancholy, from which the first natural step of escape is the denial of the idol; and with the downfall of the idol, whatever lack of positive joyousness may remain, there comes also the downfall of the whimpering and cowering mood. With evil simply taken as such, men can make short work, for their relations with it then are only practical. It looms up no longer so spectrally, it loses all its haunting and perplexing significance, as soon as the mind attacks the instances of it singly, and ceases to worry about their derivation from the ' one and only Power.'

Here, then, on this stage of mere emancipation from monistic superstition, the would-be suicide may already get encouraging answers to his question about the worth of life. There are in most men instinctive springs of vitality that respond healthily when the burden of metaphysical and infinite responsibility rolls off. The certainty that you now *may* step out of life whenever you please, and that to do so is not blasphemous or monstrous, is itself an immense relief.

The thought of suicide is now no longer a guilty challenge and obsession.

" This little life is all we must endure;
    The grave's most holy peace is ever sure," —

says Thomson; adding, " I ponder these thoughts, and they comfort me." Meanwhile we can always stand it for twenty-four hours longer, if only to see what to-morrow's newspapers will contain, or what the next postman will bring.

But far deeper forces than this mere vital curiosity are arousable, even in the pessimistically-tending mind; for where the loving and admiring impulses are dead, the hating and fighting impulses will still respond to fit appeals. This evil which we feel so deeply is something that we can also help to over-throw; for its sources, now that no ' Substance ' or ' Spirit ' is behind them, are finite, and we can deal with each of them in turn. It is, indeed, a remark-able fact that sufferings and hardships do not, as a rule, abate the love of life; they seem, on the con-trary, usually to give it a keener zest. The sovereign source of melancholy is repletion. Need and strug-gle are what excite and inspire us; our hour of tri-umph is what brings the void. Not the Jews of the captivity, but those of the days of Solomon's glory are those from whom the pessimistic utterances in our Bible come. Germany, when she lay trampled beneath the hoofs of Bonaparte's troopers, produced perhaps the most optimistic and idealistic literature that the world has seen; and not till the French ' milliards ' were distributed after 1871 did pessimism overrun the country in the shape in which we see it there to-day. The history of our own race is one long commentary on the cheerfulness that comes with fighting ills. Or take the Waldenses, of whom I lately have been reading, as examples of what strong men will endure. In 1485 a papal bull of Innocent VIII enjoined their extermination. It absolved those who should take up the crusade against them from all ecclesiastical pains and penalties, released them from any oath, legitimized their title to all property which they might have illegally acquired, and promised remission of sins to all who should kill the heretics.

" There is no town in Piedmont," says a Vaudois writer, " where some of our brethren have not been put to death. Jordan Terbano was burnt alive at Susa; Hippolite Rossiero at Turin; Michael Goneto, an octogenarian, at Sarcena; Vilermin Ambrosio hanged on the Col di Meano; Hugo Chiambs, of Fenestrelle, had his entrails torn from his living body at Turin; Peter Geymarali of Bobbio in like manner had his entrails taken out in Lucerna, and a fierce cat thrust in their place to torture him further; Maria Romano was buried alive at Rocca Patia; Magdalena Fauno underwent the same fate at San Giovanni; Susanna Michelini was bound hand and foot, and left to perish of cold and hunger on the snow at Sarcena: Bartolomeo Fache, gashed with sabres, had the wounds filled up with quicklime, and perished thus in agony at Fenile; Daniel Michelini had his tongue torn out at Bobbo for having praised God; James Baridari perished covered with sulphurous matches which had been forced into his flesh under the nails, between the fingers, in the nostrils, in the lips, and all over the body, and then lighted; Daniel Rovelli had his mouth filled with gunpowder, which, being lighted, blew his head to pieces; . . . Sara Rostignol was slit open from the legs to the bosom, and left so to perish on the road between Eyral and Lucerna; Anna Charbonnier was impaled, and carried thus on a pike from San Giovanni to La Torre." *

Und dergleichen mehr! In 1630 the plague swept away one-half of the Vaudois population, including fifteen of their seventeen pastors. The places of these were supplied from Geneva and Dauphiny, and the whole Vaudois people learned French in order to follow their services. More than once their number fell, by unremitting persecution, from the normal standard of twenty-five thousand to about four thousand. In 1686 the Duke of Savoy ordered the three thousand that remained to give up their faith or leave the country. Refusing, they fought the French and Piedmontese armies till only eighty of their fighting men remained alive or uncaptured, when they gave up, and were sent in a body to Switzerland. But in 1689, encouraged by William of Orange and led by one of their pastor-captains, between eight hundred and nine hundred of them returned to conquer their old homes again. They fought their way to Bobi, reduced to four hundred men in the first half year, and met every force sent against them; until at last the Duke of Savoy, giving up his alliance with that abomination of desolation, Louis XIV, restored them to comparative freedom, — since which time they have increased and multiplied in their barren Alpine valleys to this day.

What are our woes and sufferance compared with these? Does not the recital of such a fight so obstinately waged against such odds fill us with resolution against *our* petty powers of darkness, — machine politicians, spoilsmen, and the rest? Life is worth

* Quoted by George E. Waring in his book on Tyrol. Compare A. Bérard: Les Vaudois, Lyon, Storck, 1892.

living, no matter what it bring, if only such combats may be carried to successful terminations and one's heel set on the tyrant's throat.   To the suicide, then, in his supposed world of multifarious and immoral nature, you can appeal — and appeal in the name of the very evils that make his heart sick there — to wait and see *his* part of the battle out.   And the consent to live on, which you ask of him under these circumstances, is not the sophistical 'resignation' which devotees of cowering religions preach: it is not resignation in the sense of licking a despotic Deity's hand.   It is, on the contrary, a resignation based on manliness and pride.   So long as your would-be suicide leaves an evil of his own unremedied, so long he has strictly no concern with evil in the abstract and at large.   The submission which you demand of yourself to the general fact of evil in the world, your apparent acquiescence in it, is here nothing but the conviction that evil at large is *none of your business* until your business with your private particular evils is liquidated and settled up.   A challenge of this sort, with proper designation of detail, is one that need only be made to be accepted by men whose normal instincts are not decayed; and your reflective would-be suicide may easily be moved by it to face life with a certain interest again.   The sentiment of honor is a very penetrating thing.   When you and I, for instance, realize how many innocent beasts have had to suffer in cattle-cars and slaughter-pens and lay down their lives that we might grow up, all fattened and clad, to sit together here in comfort and carry on this discourse, it does, indeed, put our relation to the universe in a more solemn light.   "Does not," as a young Amherst philosopher (Xenos Clark, now dead) once wrote, " the acceptance of

a happy life upon such terms involve a point of
honor?" Are we not bound to take some suffering
upon ourselves, to do some self-denying service with
our lives, in return for all those lives upon which ours
are built? To hear this question is to answer it in
but one possible way, if one have a normally constituted heart.

Thus, then, we see that mere instinctive curiosity,
pugnacity, and honor may make life on a purely
naturalistic basis seem worth living from day to day
to men who have cast away all metaphysics in order
to get rid of hypochondria, but who are resolved to
owe nothing as yet to religion and its more positive
gifts. A poor half-way stage, some of you may be
inclined to say; but at least you must grant it to be
an honest stage; and no man should dare to speak
meanly of these instincts which are our nature's best
equipment, and to which religion herself must in the
last resort address her own peculiar appeals.

IV

AND now, in turning to what religion may have to
say to the question, I come to what is the soul of my
discourse. Religion has meant many things in human history; but when from now onward I use the
word I mean to use it in the supernaturalist sense, as
declaring that the so-called order of nature, which
constitutes this world's experience, is only one portion
of the total universe, and that there stretches beyond
this visible world an unseen world of which we now
know nothing positive, but in its relation to which
the true significance of our present mundane life consists. A man's religious faith (whatever more special
items of doctrine it may involve) means for me essen-

tially his faith in the existence of an unseen order of some kind in which the riddles of the natural order may be found explained. In the more developed religions the natural world has always been regarded as the mere scaffolding or vestibule of a truer, more eternal world, and affirmed to be a sphere of education, trial, or redemption. In these religions, one must in some fashion die to the natural life before one can enter into life eternal. The notion that this physical world of wind and water, where the sun rises and the moon sets, is absolutely and ultimately the divinely aimed-at and established thing, is one which we find only in very early religions, such as that of the most primitive Jews. It is this natural religion (primitive still, in spite of the fact that poets and men of science whose good-will exceeds their perspicacity keep publishing it in new editions tuned to our contemporary ears) that, as I said a while ago, has suffered definitive bankruptcy in the opinion of a circle of persons, among whom I must count myself, and who are growing more numerous every day. For such persons the physical order of nature, taken simply as science knows it, cannot be held to reveal any one harmonious spiritual intent. It is mere *weather*, as Chauncey Wright called it, doing and undoing without end.

Now, I wish to make you feel, if I can in the short remainder of this hour, that we have a right to believe the physical order to be only a partial order; that we have a right to supplement it by an unseen spiritual order which we assume on trust, if only thereby life may seem to us better worth living again. But as such a trust will seem to some of you sadly mystical and execrably unscientific, I must first say a word or two to weaken the veto which you may consider that science opposes to our act.

There is included in human nature an ingrained naturalism and materialism of mind which can only admit facts that are actually tangible. Of this sort of mind the entity called 'science' is the idol. Fondness for the word 'scientist' is one of the notes by which you may know its votaries; and its short way of killing any opinion that it disbelieves in is to call it 'unscientific.' It must be granted that there is no slight excuse for this. Science has made such glorious leaps in the last three hundred years, and extended our knowledge of nature so enormously both in general and in detail; men of science, more-over, have as a class displayed such admirable vir-tues, — that it is no wonder if the worshippers of science lose their head. In this very University, ac-cordingly, I have heard more than one teacher say that all the fundamental conceptions of truth have already been found by science, and that the future has only the details of the picture to fill in. But the slightest reflection on the real conditions will suffice to show how barbaric such notions are. They show such a lack of scientific imagination, that it is hard to see how one who is actively advancing any part of science can make a mistake so crude. Think how many absolutely new scientific conceptions have arisen in our own generation, how many new prob-lems have been formulated that were never thought of before, and then cast an eye upon the brevity of science's career. It began with Galileo, not three hundred years ago. Four thinkers since Galileo, each informing his successor of what discoveries his own lifetime had seen achieved, might have passed the torch of science into our hands as we sit here in this room. Indeed, for the matter of that, an audience much smaller than the present one, an audience of some five or six score people, if each person in it could speak for his own generation, would carry us away to the black unknown of the human species, to days without a document or monument to tell their tale. Is it credible that such a mushroom knowledge, such a growth overnight as this, *can* represent more than the minutest glimpse of what the universe will really prove to be when adequately understood? No! our science is a drop, our ignorance a sea. Whatever else be certain, this at least is certain, — that the world of our present natural knowledge *is* enveloped in a larger world of *some* sort of whose residual properties we at present can frame no positive idea.

Agnostic positivism, of course, admits this principle theoretically in the most cordial terms, but insists that we must not turn it to any practical use. We have no right, this doctrine tells us, to dream dreams, or suppose anything about the unseen part of the universe, merely because to do so may be for what we are pleased to call our highest interests. We must always wait for sensible evidence for our beliefs; and where such evidence is inaccessible we must frame no hypotheses whatever. Of course this is a safe enough position *in abstracto*. If a thinker had no stake in the unknown, no vital needs, to live or languish according to what the unseen world contained, a philosophic neutrality and refusal to believe either one way or the other would be his wisest cue. But, unfortunately, neutrality is not only inwardly difficult, it is also outwardly unrealizable, where our relations to an alternative are practical and vital.

This is because, as the psychologists tell us, belief and doubt are living attitudes, and involve conduct on our part. Our only way, for example, of doubting, or refusing to believe, that a certain thing *is,* is continuing to act as if it were *not.* If, for instance, I refuse to believe that the room is getting cold, I leave the windows open and light no fire just as if it still were warm. If I doubt that you are worthy of my confidence, I keep you uninformed of all my secrets just as if you were *un*worthy of the same. If I doubt the need of insuring my house, I leave it uninsured as much as if I believed there were no need. And so if I must not believe that the world is divine, I can only express that refusal by declining ever to act distinctively as if it were so, which can only mean acting on certain critical occasions as if it were *not* so, or in an irreligious way. There are, you see, inevitable occasions in life when inaction is a kind of action, and must count as action, and when not to be for is to be practically against; and in all such cases strict and consistent neutrality is an unattainable thing.

And, after all, is not this duty of neutrality where only our inner interests would lead us to believe, the most ridiculous of commands? Is it not sheer dogmatic folly to say that our inner interests can have no real connection with the forces that the hidden world may contain? In other cases divinations based on inner interests have proved prophetic enough. Take science itself! Without an imperious inner demand on our part for ideal logical and mathematical harmonies, we should never have attained to proving that such harmonies lie hidden between all the chinks and interstices of the crude natural world. Hardly a law has been established in science, hardly a fact ascertained, which was not first sought after, often with sweat and blood, to gratify an inner need. Whence such needs come from we do not know: we find them in us, and biological psychology so far only classes them with Darwin's 'accidental variations.' But the inner need of believing that this world of nature is a sign of something more spiritual and eternal than itself is just as strong and authoritative in those who feel it, as the inner need of uniform laws of causation ever can be in a professionally scientific head. The toil of many generations has proved the latter need prophetic. Why *may* not the former one be prophetic, too? And if needs of ours outrun the visible universe, why *may* not that be a sign that an invisible universe is there? What, in short, has authority to debar us from trusting our religious demands? Science as such assuredly has no authority, for she can only say what is, not what is not; and the agnostic " thou shalt not believe without coercive sensible evidence " is simply an expression (free to any one to make) of private personal appetite for evidence of a certain peculiar kind.

Now, when I speak of trusting our religious demands, just what do I mean by ' trusting ' ? Is the word to carry with it license to define in detail an invisible world, and to anathematize and excommunicate those whose trust is different? Certainly not! Our faculties of belief were not primarily given us to make orthodoxies and heresies withal; they were given us to live by. And to trust our religious demands means first of all to live in the light of them, and to act as if the invisible world which they suggest were real. It is a fact of human nature, that men can live and die by the help of a sort of faith that goes without a single dogma or definition. The bare assurance that this natural order is not ultimate

but a mere sign or vision, the external staging of
a many-storied universe, in which spiritual forces
have the last word and are eternal, — this bare assurance is to such men enough to make life seem worth
living in spite of every contrary presumption suggested by its circumstances on the natural plane.
Destroy this inner assurance, however, vague as it is,
and all the light and radiance of existence is extin-
guished for these persons at a stroke. Often enough
the wild-eyed look at life — the suicidal mood — will
then set in.

And now the application comes directly home to
you and me. Probably to almost every one of us
here the most adverse life would seem well worth
living, if we only could be *certain* that our bravery
and patience with it were terminating and eventuating
and bearing fruit somewhere in an unseen spiritual
world. But granting we are not certain, does it then
follow that a bare trust in such a world is a fool's
paradise and lubberland, or rather that it is a living
attitude in which we are free to indulge? Well, we
are free to trust at our own risks anything that is not
impossible, and that can bring analogies to bear in its
behalf. That the world of physics is probably not
absolute, all the converging multitude of arguments
that make in favor of idealism tend to prove; and
that our whole physical life may lie soaking in a spiritual atmosphere, a dimension of being that we at
present have no organ for apprehending, is vividly
suggested to us by the analogy of the life of our
domestic animals. Our dogs, for example, are in our
human life but not of it. They witness hourly the
outward body of events whose inner meaning cannot,
by any possible operation, be revealed to their intelligence, — events in which they themselves often play

the cardinal part. My terrier bites a teasing boy, for example, and the father demands damages. The dog may be present at every step of the negotiations, and see the money paid, without an inkling of what it all means, without a suspicion that it has anything to do with *him;* and he never *can* know in his natural dog's life. Or take another case which used greatly to impress me in my medical-student days. Consider a poor dog whom they are vivisecting in a laboratory. He lies strapped on a board and shrieking at his executioners, and to his own dark consciousness is literally in a sort of hell. He cannot see a single redeeming ray in the whole business; and yet all these diabolical-seeming events are often controlled by human intentions with which, if his poor benighted mind could only be made to catch a glimpse of them, all that is heroic in him would religiously acquiesce. Healing truth, relief to future sufferings of beast and man, are to be bought by them. It may be genuinely a process of redemption. Lying on his back on the board there he may be performing a function incalculably higher than any that prosperous canine life admits of; and yet, of the whole performance, this function is the one portion that must remain absolutely beyond his ken.

Now turn from this to the life of man. In the dog's life we see the world invisible to him because we live in both worlds. In human life, although we only see our world, and his within it, yet encompassing both these worlds a still wider world may be there, as unseen by us as our world is by him; and to believe in that world *may* be the most essential function that our lives in this world have to perform. But " *may* be! *may* be! " one now hears the positivist contemptuously exclaim; " what use can a scientific life have for maybes?" Well, I reply, the 'scientific' life itself has much to do with maybes, and human life at large has everything to do with them. So far as man stands for anything, and is productive or originative at all, his entire vital function may be said to have to deal with maybes. Not a victory is gained, not a deed of faithfulness or courage is done, except upon a maybe; not a service, not a sally of generosity, not a scientific exploration or experiment or textbook, that may not be a mistake. It is only by risking our persons from one hour to another that we live at all. And often enough our faith beforehand in an uncertified result *is the only thing that makes the result come true.* Suppose, for instance, that you are climbing a mountain, and have worked yourself into a position from which the only escape is by a terrible leap. Have faith that you can successfully make it, and your feet are nerved to its accomplishment. But mistrust yourself, and think of all the sweet things you have heard the scientists say of *maybes,* and you will hesitate so long that, at last, all unstrung and trembling, and launching yourself in a moment of despair, you roll in the abyss. In such a case (and it belongs to an enormous class), the part of wisdom as well as of courage is to *believe what is in the line of your needs,* for only by such belief is the need fulfilled. Refuse to believe, and you shall indeed be right, for you shall irretrievably perish. But believe, and again you shall be right, for you shall save yourself. You make one or the other of two possible universes true by your trust or mistrust, — both universes having been only *maybes,* in this particular, before you contributed your act.

Now, it appears to me that the question whether life is worth living is subject to conditions logically much like these. It does, indeed, depend on you *the liver*. If you surrender to the nightmare view and crown the evil edifice by your own suicide, you have indeed made a picture totally black. Pessimism, completed by your act, is true beyond a doubt, so far as your world goes. Your mistrust of life has removed whatever worth your own enduring existence might have given to it; and now, throughout the whole sphere of possible influence of that existence, the mistrust has proved itself to have had divining power. But suppose, on the other hand, that instead of giving way to the nightmare view you cling to it that this world is not the *ultimatum*. Suppose you find yourself a very well-spring, as Wordsworth says, of —

" Zeal, and the virtue to exist by faith
    As soldiers live by courage; as, by strength
    Of heart, the sailor fights with roaring seas."

Suppose, however thickly evils crowd upon you, that your unconquerable subjectivity proves to be their match, and that you find a more wonderful joy than any passive pleasure can bring in trusting ever in the larger whole. Have you not now made life worth living on these terms? What sort of a thing would life really be, with your qualities ready for a tussle with it, if it only brought fair weather and gave these higher faculties of yours no scope? Please remember that optimism and pessimism are definitions of the world, and that our own reactions on the world, small as they are in bulk, are integral parts of the whole thing, and necessarily help to determine the definition. They may even be the decisive elements in determining the definition. A large mass can have its unstable equilibrium overturned by the addition

of a feather's weight; a long phrase may have its
sense reversed by the addition of the three letters
n-o-t. This life *is* worth living, we can say, *since it
is what we make it, from the moral point of view;* and
we are determined to make it from that point of view,
so far as we have anything to do with it, a success.

Now, in this description of faiths that verify themselves I have assumed that our faith in an invisible
order is what inspires those efforts and that patience
which make this visible order good for moral men.
Our faith in the seen world's goodness (goodness now
meaning fitness for successful moral and religious life)
has verified itself by leaning on our faith in the unseen
world. But will our faith in the unseen world similarly verify itself? Who knows?

Once more it is a case of *maybe;* and once more
maybes are the essence of the situation. I confess
that I do not see why the very existence of an invisible world may not in part depend on the personal
response which any one of us may make to the religious appeal. God himself, in short, may draw vital
strength and increase of very being from our fidelity.
For my own part, I do not know what the sweat and
blood and tragedy of this life mean, if they mean anything short of this. If this life be not a real fight, in
which something is eternally gained for the universe
by success, it is no better than a game of private the-
atricals from which one may withdraw at will. But
it *feels* like a real fight, — as if there were something
really wild in the universe which we, with all our ide-
alities and faithfulnesses, are needed to redeem; and
first of all to redeem our own hearts from atheisms
and fears. For such a half-wild, half-saved universe
our nature is adapted. The deepest thing in our

nature is this *Binnenleben* (as a German doctor lately has called it), this dumb region of the heart in which we dwell alone with our willingnesses and unwillingnesses, our faiths and fears. As through the cracks and crannies of caverns those waters exude from the earth's bosom which then form the fountain-heads of springs, so in these crepuscular depths of personality the sources of all our outer deeds and decisions take their rise. Here is our deepest organ of communication with the nature of things; and compared with these concrete movements of our soul all abstract statements and scientific arguments — the veto, for example, which the strict positivist pronounces upon our faith — sound to us like mere chatterings of the teeth. For here possibilities, not finished facts, are the realities with which we have actively to deal; and to quote my friend William Salter, of the Philadelphia Ethical Society, " as the essence of courage is to stake one's life on a possibility, so the essence of faith is to believe that the possibility exists."

These, then, are my last words to you: Be not afraid of life. Believe that life *is* worth living, and your belief will help create the fact. The ' scientific proof ' that you are right may not be clear before the day of judgment (or some stage of being which that expression may serve to symbolize) is reached. But the faithful fighters of this hour, or the beings that then and there will represent them, may then turn to the faint-hearted, who here decline to go on, with words like those with which Henry IV greeted the tardy Crillon after a great victory had been gained: " Hang yourself, brave Crillon! we fought at Arques, and you were not there."

THE WILL TO BELIEVE *

IN the recently published Life by Leslie Stephen of his brother, Fitz-James, there is an account of a school to which the latter went when he was a boy. The teacher, a certain Mr. Guest, used to converse with his pupils in this wise: " Gurney, what is the difference between justification and sanctification? — Stephen, prove the omnipotence of God! " etc. In the midst of our Harvard freethinking and indifference we are prone to imagine that here at your good old orthodox College conversation continues to be somewhat upon this order; and to show you that we at Harvard have not lost all interest in these vital subjects, I have brought with me to-night something like a sermon on justification by faith to read to you, — I mean an essay in justification *of* faith, a defence of our right to adopt a believing attitude in religious matters, in spite of the fact that our merely logical

* An Address to the Philosophical Clubs of Yale and Brown Universities. Published in the New World, June, 1896.

intellect may not have been coerced. 'The Will to Believe,' accordingly, is the title of my paper.

I have long defended to my own students the lawfulness of voluntarily adopted faith; but as soon as they have got well imbued with the logical spirit, they have as a rule refused to admit my contention to be lawful philosophically, even though in point of fact they were personally all the time chock-full of some faith or other themselves. I am all the while, however, so profoundly convinced that my own position is correct, that your invitation has seemed to me a good occasion to make my statements more clear. Perhaps your minds will be more open than those with which I have hitherto had to deal. I will be as little technical as I can, though I must begin by setting up some technical distinctions that will help us in the end.

I

LET us give the name of *hypothesis* to anything that may be proposed to our belief; and just as the electricians speak of live and dead wires, let us speak of any hypothesis as either *live* or *dead*. A live hypothesis is one which appeals as a real possibility to him to whom it is proposed. If I ask you to believe in the Mahdi, the notion makes no electric connection with your nature, — it refuses to scintillate with any credibility at all. As an hypothesis it is completely dead. To an Arab, however (even if he be not one of the Mahdi's followers), the hypothesis is among the mind's possibilities: it is alive. This shows that deadness and liveness in an hypothesis are not intrinsic properties, but relations to the individual thinker. They are measured by his willingness to act. The maximum of liveness in an hypothesis means willingness to act irrevocably. Practically, that means belief; but there is some believing tendency wherever there is willingness to act at all.

Next, let us call the decision between two hypotheses an *option*. Options may be of several kinds. They may be — 1, *living* or *dead;* 2, *forced* or *avoidable;* 3, *momentous* or *trivial;* and for our purposes we may call an option a *genuine* option when it is of the forced, living, and momentous kind.

1. A living option is one in which both hypotheses are live ones. If I say to you: " Be a theosophist or be a Mohammedan," it is probably a dead option, because for you neither hypothesis is likely to be alive. But if I say: " Be an agnostic or be a Christian," it is otherwise: trained as you are, each hypothesis makes some appeal, however small, to your belief.

2. Next, if I say to you: " Choose between going out with your umbrella or without it," I do not offer you a genuine option, for it is not forced. You can easily avoid it by not going out at all. Similarly, if I say, " Either love me or hate me," " Either call my theory true or call it false," your option is avoidable. You may remain indifferent to me, neither loving nor hating, and you may decline to offer any judgment as to my theory. But if I say, " Either accept this truth or go without it," I put on you a forced option, for there is no standing place outside of the alternative. Every dilemma based on a complete logical disjunction, with no possibility of not choosing, is an option of this forced kind.

3. Finally, if I were Dr. Nansen and proposed to you to join my North Pole expedition, your option would be momentous; for this would probably be your only similar opportunity, and your choice now would either exclude you from the North Pole sort of immortality altogether or put at least the chance of it into your hands. He who refuses to embrace a unique opportunity loses the prize as surely as if he tried and failed. *Per contra,* the option is trivial when the opportunity is not unique, when the stake is insignificant, or when the decision is reversible if it later prove unwise. Such trivial options abound in the scientific life. A chemist finds an hypothesis live enough to spend a year in its verification: he believes in it to that extent. But if his experiments prove inconclusive either way, he is quit for his loss of time, no vital harm being done.

It will facilitate our discussion if we keep all these distinctions well in mind.

II

THE next matter to consider is the actual psychology of human opinion. When we look at certain facts, it seems as if our passional and volitional nature lay at the root of all our convictions. When we look at others, it seems as if they could do nothing when the intellect had once said its say. Let us take the latter facts up first.

Does it not seem preposterous on the very face of it to talk of our opinions being modifiable at will? Can our will either help or hinder our intellect in its perceptions of truth? Can we, by just willing it, believe that Abraham Lincoln's existence is a myth, and that the portraits of him in McClure's Magazine are all of some one else? Can we, by any effort of our will, or by any strength of wish that it were true, believe ourselves well and about when we are roaring with rheumatism in bed, or feel certain that the sum of the two one-dollar bills in our pocket must be a hundred dollars? We can *say* any of these things, but we are absolutely impotent to believe them; and of just such things is the whole fabric of the truths that we do believe in made up, — matters of fact, immediate or remote, as Hume said, and relations between ideas, which are either there or not there for us if we see them so, and which if not there cannot be put there by any action of our own.

In Pascal's Thoughts there is a celebrated passage known in literature as Pascal's wager. In it he tries to force us into Christianity by reasoning as if our concern with truth resembled our concern with the stakes in a game of chance. Translated freely his words are these: You must either believe or not believe that God is — which will you do? Your human reason cannot say. A game is going on between you and the nature of things which at the day of judgment will bring out either heads or tails. Weigh what your gains and your losses would be if you should stake all you have on heads, or God's existence: if you win in such case, you gain eternal beatitude; if you lose, you lose nothing at all. If there were an infinity of chances, and only one for God in this wager, still you ought to stake your all on God; for though you surely risk a finite loss by this procedure, any finite loss is reasonable, even a certain one is reasonable, if there is but the possibility of infinite gain. Go, then, and take holy water, and have masses said; belief will come and stupefy your scruples, — *Cela vous fera croire et vous abêtira.* Why should you not? At bottom, what have you to lose?

You probably feel that when religious faith expresses itself thus, in the language of the gaming-table, it is put to its last trumps. Surely Pascal's own personal belief in masses and holy water had far other springs; and this celebrated page of his is but an argument for others, a last desperate snatch at a weapon against the hardness of the unbelieving heart. We feel that a faith in masses and holy water adopted wilfully after such a mechanical calculation would lack the inner soul of faith's reality; and if we were ourselves in the place of the Deity, we should probably take particular pleasure in cutting off believers of this pattern from their infinite reward. It is evident that unless there be some pre-existing tendency to believe in masses and holy water, the option offered to the will by Pascal is not a living option. Certainly no Turk ever took to masses and holy water on its account; and even to us Protestants these means of salvation seem such foregone impossibilities that Pascal's logic, invoked for them specifically, leaves us unmoved. As well might the Mahdi write to us, saying, " I am the Expected One whom God has created in his effulgence. You shall be infinitely happy if you confess me; otherwise you shall be cut off from the light of the sun. Weigh, then, your infinite gain if I am genuine against your finite sacrifice if I am not! " His logic would be that of Pascal; but he would vainly use it on us, for the hypothesis he offers us is dead. No tendency to act on it exists in us to any degree.

The talk of believing by our volition seems, then, from one point of view, simply silly. From another point of view it is worse than silly, it is vile. When one turns to the magnificent edifice of the physical sciences, and sees how it was reared; what thousands of disinterested moral lives of men lie buried in its mere foundations; what patience and postponement, what choking down of preference, what submission to the icy laws of outer fact are wrought into its very stones and mortar; how absolutely impersonal it stands in its vast augustness, — then how besotted and contemptible seems every little sentimentalist who comes blowing his voluntary smoke-wreaths, and pretending to decide things from out of his private dream! Can we wonder if those bred in the rugged and manly school of science should feel like spewing such subjectivism out of their mouths? The whole system of loyalties which grow up in the schools of science go dead against its toleration; so that it is only natural that those who have caught the scientific fever should pass over to the opposite extreme, and write sometimes as if the incorruptibly truthful intellect ought positively to prefer bitterness and unacceptableness to the heart in its cup.

> It fortifies my soul to know
> That, though I perish, Truth is so —

sings Clough, while Huxley exclaims: "My only consolation lies in the reflection that, however bad our posterity may become, so far as they hold by the plain rule of not pretending to believe what they have no reason to believe, because it may be to their advantage so to pretend [the word 'pretend' is surely here redundant], they will not have reached the lowest depth of immorality." And that delicious *enfant terrible* Clifford writes: "Belief is desecrated when given to unproved and unquestioned statements for the solace and private pleasure of the believer. . . . Whoso would deserve well of his fellows in this matter will guard the purity of his belief with a very fanaticism of jealous care, lest at any time it should rest on an unworthy object, and catch a stain which can never be wiped away. . . . If [a] belief has been accepted on insufficient evidence [even though the belief be true, as Clifford on the same page explains] the pleasure is a stolen one. . . . It is sinful because it is stolen in defiance of our duty to mankind. That duty is to guard ourselves from such beliefs as from a pestilence which may shortly master our own body and then spread to the rest of the town. . . . It is wrong always, everywhere, and for every one, to believe anything upon insufficient evidence."

III

ALL this strikes one as healthy, even when expressed, as by Clifford, with somewhat too much of robustious pathos in the voice. Free-will and simple wishing do seem, in the matter of our credences, to be only fifth wheels to the coach. Yet if any one should thereupon assume that intellectual insight is what remains after wish and will and sentimental preference have taken wing, or that pure reason is what then settles our opinions, he would fly quite as directly in the teeth of the facts.

It is only our already dead hypotheses that our willing nature is unable to bring to life again. But what has made them dead for us is for the most part

a previous action of our willing nature of an antago-
nistic kind.   When I say 'willing nature,' I do not
mean only such deliberate volitions as may have set
up habits of belief that we cannot now escape from, —
I mean all such factors of belief as fear and hope,
prejudice and passion, imitation and partisanship,
the circumpressure of our caste and set.   As a matter of fact we find ourselves believing, we hardly
know how or why.   Mr. Balfour gives the name of
' authority' to all those influences, born of the intellectual climate, that make hypotheses possible or
impossible for us, alive or dead.   Here in this room,
we all of us believe in molecules and the conserva-
tion of energy, in democracy and necessary progress,
in Protestant Christianity and the duty of fighting for
' the doctrine of the immortal Monroe,' all for no reasons worthy of the name.   We see into these matters with no more inner clearness, and probably with
much less, than any disbeliever in them might possess.   His unconventionality would probably have
some grounds to show for its conclusions; but for
us, not insight, but the *prestige* of the opinions, is
what makes the spark shoot from them and light up
our sleeping magazines of faith.   Our reason is quite
satisfied, in nine hundred and ninety-nine cases out of
every thousand of us, if it can find a few arguments
that will do to recite in case our credulity is criticised
by some one else.   Our faith is faith in some one else's
faith, and in the greatest matters this is most the case.
Our belief in truth itself, for instance, that there is a
truth, and that our minds and it are made for each
other, — what is it but a passionate affirmation of
desire, in which our social system backs us up?   We
want to have a truth; we want to believe that our

experiments and studies and discussions must put us in a continually better and better position towards it; and on this line we agree to fight out our thinking lives. But if a pyrrhonistic sceptic asks us *how we know* all this, can our logic find a reply? No! certainly it cannot. It is just one volition against another, — we willing to go in for life upon a trust or assumption which he, for his part, does not care to make.*

As a rule we disbelieve all facts and theories for which we have no use. Clifford's cosmic emotions find no use for Christian feelings. Huxley belabors the bishops because there is no use for sacerdotalism in his scheme of life. Newman, on the contrary, goes over to Romanism, and finds all sorts of reasons good for staying there, because a priestly system is for him an organic need and delight. Why do so few ' scientists ' even look at the evidence for telepathy, so called? Because they think, as a leading biologist, now dead, once said to me, that even if such a thing were true, scientists ought to band together to keep it suppressed and concealed. It would undo the uniformity of Nature and all sorts of other things without which scientists cannot carry on their pursuits. But if this very man had been shown something which as a scientist he might *do* with telepathy, he might not only have examined the evidence, but even have found it good enough. This very law which the logicians would impose upon us — if I may give the name of logicians to those who would rule out our willing nature here — is based on nothing but their own natural wish to exclude all elements for

* Compare the admirable page 310 in S. H. Hodgson's " Time and Space," London, 1865.

which they, in their professional quality of logicians, can find no use.

Evidently, then, our non-intellectual nature does influence our convictions. There are passional tendencies and volitions which run before and others which come after belief, and it is only the latter that are too late for the fair; and they are not too late when the previous passional work has been already in their own direction. Pascal's argument, instead of being powerless, then seems a regular clincher, and is the last stroke needed to make our faith in masses and holy water complete. The state of things is evidently far from simple; and pure insight and logic, whatever they might do ideally, are not the only things that really do produce our creeds.

IV

OUR next duty, having recognized this mixed-up state of affairs, is to ask whether it be simply reprehensible and pathological, or whether, on the contrary, we must treat it as a normal element in making up our minds. The thesis I defend is, briefly stated, this: *Our passional nature not only lawfully may, but must, decide an option between propositions, whenever it is a genuine option that cannot by its nature be decided on intellectual grounds; for to say, under such circumstances, " Do not decide, but leave the question open," is itself a passional decision, — just like deciding yes or no, — and is attended with the same risk of losing the truth.* The thesis thus abstractly expressed will, I trust, soon become quite clear. But I must first indulge in a bit more of preliminary work.

V

It will be observed that for the purposes of this discussion we are on 'dogmatic' ground, — ground, I mean, which leaves systematic philosophical scepticism altogether out of account. The postulate that there is truth, and that it is the destiny of our minds to attain it, we are deliberately resolving to make, though the sceptic will not make it. We part company with him, therefore, absolutely, at this point. But the faith that truth exists, and that our minds can find it, may be held in two ways. We may talk of the *empiricist* way and of the *absolutist* way of believing in truth. The absolutists in this matter say that we not only can attain to knowing truth, but we can *know when* we have attained to knowing it; while the empiricists think that although we may attain it, we cannot infallibly know when. To *know* is one thing, and to know for certain *that* we know is another. One may hold to the first being possible without the second; hence the empiricists and the absolutists, although neither of them is a sceptic in the usual philosophic sense of the term, show very different degrees of dogmatism in their lives.

If we look at the history of opinions, we see that the empiricist tendency has largely prevailed in science, while in philosophy the absolutist tendency has had everything its own way. The characteristic sort of happiness, indeed, which philosophies yield has mainly consisted in the conviction felt by each successive school or system that by it bottom-certitude had been attained. "Other philosophies are collections of opinions, mostly false; *my* philosophy gives standing-ground forever," — who does not recognize in this the key-note of every system worthy of the name? A system, to be a system at all, must come as a *closed* system, reversible in this or that detail, perchance, but in its essential features never!

Scholastic orthodoxy, to which one must always go when one wishes to find perfectly clear statement, has beautifully elaborated this absolutist conviction in a doctrine which it calls that of ' objective evidence.' If, for example, I am unable to doubt that I now exist before you, that two is less than three, or that if all men are mortal then I am mortal too, it is because these things illumine my intellect irresistibly. The final ground of this objective evidence possessed by certain propositions is the *adæquatio intellectûs nostri cum rê.* The certitude it brings involves an *aptitudinem ad extorquendum certum assensum* on the part of the truth envisaged, and on the side of the subject a *quietem in cognitione,* when once the object is mentally received, that leaves no possibility of doubt behind; and in the whole transaction nothing operates but the *entitas ipsa* of the object and the *entitas ipsa* of the mind. We slouchy modern thinkers dislike to talk in Latin, — indeed, we dislike to talk in set terms at all; but at bottom our own state of mind is very much like this whenever we uncritically abandon ourselves: You believe in objective evidence, and I do. Of some things we feel that we are certain: we know, and we know that we do know. There is something that gives a click inside of us, a bell that strikes twelve, when the hands of our mental clock have swept the dial and meet over the meridian hour. The greatest empiricists among us are only empiricists on reflection: when

left to their instincts, they dogmatize like infallible
popes.   When the Cliffords tell us how sinful it is to
be Christians on such ' insufficient evidence,' insufficiency is really the last thing they have in mind.
For them the evidence is absolutely sufficient, only
it makes the other way.   They believe so completely
in an anti-christian order of the universe that there
is no living option: Christianity is a dead hypothesis from the start.

VI

BUT now, since we are all such absolutists by instinct, what in our quality of students of philosophy
ought we to do about the fact?   Shall we espouse
and indorse it?   Or shall we treat it as a weakness
of our nature from which we must free ourselves, if
we can?

I sincerely believe that the latter course is the only
one we can follow as reflective men.   Objective evidence and certitude are doubtless very fine ideals to
play with, but where on this moonlit and dream-
visited planet are they found?   I am, therefore, myself a complete empiricist so far as my theory of
human knowledge goes.   I live, to be sure, by the
practical faith that we must go on experiencing and
thinking over our experience, for only thus can our
opinions grow more true; but to hold any one of
them — I absolutely do not care which — as if it never
could be reinterpretable or corrigible, I believe to be
a tremendously mistaken attitude, and I think that the
whole history of philosophy will bear me out.   There
is but one indefectibly certain truth, and that is the
truth that pyrrhonistic scepticism itself leaves stand-

ing, — the truth that the present phenomenon of
consciousness exists.   That, however, is the bare
starting-point of knowledge, the mere admission of
a stuff to be philosophized about.   The various philosophies are but so many attempts at expressing
what this stuff really is.   And if we repair to our
libraries what disagreement do we discover!   Where
is a certainly true answer found?   Apart from abstract propositions of comparison (such as two and
two are the same as four), propositions which tell
us nothing by themselves about concrete reality, we
find no proposition ever regarded by any one as evidently certain that has not either been called a falsehood, or at least had its truth sincerely questioned
by some one else.   The transcending of the axioms
of geometry, not in play but in earnest, by certain of
our contemporaries (as Zöllner and Charles H.
Hinton), and the rejection of the whole Aristotelian
logic by the Hegelians, are striking instances in
point.

No concrete test of what is really true has ever
been agreed upon.   Some make the criterion external to the moment of perception, putting it either
in revelation, the *consensus gentium,* the instincts of
the heart, or the systematized experience of the race.
Others make the perceptive moment its own test, —
Descartes, for instance, with his clear and distinct
ideas guaranteed by the veracity of God; Reid with
his ' common-sense; ' and Kant with his forms of
synthetic judgment *a priori.*   The inconceivability
of the opposite; the capacity to be verified by sense;
the possession of complete organic unity or self-rela-
tion, realized when a thing is its own other, — are
standards which, in turn, have been used.   The much

lauded objective evidence is never triumphantly there; it is a mere aspiration or *Grenzbegriff*, marking the infinitely remote ideal of our thinking life. To claim that certain truths now possess it, is simply to say that when you think them true and they *are* true, then their evidence is objective, otherwise it is not. But practically one's conviction that the evidence one goes by is of the real objective brand, is only one more subjective opinion added to the lot. For what a contradictory array of opinions have objective evidence and absolute certitude been claimed! The world is rational through and through, — its existence is an ultimate brute fact; there is a personal God, — a personal God is inconceivable; there is an extra-mental physical world immediately known, — the mind can only know its own ideas; a moral imperative exists, — obligation is only the resultant of desires; a permanent spiritual principle is in every one, — there are only shifting states of mind; there is an endless chain of causes, — there is an absolute first cause; an eternal necessity, — a freedom; a purpose, — no purpose; a primal One, — a primal Many; a universal continuity, — an essential discontinuity in things; an infinity, — no infinity. There is this, — there is that; there is indeed nothing which some one has not thought absolutely true, while his neighbor deemed it absolutely false; and not an absolutist among them seems ever to have considered that the trouble may all the time be essential, and that the intellect, even with truth directly in its grasp, may have no infallible signal for knowing whether it be truth or no. When, indeed, one remembers that the most striking practical application to life of the doctrine of objective certitude has been the conscientious labors of the Holy Office of the Inquisition, one feels less tempted than ever to lend the doctrine a respectful ear.

But please observe, now, that when as empiricists we give up the doctrine of objective certitude, we do not thereby give up the quest or hope of truth itself. We still pin our faith on its existence, and still believe that we gain an ever better position towards it by systematically continuing to roll up experiences and think. Our great difference from the scholastic lies in the way we face. The strength of his system lies in the principles, the origin, the *terminus a quo* of his thought; for us the strength is in the outcome, the upshot, the *terminus ad quem*. Not where it comes from but what it leads to is to decide. It matters not to an empiricist from what quarter an hypothesis may come to him: he may have acquired it by fair means or by foul; passion may have whispered or accident suggested it; but if the total drift of thinking continues to confirm it, that is what he means by its being true.

VII

ONE more point, small but important, and our preliminaries are done. There are two ways of looking at our duty in the matter of opinion, — ways entirely different, and yet ways about whose difference the theory of knowledge seems hitherto to have shown very little concern. *We must know the truth;* and *we must avoid error,* — these are our first and great commandments as would-be knowers; but they are not two ways of stating an identical commandment, they are two separable laws. Although it may indeed happen that when we believe the truth *A,* we escape

as an incidental consequence from believing the falsehood *B*, it hardly ever happens that by merely disbelieving *B* we necessarily believe *A*. We may in
escaping *B* fall into believing other falsehoods, *C* or
D, just as bad as *B*; or we may escape *B* by not
believing anything at all, not even *A*.

Believe truth! Shun error! — these, we see, are
two materially different laws; and by choosing between them we may end by coloring differently our
whole intellectual life. We may regard the chase
for truth as paramount, and the avoidance of error as
secondary; or we may, on the other hand, treat the
avoidance of error as more imperative, and let truth
take its chance. Clifford, in the instructive passage
which I have quoted, exhorts us to the latter course.
Believe nothing, he tells us, keep your mind in suspense forever, rather than by closing it on insufficient
evidence incur the awful risk of believing lies. You,
on the other hand, may think that the risk of being in
error is a very small matter when compared with the
blessings of real knowledge, and be ready to be duped
many times in your investigation rather than post-
pone indefinitely the chance of guessing true. I
myself find it impossible to go with Clifford. We
must remember that these feelings of our duty about
either truth or error are in any case only expressions
of our passional life. Biologically considered, our
minds are as ready to grind out falsehood as veracity,
and he who says, " Better go without belief forever
than believe a lie! " merely shows his own prepon-
derant private horror of becoming a dupe. He may
be critical of many of his desires and fears, but this
fear he slavishly obeys. He cannot imagine any one
questioning its binding force. For my own part, I

have also a horror of being duped; but I can believe that worse things than being duped may happen to a man in this world: so Clifford's exhortation has to my ears a thoroughly fantastic sound. It is like a general informing his soldiers that it is better to keep out of battle forever than to risk a single wound. Not so are victories either over enemies or over nature gained. Our errors are surely not such awfully solemn things. In a world where we are so certain to incur them in spite of all our caution, a certain lightness of heart seems healthier than this excessive nervousness on their behalf. At any rate, it seems the fittest thing for the empiricist philosopher.

VIII

AND now, after all this introduction, let us go straight at our question. I have said, and now repeat it, that not only as a matter of fact do we find our passional nature influencing us in our opinions, but that there are some options between opinions in which this influence must be regarded both as an inevitable and as a lawful determinant of our choice.

I fear here that some of you my hearers will begin to scent danger, and lend an inhospitable ear. Two first steps of passion you have indeed had to admit as necessary, — we must think so as to avoid dupery, and we must think so as to gain truth; but the surest path to those ideal consummations, you will probably consider, is from now onwards to take no further passional step.

Well, of course, I agree as far as the facts will allow. Wherever the option between losing truth and gaining it is not momentous, we can throw the chance of *gaining truth* away, and at any rate save ourselves from any chance of *believing falsehood,* by not making up our minds at all till objective evidence has come. In scientific questions, this is almost always the case; and even in human affairs in general, the need of acting is seldom so urgent that a false belief to act on is better than no belief at all. Law courts, indeed, have to decide on the best evidence attainable for the moment, because a judge's duty is to make law as well as to ascertain it, and (as a learned judge once said to me) few cases are worth spending much time over: the great thing is to have them decided on *any* acceptable principle, and got out of the way. But in our dealings with objective nature we obviously are recorders, not makers, of the truth; and decisions for the mere sake of deciding promptly and getting on to the next business would be wholly out of place. Throughout the breadth of physical nature facts are what they are quite independently of us, and seldom is there any such hurry about them that the risks of being duped by believing a premature theory need be faced. The questions here are always trivial options, the hypotheses are hardly living (at any rate not living for us spectators), the choice between believing truth or falsehood is seldom forced. The attitude of sceptical balance is therefore the absolutely wise one if we would escape mistakes. What difference, indeed, does it make to most of us whether we have or have not a theory of the Röntgen rays, whether we believe or not in mind-stuff, or have a conviction about the causality of conscious states? It makes no difference. Such options are not forced on us. On every account it is better not to make them, but still keep weighing reasons *pro et contra* with an indifferent hand.

I speak, of course, here of the purely judging mind. For purposes of discovery such indifference is to be less highly recommended, and science would be far less advanced than she is if the passionate desires of individuals to get their own faiths confirmed had been kept out of the game. See for example the sagacity which Spencer and Weismann now display. On the other hand, if you want an absolute duffer in an investigation, you must, after all, take the man who has no interest whatever in its results: he is the warranted incapable, the positive fool. The most useful investigator, because the most sensitive observer, is always he whose eager interest in one side of the question is balanced by an equally keen nervousness lest he become deceived.* Science has organized this nervousness into a regular *technique,* her so-called method of verification; and she has fallen so deeply in love with the method that one may even say she has ceased to care for truth by itself at all. It is only truth as technically verified that interests her. The truth of truths might come in merely affirmative form, and she would decline to touch it. Such truth as that, she might repeat with Clifford, would be stolen in defiance of her duty to mankind. Human passions, however, are stronger than technical rules. " Le cœur a ses raisons," as Pascal says, " que la raison ne connaît pas; " and however indifferent to all but the bare rules of the game the umpire, the abstract intellect, may be, the concrete players who furnish him the materials to judge of are usually, each one of them, in love with some pet ' live hypothesis ' of his own. Let us agree, however, that wherever there is no forced option, the

---

* Compare Wilfrid Ward's Essay, "The Wish to Believe," in his *Witnesses to the Unseen,* Macmillan & Co., 1893.

dispassionately judicial intellect with no pet hypothesis, saving us, as it does, from dupery at any rate, ought to be our ideal.

The question next arises: Are there not somewhere forced options in our speculative questions, and can we (as men who may be interested at least as much in positively gaining truth as in merely escaping dupery) always wait with impunity till the coercive evidence shall have arrived? It seems *a priori* improbable that the truth should be so nicely adjusted to our needs and powers as that. In the great boarding-house of nature, the cakes and the butter and the syrup seldom come out so even and leave the plates so clean. Indeed, we should view them with scientific suspicion if they did.

IX

Moral questions immediately present themselves as questions whose solution cannot wait for sensible proof. A moral question is a question not of what sensibly exists, but of what is good, or would be good if it did exist. Science can tell us what exists; but to compare the *worths,* both of what exists and of what does not exist, we must consult not science, but what Pascal calls our heart. Science herself consults her heart when she lays it down that the infinite ascertainment of fact and correction of false belief are the supreme goods for man. Challenge the statement, and science can only repeat it oracularly, or else prove it by showing that such ascertainment and correction bring man all sorts of other goods which man's heart in turn declares. The question of having moral beliefs at all or not having them is decided by

our will. Are our moral preferences true or false,
or are they only odd biological phenomena, making
things good or bad for *us,* but in themselves indifferent? How can your pure intellect decide? If your
heart does not *want* a world of moral reality, your
head will assuredly never make you believe in one.
Mephistophelian scepticism, indeed, will satisfy the
head's play-instincts much better than any rigor-
ous idealism can. Some men (even at the student
age) are so naturally cool-hearted that the moralistic
hypothesis never has for them any pungent life, and
in their supercilious presence the hot young moralist
always feels strangely ill at ease. The appearance of
knowingness is on their side, of *naïveté* and gullibility
on his. Yet, in the inarticulate heart of him, he clings
to it that he is not a dupe, and that there is a realm
in which (as Emerson says) all their wit and intellectual superiority is no better than the cunning of
a fox. Moral scepticism can no more be refuted or
proved by logic than intellectual scepticism can.
When we stick to it that there *is* truth (be it of either
kind), we do so with our whole nature, and resolve to
stand or fall by the results. The sceptic with his
whole nature adopts the doubting attitude; but which
of us is the wiser, Omniscience only knows.

Turn now from these wide questions of good to a
certain class of questions of fact, questions concerning
personal relations, states of mind between one man
and another. *Do you like me or not?* — for example.
Whether you do or not depends, in countless instances, on whether I meet you half-way, am willing
to assume that you must like me, and show you trust
and expectation. The previous faith on my part in
your liking's existence is in such cases what makes

your liking come. But if I stand aloof, and refuse to budge an inch until I have objective evidence, until you shall have done something apt, as the absolutists say, *ad extorquendum assensum meum,* ten to one your liking never comes. How many women's hearts are vanquished by the mere sanguine insistence of some man that they *must* love him! he will not consent to the hypothesis that they cannot. The desire for a certain kind of truth here brings about that special truth's existence; and so it is in innumerable cases of other sorts. Who gains promotions, boons, appointments, but the man in whose life they are seen to play the part of live hypotheses, who discounts them, sacrifices other things for their sake before they have come, and takes risks for them in advance? His faith acts on the powers above him as a claim, and creates its own verification.

A social organism of any sort whatever, large or small, is what it is because each member proceeds to his own duty with a trust that the other members will simultaneously do theirs. Wherever a desired result is achieved by the co-operation of many independent persons, its existence as a fact is a pure consequence of the precursive faith in one another of those immediately concerned. A government, an army, a commercial system, a ship, a college, an athletic team, all exist on this condition, without which not only is nothing achieved, but nothing is even attempted. A whole train of passengers (individually brave enough) will be looted by a few highwaymen, simply because the latter can count on one another, while each passenger fears that if he makes a movement of resistance, he will be shot before any one else backs him up. If we believed that the whole car-full would rise

at once with us, we should each severally rise, and
train-robbing would never even be attempted. There
are, then, cases where a fact cannot come at all unless
a preliminary faith exists in its coming. *And where
faith in a fact can help create the fact,* that would be
an insane logic which should say that faith running
ahead of scientific evidence is the 'lowest kind of
immorality' into which a thinking being can fall. Yet
such is the logic by which our scientific absolutists
pretend to regulate our lives!

X

In truths dependent on our personal action, then,
faith based on desire is certainly a lawful and possibly an indispensable thing.

But now, it will be said, these are all childish human cases, and have nothing to do with great cosmi-
cal matters, like the question of religious faith. Let
us then pass on to that. Religions differ so much
in their accidents that in discussing the religious
question we must make it very generic and broad.
What then do we now mean by the religious hypothesis? Science says things are; morality says some
things are better than other things; and religion says
essentially two things.

First, she says that the best things are the more
eternal things, the overlapping things, the things in
the universe that throw the last stone, so to speak,
and say the final word. "Perfection is eternal," —
this phrase of Charles Secrétan seems a good way of
putting this first affirmation of religion, an affirmation
which obviously cannot yet be verified scientifically
at all.

The second affirmation of religion is that we are better off even now if we believe her first affirmation to be true.

Now, let us consider what the logical elements of this situation are *in case the religious hypothesis in both its branches be really true.* (Of course, we must admit that possibility at the outset. If we are to discuss the question at all, it must involve a living option. If for any of you religion be a hypothesis that cannot, by any living possibility be true, then you need go no farther. I speak to the 'saving remnant' alone.) So proceeding, we see, first that religion offers itself as a *momentous* option. We are supposed to gain, even now, by our belief, and to lose by our non-belief, a certain vital good. Secondly, religion is a *forced* option, so far as that good goes. We cannot escape the issue by remaining sceptical and waiting for more light, because, although we do avoid error in that way *if religion be untrue,* we lose the good, *if it be true,* just as certainly as if we positively chose to disbelieve. It is as if a man should hesitate indefinitely to ask a certain woman to marry him because he was not perfectly sure that she would prove an angel after he brought her home. Would he not cut himself off from that particular angel-possibility as decisively as if he went and married some one else? Scepticism, then, is not avoidance of option; it is option of a certain particular kind of risk. *Better risk loss of truth than chance of error,* — that is your faith-vetoer's exact position. He is actively playing his stake as much as the believer is; he is backing the field against the religious hypothesis, just as the believer is backing the religious hypothesis against the field. To preach scepticism to us as a duty until

'sufficient evidence' for religion be found, is tanta-
mount therefore to telling us, when in presence of the
religious hypothesis, that to yield to our fear of its
being error is wiser and better than to yield to our
hope that it may be true. It is not intellect against
all passions, then; it is only intellect with one passion laying down its law. And by what, forsooth,
is the supreme wisdom of this passion warranted?
Dupery for dupery, what proof is there that dupery
through hope is so much worse than dupery through
fear? I, for one, can see no proof; and I simply
refuse obedience to the scientist's command to imitate his kind of option, in a case where my own stake
is important enough to give me the right to choose
my own form of risk. If religion be true and the
evidence for it be still insufficient, I do not wish, by
putting your extinguisher upon my nature (which
feels to me as if it had after all some business in this
matter), to forfeit my sole chance in life of getting
upon the winning side, — that chance depending, of
course, on my willingness to run the risk of acting
as if my passional need of taking the world religiously
might be prophetic and right.

All this is on the supposition that it really may
be prophetic and right, and that, even to us who are
discussing the matter, religion is a live hypothesis
which may be true. Now, to most of us religion
comes in a still further way that makes a veto on
our active faith even more illogical. The more perfect and more eternal aspect of the universe is represented in our religions as having personal form.
The universe is no longer a mere *It* to us, but a *Thou*,
if we are religious; and any relation that may be
possible from person to person might be possible

here. For instance, although in one sense we are passive portions of the universe, in another we show a curious autonomy, as if we were small active centres on our own account. We feel, too, as if the appeal of religion to us were made to our own active good-will, as if evidence might be forever withheld from us unless we met the hypothesis half-way. To take a trivial illustration: just as a man who in a company of gentlemen made no advances, asked a warrant for every concession, and believed no one's word without proof, would cut himself off by such churlishness from all the social rewards that a more trusting spirit would earn, — so here, one who should shut himself up in snarling logicality and try to make the gods extort his recognition willy-nilly, or not get it at all, might cut himself off forever from his only opportunity of making the gods' acquaintance. This feeling, forced on us we know not whence, that by obstinately believing that there are gods (although not to do so would be so easy both for our logic and our life) we are doing the universe the deepest service we can, seems part of the living essence of the religious hypothesis. If the hypothesis *were* true in all its parts, including this one, then pure intellectualism, with its veto on our making willing advances, would be an absurdity; and some participation of our sympathetic nature would be logically required. I, therefore, for one, cannot see my way to accepting the agnostic rules for truth-seeking, or wilfully agree to keep my willing nature out of the game. I cannot do so for this plain reason, that *a rule of thinking which would absolutely prevent me from acknowledging certain kinds of truth if those kinds of truth were really there, would be an irrational rule.* That for me is the long and short of the formal logic of the situation, no matter what the kinds of truth might materially be.

I confess I do not see how this logic can be escaped. But sad experience makes me fear that some of you may still shrink from radically saying with me, *in abstracto,* that we have the right to believe at our own risk any hypothesis that is live enough to tempt our will. I suspect, however, that if this is so, it is because you have got away from the abstract logical point of view altogether, and are thinking (perhaps without realizing it) of some particular religious hypothesis which for you is dead. The freedom to ' believe what we will ' you apply to the case of some patent superstition; and the faith you think of is the faith defined by the schoolboy when he said, " Faith is when you believe something that you know ain't true." I can only repeat that this is misapprehension. *In concreto,* the freedom to believe can only cover living options which the intellect of the individual cannot by itself resolve; and living options never seem absurdities to him who has them to consider. When I look at the religious question as it really puts itself to concrete men, and when I think of all the possibilities which both practically and theoretically it involves, then this command that we shall put a stopper on our heart, instincts, and courage, and *wait* — acting of course meanwhile more or less as if religion were *not* true * —

* Since belief is measured by action, he who forbids us to believe religion to be true, necessarily also forbids us to act as we should if we did believe it to be true. The whole defence of religious faith hinges upon action. If the action required or inspired by the reli-

till doomsday, or till such time as our intellect and senses working together may have raked in evidence enough, — this command, I say, seems to me the queerest idol ever manufactured in the philosophic cave. Were we scholastic absolutists, there might be more excuse. If we had an infallible intellect with its objective certitudes, we might feel ourselves disloyal to such a perfect organ of knowledge in not trusting to it exclusively, in not waiting for its releasing word. But if we are empiricists, if we believe that no bell in us tolls to let us know for certain when truth is in our grasp, then it seems a piece of idle fantasticality to preach so solemnly our duty of waiting for the bell. Indeed we *may* wait if we will, — I hope you do not think that I am denying that, — but if we do so, we do so at our peril as much as if we believed. In either case we *act,* taking our life in our hands. No one of us ought to issue vetoes to the other, nor should we bandy words of abuse. We ought, on the contrary, delicately and profoundly to respect one another's mental freedom: then only shall we bring about the intellectual republic; then only shall we have that spirit of inner tolerance without which all our outer tolerance is soulless, and which is empiricism's glory; then only shall we live and let live, in speculative as well as in practical things.

---

gious hypothesis is in no way different from that dictated by the naturalistic hypothesis, then religious faith is a pure superfluity, better pruned away, and controversy about its legitimacy is a piece of idle trifling, unworthy of serious minds. I myself believe, of course, that the religious hypothesis gives to the world an expression which specifically determines our reactions, and makes them in a large part unlike what they might be on a purely naturalistic scheme of belief.

I began by a reference to Fitz James Stephen; let me end by a quotation from him. "What do you think of yourself? What do you think of the world? . . . These are questions with which all must deal as it seems good to them. They are riddles of the Sphinx, and in some way or other we must deal with them. . . . In all important transactions of life we have to take a leap in the dark. . . . If we decide to leave the riddles unanswered, that is a choice; if we waver in our answer, that, too, is a choice: but whatever choice we make, we make it at our peril. If a man chooses to turn his back altogether on God and the future, no one can prevent him; no one can show beyond reasonable doubt that he is mistaken. If a man thinks otherwise and acts as he thinks, I do not see that any one can prove that *he* is mistaken. Each must act as he thinks best; and if he is wrong, so much the worse for him. We stand on a mountain pass in the midst of whirling snow and blinding mist, through which we get glimpses now and then of paths which may be deceptive. If we stand still we shall be frozen to death. If we take the wrong road we shall be dashed to pieces. We do not certainly know whether there is any right one. What must we do? 'Be strong and of a good courage.' Act for the best, hope for the best, and take what comes. . . . If death ends all, we cannot meet death better." *

* Liberty, Equality, Fraternity, p. 353, 2d edition. London, 1874.

THE SENTIMENT OF RATIONALITY *

I

WHAT is the task which philosophers set themselves to perform; and why do they philosophize at all? Almost every one will immediately reply: They desire to attain a conception of the frame of things which shall on the whole be more rational than that somewhat chaotic view which every one by nature carries about with him under his hat. But suppose this rational conception attained, how is the philosopher to recognize it for what it is, and not let it slip through ignorance? The only answer can be that he will recognize its rationality as he recognizes everything else, by certain subjective marks with which it affects him. When he gets the marks, he may know that he has got the rationality.

What, then, are the marks? A strong feeling of ease, peace, rest, is one of them. The transition from a state of puzzle and perplexity to rational comprehension is full of lively relief and pleasure.

But this relief seems to be a negative rather than a positive character. Shall we then say that the feeling of rationality is constituted merely by the absence

___

* This essay as far as page 75 consists of extracts from an article printed in Mind for July, 1879. Thereafter it is a reprint of an address to the Harvard Philosophical Club, delivered in 1880, and published in the Princeton Review, July, 1882.

of any feeling of irrationality? I think there are very good grounds for upholding such a view. All feeling whatever, in the light of certain recent psychological speculations, seems to depend for its physical condition not on simple discharge of nerve-currents, but on their discharge under arrest, impediment, or resistance. Just as we feel no particular pleasure when we breathe freely, but a very intense feeling of distress when the respiratory motions are prevented, — so any unobstructed tendency to action discharges itself without the production of much cogitative accompaniment, and any perfectly fluent course of thought awakens but little feeling; but when the movement is inhibited, or when the thought meets with difficulties, we experience distress. It is only when the distress is upon us that we can be said to strive, to crave, or to aspire. When enjoying plenary freedom either in the way of motion or of thought, we are in a sort of anæsthetic state in which we might say with Walt Whitman, if we cared to say anything about ourselves at such times, " I am sufficient as I am." This feeling of the sufficiency of the present moment, of its absoluteness, — this absence of all need to explain it, account for it, or justify it, — is what I call the Sentiment of Rationality. As soon, in short, as we are enabled from any cause whatever to think with perfect fluency, the thing we think of seems to us *pro tanto* rational.

Whatever modes of conceiving the cosmos facilitate this fluency, produce the sentiment of rationality. Conceived in such modes, being vouches for itself and needs no further philosophic formulation. But this fluency may be obtained in various ways; and first I will take up the theoretic way.

The facts of the world in their sensible diversity are always before us, but our theoretic need is that they should be conceived in a way that reduces their manifoldness to simplicity. Our pleasure at finding that a chaos of facts is the expression of a single underlying fact is like the relief of the musician at resolving a confused mass of sound into melodic or harmonic order. The simplified result is handled with far less mental effort than the original data; and a philosophic conception of nature is thus in no metaphorical sense a labor-saving contrivance. The passion for parsimony, for economy of means in thought, is the philosophic passion *par excellence;* and any character or aspect of the world's phenomena which gathers up their diversity into monotony will gratify that passion, and in the philosopher's mind stand for that essence of things compared with which all their other determinations may by him be overlooked.

More universality or extensiveness is, then, one mark which the philosopher's conceptions must possess. Unless they apply to an enormous number of cases they will not bring him relief. The knowledge of things by their causes, which is often given as a definition of rational knowledge, is useless to him unless the causes converge to a minimum number, while still producing the maximum number of effects. The more multiple then are the instances, the more flowingly does his mind rove from fact to fact. The phenomenal transitions are no real transitions; each item is the same old friend with a slightly altered dress.

Who does not feel the charm of thinking that the moon and the apple are, as far as their relation to the earth goes, identical; of knowing respiration and combustion to be one; of understanding that the balloon rises by the same law whereby the stone sinks; of feeling that the warmth in one's palm when one rubs one's sleeve is identical with the motion which the friction checks; of recognizing the difference between beast and fish to be only a higher degree of that between human father and son; of believing our strength when we climb the mountain or fell the tree to be no other than the strength of the sun's rays which made the corn grow out of which we got our morning meal?

But alongside of this passion for simplification there exists a sister passion, which in some minds — though they perhaps form the minority — is its rival. This is the passion for distinguishing; it is the impulse to be *acquainted* with the parts rather than to comprehend the whole. Loyalty to clearness and integrity of perception, dislike of blurred outlines, of vague identifications, are its characteristics. It loves to recognize particulars in their full completeness, and the more of these it can carry the happier it is. It prefers any amount of incoherence, abruptness, and fragmentariness (so long as the literal details of the separate facts are saved) to an abstract way of conceiving things that, while it simplifies them, dissolves away at the same time their concrete fulness. Clearness and simplicity thus set up rival claims, and make a real dilemma for the thinker.

A man's philosophic attitude is determined by the balance in him of these two cravings. No system of philosophy can hope to be universally accepted among men which grossly violates either need, or entirely subordinates the one to the other. The fate of Spinosa, with his barren union of all things in one substance, on the one hand; that of Hume, with his equally barren 'looseness and separateness' of everything, on the other, — neither philosopher owning any strict and systematic disciples to-day, each being to posterity a warning as well as a stimulus, — show us that the only possible philosophy must be a compromise between an abstract monotony and a concrete heterogeneity. But the only way to mediate between diversity and unity is to class the diverse items as cases of a common essence which you discover in them. Classification of things into extensive 'kinds' is thus the first step; and classification of their relations and conduct into extensive 'laws' is the last step, in their philosophic unification. A completed theoretic philosophy can thus never be anything more than a completed classification of the world's ingredients; and its results must always be abstract, since the basis of every classification is the abstract essence embedded in the living fact, — the rest of the living fact being for the time ignored by the classifier. This means that none of our explanations are complete. They subsume things under heads wider or more familiar; but the last heads, whether of things or of their connections, are mere abstract genera, data which we just find in things and write down.

When, for example, we think that we have rationally explained the connection of the facts A and B by classing both under their common attribute x, it is obvious that we have really explained only so much of these items as is x. To explain the connection of choke-damp and suffocation by the lack of oxygen is to leave untouched all the other peculiarities both of choke-damp and of suffocation, — such as convulsions and agony on the one hand, density and explosibility on the other. In a word, so far as A and B contain l, m, n, and o, p, q, respectively, in addition to x, they are not explained by x. Each additional particularity makes its distinct appeal. A single explanation of a fact only explains it from a single point of view. The entire fact is not accounted for until each and all of its characters have been classed with their likes elsewhere. To apply this now to the case of the universe, we see that the explanation of the world by molecular movements explains it only so far as it actually *is* such movements. To invoke the 'Unknowable' explains only so much as is unknowable, 'Thought' only so much as is thought, 'God' only so much as is God. *Which* thought? *Which* God? — are questions that have to be answered by bringing in again the residual data from which the general term was abstracted. All those data that cannot be analytically identified with the attribute invoked as universal principle, remain as independent kinds or natures, associated empirically with the said attribute but devoid of rational kinship with it.

Hence the unsatisfactoriness of all our speculations. On the one hand, so far as they retain any multiplicity in their terms, they fail to get us out of the empirical sand-heap world; on the other, so far as they eliminate multiplicity the practical man despises their empty barrenness. The most they can say is that the elements of the world are such and such, and that each is identical with itself wherever found; but the question Where is it found? the practical man is left to answer by his own wit. Which, of all the

essences, shall here and now be held the essence of
this concrete thing, the fundamental philosophy never
attempts to decide. We are thus led to the conclusion that the simple classification of things is, on
the one hand, the best possible theoretic philosophy,
but is, on the other, a most miserable and inadequate
substitute for the fulness of the truth. It is a monstrous abridgment of life, which, like all abridgments
is got by the absolute loss and casting out of real
matter. This is why so few human beings truly care
for philosophy. The particular determinations which
she ignores are the real matter exciting needs, quite
as potent and authoritative as hers. What does the
moral enthusiast care for philosophical ethics? Why
does the *Æsthetik* of every German philosopher appear to the artist an abomination of desolation?

> Grau, theurer Freund, ist alle Theorie
> Und grün des Lebens goldner Baum.

The entire man, who feels all needs by turns, will take
nothing as an equivalent for life but the fulness of
living itself. Since the essences of things are as a
matter of fact disseminated through the whole extent
of time and space, it is in their spread-outness and
alternation that he will enjoy them. When weary of
the concrete clash and dust and pettiness, he will refresh himself by a bath in the eternal springs, or
fortify himself by a look at the immutable natures.
But he will only be a visitor, not a dweller in the
region; he will never carry the philosophic yoke
upon his shoulders, and when tired of the gray monotony of her problems and insipid spaciousness of
her results, will always escape gleefully into the teem-
ing and dramatic richness of the concrete world.

So our study turns back here to its beginning.
Every way of classifying a thing is but a way of
handling it for some particular purpose. Conceptions, 'kinds,' are teleological instruments. No abstract concept can be a valid substitute for a concrete
reality except with reference to a particular interest
in the conceiver. The interest of theoretic rationality,
the relief of identification, is but one of a thousand
human purposes. When others rear their heads, it
must pack up its little bundle and retire till its turn
recurs. The exaggerated dignity and value that
philosophers have claimed for their solutions is thus
greatly reduced. The only virtue their theoretic conception need have is simplicity, and a simple conception is an equivalent for the world only so far as the
world is simple, — the world meanwhile, whatever
simplicity it may harbor, being also a mightily complex affair. Enough simplicity remains, however,
and enough urgency in our craving to reach it, to
make the theoretic function one of the most invincible
of human impulses. The quest of the fewest elements of things is an ideal that some will follow, as
long as there are men to think at all.

But suppose the goal attained. Suppose that at
last we have a system unified in the sense that has
been explained. Our world can now be conceived
simply, and our mind enjoys the relief. Our universal concept has made the concrete chaos rational.
But now I ask, Can that which is the ground of rationality in all else be itself properly called rational?
It would seem at first sight that it might. One is
tempted at any rate to say that, since the craving for
rationality is appeased by the identification of one
thing with another, a datum which left nothing else

outstanding might quench that craving definitively, or be rational *in se.* No otherness being left to annoy us, we should sit down at peace. In other words, as the theoretic tranquillity of the boor results from his spinning no further considerations about his chaotic universe, so any datum whatever (provided it were simple, clear, and ultimate) ought to banish puzzle from the universe of the philosopher and confer peace, inasmuch as there would then be for him absolutely no further considerations to spin.

This in fact is what some persons think. Professor Bain says, —

" A difficulty is solved, a mystery unriddled, when it can be shown to resemble something else; to be an example of a fact already known. Mystery is isolation, exception, or it may be apparent contradiction: the resolution of the mystery is found in assimilation, identity, fraternity. When all things are assimilated, so far as assimilation can go, so far as likeness holds, there is an end to explanation; there is an end to what the mind can do, or can intelligently desire. . . . The path of science as exhibited in modern ages is toward generality, wider and wider, until we reach the highest, the widest laws of every department of things; there explanation is finished, mystery ends, perfect vision is gained."

But, unfortunately, this first answer will not hold. Our mind is so wedded to the process of seeing an *other* beside every item of its experience, that when the notion of an absolute datum is presented to it, it goes through its usual procedure and remains pointing at the void beyond, as if in that lay further matter for contemplation. In short, it spins for itself the further positive consideration of a nonentity envel-

oping the being of its datum; and as that leads nowhere, back recoils the thought toward its datum
again. But there is no natural bridge between nonentity and this particular datum, and the thought stands
oscillating to and fro, wondering " Why was there anything but nonentity; why just this universal datum
and not another? " and finds no end, in wandering
mazes lost. Indeed, Bain's words are so untrue that
in reflecting men it is just when the attempt to fuse
the manifold into a single totality has been most
successful, when the conception of the universe as a
unique fact is nearest its perfection, that the craving
for further explanation, the ontological wonder-sick-
ness, arises in its extremest form. As Schopenhauer
says, " The uneasiness which keeps the never-resting
clock of metaphysics in motion, is the consciousness
that the non-existence of this world is just as possible
as its existence."

The notion of nonentity may thus be called the
parent of the philosophic craving in its subtilest and
profoundest sense. Absolute existence is absolute
mystery, for its relations with the nothing remain
unmediated to our understanding. One philosopher
only has pretended to throw a logical bridge over
this chasm. Hegel, by trying to show that nonentity and concrete being are linked together by a
series of identities of a synthetic kind, binds everything conceivable into a unity, with no outlying notion to disturb the free rotary circulation of the mind
within its bounds. Since such unchecked movement
gives the feeling of rationality, he must be held, if
he has succeeded, to have eternally and absolutely
quenched all rational demands.

But for those who deem Hegel's heroic effort to

have failed, nought remains but to confess that when all things have been unified to the supreme degree, the notion of a possible other than the actual may still haunt our imagination and prey upon our system. The bottom of being is left logically opaque to us, as something which we simply come upon and find, and about which (if we wish to act) we should pause and wonder as little as possible. The philosopher's logical tranquillity is thus in essence no other than the boor's. They differ only as to the point at which each refuses to let further considerations upset the absoluteness of the data he assumes. The boor does so immediately, and is liable at any moment to the ravages of many kinds of doubt. The philosopher does not do so till unity has been reached, and is warranted against the inroads of those considerations, but only practically, not essentially, secure from the blighting breath of the ultimate Why? If he cannot exorcise this question, he must ignore or blink it, and, assuming the data of his system as something given, and the gift as ultimate, simply proceed to a life of contemplation or of action based on it. There is no doubt that this acting on an opaque necessity is accompanied by a certain pleasure. See the reverence of Carlyle for brute fact: "There is an infinite significance in fact." "Necessity," says Dühring, and he means not rational but given necessity, "is the last and highest point that we can reach. . . . It is not only the interest of ultimate and definitive knowledge, but also that of the feelings, to find a last repose and an ideal equilibrium in an uttermost datum which can simply not be other than it is."

Such is the attitude of ordinary men in their theism, God's fiat being in physics and morals such an uttermost datum. Such also is the attitude of all hard-minded analysts and *Verstandesmenschen.* Lotze, Renouvier, and Hodgson promptly say that of experience as a whole no account can be given, but neither seek to soften the abruptness of the confession nor to reconcile us with our impotence.

But mediating attempts may be made by more mystical minds. The peace of rationality may be sought through ecstasy when logic fails. To religious persons of every shade of doctrine moments come when the world, as it is, seems so divinely orderly, and the acceptance of it by the heart so rapturously complete, that intellectual questions vanish; nay, the intellect itself is hushed to sleep, — as Wordsworth says, " thought is not; in enjoyment it expires." Ontological emotion so fills the soul that ontological speculation can no longer overlap it and put her girdle of interrogation-marks round existence. Even the least religious of men must have felt with Walt Whitman, when loafing on the grass on some transparent summer morning, that " swiftly arose and spread round him the peace and knowledge that pass all the argument of the earth." At such moments of energetic living we feel as if there were something diseased and contemptible, yea vile, in theoretic grubbing and brooding. In the eye of healthy sense the philosopher is at best a learned fool.

Since the heart can thus wall out the ultimate irrationality which the head ascertains, the erection of its procedure into a systematized method would be a philosophic achievement of first-rate importance. But as used by mystics hitherto it has lacked universality, being available for few persons and at few times, and even in these being apt to be followed by fits of reaction and dryness; and if men should agree that the mystical method is a subterfuge without logical pertinency, a plaster but no cure, and that the idea of nonentity can never be exorcised, empiricism will be the ultimate philosophy. Existence then will be a brute fact to which as a whole the emotion of ontologic wonder shall rightfully cleave, but remain eternally unsatisfied. Then wonderfulness or mysteriousness will be an essential attribute of the nature of things, and the exhibition and emphasizing of it will continue to be an ingredient in the philosophic industry of the race. Every generation will produce its Job, its Hamlet, its Faust, or its Sartor Resartus.

With this we seem to have considered the possibilities of purely theoretic rationality. But we saw at the outset that rationality meant only unimpeded mental function. Impediments that arise in the theoretic sphere might perhaps be avoided if the stream of mental action should leave that sphere betimes and pass into the practical. Let us therefore inquire what constitutes the feeling of rationality in its *practical* aspect. If thought is not to stand forever pointing at the universe in wonder, if its movement is to be diverted from the issueless channel of purely theoretic contemplation, let us ask what conception of the universe will awaken active impulses capable of effecting this diversion. A definition of the world which will give back to the mind the free motion which has been blocked in the purely contemplative path may so far make the world seem rational again.

Well, of two conceptions equally fit to satisfy the logical demand, that one which awakens the active impulses, or satisfies other æsthetic demands better than the other, will be accounted the more rational conception, and will deservedly prevail.

There is nothing improbable in the supposition that an analysis of the world may yield a number of formulæ, all consistent with the facts. In physical science different formulæ may explain the phenomena equally well, — the one-fluid and the two-fluid theories of electricity, for example. Why may it not be so with the world? Why may there not be different points of view for surveying it, within each of which all data harmonize, and which the observer may therefore either choose between, or simply cumulate one upon another? A Beethoven string-quartet is truly, as some one has said, a scraping of horses' tails on cats' bowels, and may be exhaustively described in such terms; but the application of this description in no way precludes the simultaneous applicability of an entirely different description. Just so a thorough-going interpretation of the world in terms of mechanical sequence is compatible with its being interpreted teleologically, for the mechanism itself may be designed.

If, then, there were several systems excogitated, equally satisfying to our purely logical needs, they would still have to be passed in review, and approved or rejected by our æsthetic and practical nature. Can we define the tests of rationality which these parts of our nature would use?

Philosophers long ago observed the remarkable fact that mere familiarity with things is able to produce a feeling of their rationality. The empiricist school has been so much struck by this circumstance as to have laid it down that the feeling of rationality and the feeling of familiarity are one and the same thing, and that no other kind of rationality than this exists. The daily contemplation of phenomena juxtaposed in a certain order begets an acceptance of their connection, as absolute as the repose engendered by theoretic insight into their coherence. To explain a thing is to pass easily back to its antecedents; to know it is easily to foresee its consequents. Custom, which lets us do both, is thus the source of whatever rationality the thing may gain in our thought.

In the broad sense in which rationality was defined at the outset of this essay, it is perfectly apparent that custom must be one of its factors. We said that any perfectly fluent and easy thought was devoid of the sentiment of irrationality. Inasmuch then as custom acquaints us with all the relations of a thing, it teaches us to pass fluently from that thing to others, and *pro tanto* tinges it with the rational character.

Now, there is one particular relation of greater practical importance than all the rest, — I mean the relation of a thing to its future consequences. So long as an object is unusual, our expectations are baffled; they are fully determined as soon as it becomes familiar. I therefore propose this as the first practical requisite which a philosophic conception must satisfy: *It must, in a general way at least, banish uncertainty from the future.* The permanent presence of the sense of futurity in the mind has been strangely ignored by most writers, but the fact is that our consciousness at a given moment is never free from the ingredient of expectancy. Every one knows how when a painful thing has to be undergone in the near future, the vague feeling that it is impending penetrates all our thought with uneasiness and subtly vitiates our mood even when it does not control our attention; it keeps us from being at rest, at home in the given present. The same is true when a great happiness awaits us. But when the future is neutral and perfectly certain, ' we do not mind it,' as we say, but give an undisturbed attention to the actual. Let now this haunting sense of futurity be thrown off its bearings or left without an object, and immediately uneasiness takes possession of the mind. But in every novel or unclassified experience this is just what occurs; we do not know what will come next; and novelty *per se* becomes a mental irritant, while custom *per se* is a mental sedative, merely because the one baffles while the other settles our expectations.

Every reader must feel the truth of this. What is meant by coming ' to feel at home ' in a new place, or with new people? It is simply that, at first, when we take up our quarters in a new room, we do not know what draughts may blow in upon our back, what doors may open, what forms may enter, what interesting objects may be found in cupboards and corners. When after a few days we have learned the range of all these possibilities, the feeling of strangeness disappears. And so it does with people, when we have got past the point of expecting any essentially new manifestations from their character.

The utility of this emotional effect of expectation is perfectly obvious; ' natural selection,' in fact, was bound to bring it about sooner or later. It is of the utmost practical importance to an animal that he should have prevision of the qualities of the objects that surround him, and especially that he should not come to rest in presence of circumstances that might be fraught either with peril or advantage, — go to sleep, for example, on the brink of precipices, in the dens of enemies, or view with indifference some new-appearing object that might, if chased, prove an important addition to the larder. Novelty *ought* to irritate him. All curiosity has thus a practical genesis. We need only look at the physiognomy of a dog or a horse when a new object comes into his view, his mingled fascination and fear, to see that the element of conscious insecurity or perplexed expectation lies at the root of his emotion. A dog's curiosity about the movements of his master or a strange object only extends as far as the point of deciding what is going to happen next. That settled, curiosity is quenched. The dog quoted by Darwin, whose behavior in presence of a newspaper moved by the wind seemed to testify to a sense 'of the supernatural,' was merely exhibiting the irritation of an uncertain future. A newspaper which could move spontaneously was in itself so unexpected that the poor brute could not tell what new wonders the next moment might bring forth.

To turn back now to philosophy. An ultimate datum, even though it be logically unrationalized, will, if its quality is such as to define expectancy, be peacefully accepted by the mind; while if it leave the least opportunity for ambiguity in the future, it will to that extent cause mental uneasiness if not distress. Now, in the ultimate explanations of the universe which the craving for rationality has elicited from the human mind, the demands of expectancy to be satisfied have always played a fundamental part.

The term set up by philosophers as primordial has been one which banishes the incalculable. 'Substance,' for example, means, as Kant says, *das Beharrliche*, which will be as it has been, because its being is essential and eternal. And although we may not be able to prophesy in detail the future phenomena to which the substance shall give rise, we may set our minds at rest in a general way, when we have called the substance God, Perfection, Love, or Reason, by the reflection that whatever is in store for us can never at bottom be inconsistent with the character of this term; so that our attitude even toward the unexpected is in a general sense defined. Take again the notion of immortality, which for common people seems to be the touchstone of every philosophic or religious creed: what is this but a way of saying that the determination of expectancy is the essential factor of rationality? The wrath of science against miracles, of certain philosophers against the doctrine of free-will, has precisely the same root, — dislike to admit any ultimate factor in things which may rout our prevision or upset the stability of our outlook.

Anti-substantialist writers strangely overlook this function in the doctrine of substance: " If there be such a *substratum*," says Mill, "suppose it at this instant miraculously annihilated, and let the sensations continue to occur in the same order, and how would the *substratum* be missed? By what signs should we be able to discover that its existence had terminated? Should we not have as much reason to believe that it still existed as we now have? And if we should not then be warranted in believing it, how can we be so now?" Truly enough, if we have already securely bagged our facts in a certain order, we can dispense with any further warrant for that order. But with regard to the facts yet to come the case is far different. It does not follow that if substance may be dropped from our conception of the irrecoverably past, it need be an equally empty complication to our notions of the future. Even if it were true that, for aught we know to the contrary, the substance might develop at any moment a wholly new set of attributes, the mere logical form of referring things to a substance would still (whether rightly or wrongly) remain accompanied by a feeling of rest and future confidence. In spite of the acutest nihilistic criticism, men will therefore always have a liking for any philosophy which explains things *per substantiam.*

A very natural reaction against the theosophizing conceit and hide-bound confidence in the upshot of things, which vulgarly optimistic minds display, has formed one factor of the scepticism of empiricists, who never cease to remind us of the reservoir of possibilities alien to our habitual experience which the cosmos may contain, and which, for any warrant we have to the contrary, may turn it inside out to-morrow. Agnostic substantialism like that of Mr. Spencer, whose Unknowable is not merely the unfathomable but the absolute-irrational, on which, if consistently represented in thought, it is of course impossible to count, performs the same function of rebuking a certain stagnancy and smugness in the manner in which the ordinary philistine feels his security. But considered as anything else than as reactions against an opposite excess, these philosophies of uncertainty cannot be acceptable; the general mind will fail to come to rest in their presence, and will seek for solutions of a more reassuring kind.

We may then, I think, with perfect confidence lay down as a first point gained in our inquiry, that a prime factor in the philosophic craving is the desire to have expectancy defined; and that no philosophy will definitively triumph which in an emphatic manner denies the possibility of gratifying this need.

We pass with this to the next great division of our topic. It is not sufficient for our satisfaction merely to know the future as determined, for it may be determined in either of many ways, agreeable or disagreeable. For a philosophy to succeed on a universal scale it must define the future *congruously with our spontaneous powers*. A philosophy may be unimpeachable in other respects, but either of two defects will be fatal to its universal acceptance. First, its ultimate principle must not be one that essentially baffles and disappoints our dearest desires and most cherished powers. A pessimistic principle like Schopenhauer's incurably vicious Will-substance, or Hartmann's wicked jack-of-all-trades the Unconscious, will perpetually call forth essays at other philosophies. Incompatibility of the future with their desires and active tendencies is, in fact, to most men a source of more fixed disquietude than uncertainty itself. Witness the attempts to overcome the ' problem of evil,' the ' mystery of pain.' There is no ' problem of good.'

But a second and worse defect in a philosophy than that of contradicting our active propensities is to give them no object whatever to press against. A philosophy whose principle is so incommensurate with our most intimate powers as to deny them all relevancy in universal affairs, as to annihilate their motives at one blow, will be even more unpopular than pessimism. Better face the enemy than the eternal Void! This is why materialism will always fail of universal adoption, however well it may fuse things into an atomistic unity, however clearly it may prophesy the future eternity. For materialism denies reality to the objects of almost all the impulses which we most cherish. The real *meaning* of the impulses, it says, is something which has no emotional interest for us whatever. Now, what is called 'extradition' is quite as characteristic of our emotions as of our senses: both point to an object as the cause of the present feeling. What an intensely objective reference lies in fear! In like manner an enraptured man and a dreary-feeling man are not simply aware of their subjective states; if they were, the force of their feelings would all evaporate. Both believe there is outward cause why they should feel as they do: either, " It is a glad world! how good life is! " or, " What a loathsome tedium is existence! " Any philosophy which annihilates the validity of the reference by explaining away its objects or translating them into terms of no emotional pertinency, leaves the mind with little to care or act for. This is the opposite condition from that of nightmare, but when acutely brought home to consciousness it produces a kindred horror. In nightmare we have motives to act, but no power; here we have powers, but no motives. A nameless *unheimlichkeit* comes over us at the thought of there being nothing eternal in our final purposes, in the objects of those loves and aspirations which are our deepest energies. The monstrously lopsided equation of the universe and its knower, which we postulate as the ideal of cognition, is perfectly paralleled by the no less lopsided equation of the universe and the *doer*. We demand in it a character for which our emotions and active propensities shall be a match. Small as we are, minute as is the point by which the cosmos impinges upon each one of us, each one desires to feel that his reaction at that point is congruous with the demands of the vast whole, — that he balances the latter, so to speak, and is able to do what it expects of him. But as his abilities to do lie wholly in the line of his natural propensities; as he enjoys reacting with such emotions as fortitude, hope, rapture, admiration, earnestness, and the like; and as he very unwillingly reacts with fear, disgust, despair, or doubt, — a philosophy which should only legitimate emotions of the latter sort would be sure to leave the mind a prey to discontent and craving.

It is far too little recognized how entirely the intellect is built up of practical interests. The theory of evolution is beginning to do very good service by its reduction of all mentality to the type of reflex action. Cognition, in this view, is but a fleeting moment, a cross-section at a certain point, of what in its totality is a motor phenomenon. In the lower forms of life no one will pretend that cognition is anything more than a guide to appropriate action. The germinal question concerning things brought for the first time before consciousness is not the theoretic 'What is that?' but the practical 'Who goes there?' or rather, as Horwicz has admirably put it, 'What is to be done?' — 'Was fang' ich an?' In all our discussions about the intelligence of lower animals, the only test we use is that of their *acting* as if for a purpose.

Cognition, in short, is incomplete until discharged in act; and although it is true that the later mental development, which attains its maximum through the hypertrophied cerebrum of man, gives birth to a vast amount of theoretic activity over and above that which is immediately ministerial to practice, yet the earlier claim is only postponed, not effaced, and the active nature asserts its rights to the end.

When the cosmos in its totality is the object offered to consciousness, the relation is in no whit altered. React on it we must in some congenial way. It was a deep instinct in Schopenhauer which led him to reinforce his pessimistic argumentation by a running volley of invective against the practical man and his requirements. No hope for pessimism unless he is slain!

Helmholtz's immortal works on the eye and ear are to a great extent little more than a commentary on the law that practical utility wholly determines which parts of our sensations we shall be aware of, and which parts we shall ignore. We notice or discriminate an ingredient of sense only so far as we depend upon it to modify our actions. We *comprehend* a thing when we synthetize it by identity with another thing. But the other great department of our understanding, *acquaintance* (the two departments being recognized in all languages by the antithesis of such words as *wissen* and *kennen; scire* and *noscere,* etc.) , what is that also but a synthesis, — a synthesis of a passive perception with a certain tendency to reaction? We are acquainted with a thing as soon as we have learned how to behave towards it, or how to meet the behavior which we expect from it. Up to that point it is still ' strange ' to us.

If there be anything at all in this view, it follows that however vaguely a philosopher may define the ultimate universal datum, he cannot be said to leave it unknown to us so long as he in the slightest degree pretends that our emotional or active attitude toward it should be of one sort rather than another. He who says " life is real, life is earnest," however much he may speak of the fundamental mysteriousness of things, gives a distinct definition to that mysteriousness by ascribing to it the right to claim from us the particular mood called seriousness, — which means the willingness to live with energy, though energy bring pain. The same is true of him who says that all is vanity. For indefinable as the predicate ' vanity ' may be *in se,* it is clearly something that permits anæsthesia, mere escape from suffering, to be our rule of life. There can be no greater incongruity than for a disciple of Spencer to proclaim with one breath that the substance of things is unknowable, and with the next that the thought of it should inspire us with awe, reverence, and a willingness to add our co-operative push in the direction toward which its manifestations seem to be drifting. The unknowable may be unfathomed, but if it make such distinct demands upon our activity we surely are not ignorant of its essential quality.

If we survey the field of history and ask what feature all great periods of revival, of expansion of the human mind, display in common, we shall find, I think, simply this: that each and all of them have said to the human being, " The inmost nature of the reality is congenial to *powers* which you possess." In what did the emancipating message of primitive Christianity consist but in the announcement that

God recognizes those weak and tender impulses which paganism had so rudely overlooked? Take repentance: the man who can do nothing rightly can at least repent of his failures. But for paganism this faculty of repentance was a pure supernumerary, a straggler too late for the fair. Christianity took it, and made it the one power within us which appealed straight to the heart of God. And after the night of the middle ages had so long branded with obloquy even the generous impulses of the flesh, and defined the reality to be such that only slavish natures could commune with it, in what did the *sursum corda* of the platonizing renaissance lie but in the proclamation that the archetype of verity in things laid claim on the widest activity of our whole æsthetic being? What were Luther's mission and Wesley's but appeals to powers which even the meanest of men might carry with them, — faith and self-despair, — but which were personal, requiring no priestly intermediation, and which brought their owner face to face with God? What caused the wildfire influence of Rousseau but the assurance he gave that man's nature was in harmony with the nature of things, if only the paralyzing corruptions of custom would stand from between? How did Kant and Fichte, Goethe and Schiller, inspire their time with cheer, except by saying, " Use all your powers; that is the only obedience the universe exacts " ? And Carlyle with his gospel of work, of fact, of veracity, how does he move us except by saying that the universe imposes no tasks upon us but such as the most humble can perform? Emerson's creed that everything that ever was or will be is here in the enveloping now; that man has but to obey himself, — " He who will rest in what he *is*, is a part of destiny," — is in like manner nothing but an exorcism of all scepticism as to the pertinency of one's natural faculties.

In a word, " Son of Man, *stand upon thy feet* and I will speak unto thee!" is the only revelation of truth to which the solving epochs have helped the disciple. But that has been enough to satisfy the greater part of his rational need. *In se* and *per se* the universal essence has hardly been more defined by any of these formulas than by the agnostic x, but the mere assurance that my powers, such as they are, are not irrelevant to it, but pertinent; that it speaks to them and will in some way recognize their reply; that I can be a match for it if I will, and not a footless waif, — suffices to make it rational to my feeling in the sense given above. Nothing could be more absurd than to hope for the definitive triumph of any philosophy which should refuse to legitimate, and to legitimate in an emphatic manner, the more powerful of our emotional and practical tendencies. Fatalism, whose solving word in all crises of behavior is " all striving is vain," will never reign supreme, for the impulse to take life strivingly is indestructible in the race. Moral creeds which speak to that impulse will be widely successful in spite of inconsistency, vagueness, and shadowy determination of expectancy. Man needs a rule for his will, and will invent one if one be not given him.

But now observe a most important consequence. Men's active impulses are so differently mixed that a philosophy fit in this respect for Bismarck will almost certainly be unfit for a valetudinarian poet. In other words, although one can lay down in advance the

rule that a philosophy which utterly denies all fundamental ground for seriousness, for effort, for hope,
which says the nature of things is radically alien to
human nature, can never succeed, — one cannot in
advance say what particular dose of hope, or of gnosticism of the nature of things, the definitely successful
philosophy shall contain. In short, it is almost certain
that personal temperament will here make itself felt,
and that although all men will insist on being spoken
to by the universe in some way, few will insist on being
spoken to in just the same way. We have here, in
short, the sphere of what Matthew Arnold likes to
call *Aberglaube*, legitimate, inexpugnable, yet doomed
to eternal variations and disputes.

Take idealism and materialism as examples of what
I mean, and suppose for a moment that both give a
conception of equal theoretic clearness and consistency, and that both determine our expectations
equally well. Idealism will be chosen by a man of one
emotional constitution, materialism by another. At
this very day all sentimental natures, fond of conciliation and intimacy, tend to an idealistic faith. Why?
Because idealism gives to the nature of things such kinship with our personal selves. Our own thoughts are
what we are most at home with, what we are least
afraid of. To say then that the universe essentially is
thought, is to say that I myself, potentially at least,
am all. There is no radically alien corner, but an all-
pervading *intimacy*. Now, in certain sensitively ego-
tistic minds this conception of reality is sure to put
on a narrow, close, sick-room air. Everything sentimental and priggish will be consecrated by it. That
element in reality which every strong man of common-sense willingly feels there because it calls forth

powers that he owns — the rough, harsh, sea-wave,
north-wind element, the denier of persons, the democ-
ratizer — is banished because it jars too much on the
desire for communion. Now, it is the very enjoyment
of this element that throws many men upon the materialistic or agnostic hypothesis, as a polemic reaction
against the contrary extreme. They sicken at a life
wholly constituted of intimacy. There is an over-
powering desire at moments to escape personality, to
revel in the action of forces that have no respect for
our ego, to let the tides flow, even though they flow
over us. The strife of these two kinds of mental temper will, I think, always be seen in philosophy. Some
men will keep insisting on the reason, the atonement,
that lies in the heart of things, and that we can act
with; others, on the opacity of brute fact that we
must react *against.*

Now, there is one element of our active nature
which the Christian religion has emphatically recognized, but which philosophers as a rule have with
great insincerity tried to huddle out of sight in their
pretension to found systems of absolute certainty. I
mean the element of faith. Faith means belief in
something concerning which doubt is still theoretically possible; and as the test of belief is willingness
to act, one may say that faith is the readiness to act
in a cause the prosperous issue of which is not certified
to us in advance. It is in fact the same moral quality
which we call courage in practical affairs; and there
will be a very widespread tendency in men of vigorous nature to enjoy a certain amount of uncertainty
in their philosophic creed, just as risk lends a zest to
worldly activity. Absolutely certified philosophies

seeking the *inconcussum* are fruits of mental natures in which the passion for identity (which we saw to be but one factor of the rational appetite) plays an abnormally exclusive part. In the average man, on the contrary, the power to trust, to risk a little beyond the literal evidence, is an essential function. Any mode of conceiving the universe which makes an appeal to this generous power, and makes the man seem as if he were individually helping to create the actuality of the truth whose metaphysical reality he is willing to assume, will be sure to be responded to by large numbers.

The necessity of faith as an ingredient in our mental attitude is strongly insisted on by the scientific philosophers of the present day; but by a singularly arbitrary caprice they say that it is only legitimate when used in the interests of one particular proposition, — the proposition, namely, that the course of nature is uniform. That nature will follow to-morrow the same laws that she follows to-day is, they all admit, a truth which no man can *know;* but in the interests of cognition as well as of action we must postulate or assume it. As Helmholtz says: " Hier gilt nur der eine Rath: vertraue und handle! " And Professor Bain urges: " Our only error is in proposing to give any reason or justification of the postulate, or to treat it as otherwise than begged at the very outset."

With regard to all other possible truths, however, a number of our most influential contemporaries think that an attitude of faith is not only illogical but shameful. Faith in a religious dogma for which there is no outward proof, but which we are tempted to postulate for our emotional interests, just as we postulate the uniformity of nature for our intellectual interests, is branded by Professor Huxley as "the lowest depth of immorality." Citations of this kind from leaders of the modern *Aufklärung* might be multiplied almost indefinitely. Take Professor Clifford's article on the 'Ethics of Belief.' He calls it 'guilt' and 'sin' to believe even the truth without 'scientific evidence.' But what is the use of being a genius, unless *with the same scientific evidence* as other men, one can reach more truth than they? Why does Clifford fearlessly proclaim his belief in the conscious-automaton theory, although the 'proofs' before him are the same which make Mr. Lewes reject it? Why does he believe in primordial units of 'mind-stuff' on evidence which would seem quite worthless to Professor Bain? Simply because, like every human being of the slightest mental originality, he is peculiarly sensitive to evidence that bears in some one direction. It is utterly hopeless to try to exorcise such sensitiveness by calling it the disturbing subjective factor, and branding it as the root of all evil. 'Subjective' be it called! and 'disturbing' to those whom it foils! But if it helps those who, as Cicero says, "vim naturæ magis sentiunt," it is good and not evil. Pretend what we may, the whole man within us is at work when we form our philosophical opinions. Intellect, will, taste, and passion co-operate just as they do in practical affairs; and lucky it is if the passion be not something as petty as a love of personal conquest over the philosopher across the way. The absurd abstraction of an intellect verbally formulating all its evidence and carefully estimating the probability thereof by a vulgar fraction by the size of whose denominator and numerator alone it is swayed, is

ideally as inept as it is actually impossible. It is almost incredible that men who are themselves working
philosophers should pretend that any philosophy can
be, or ever has been, constructed without the help of
personal preference, belief, or divination. How have
they succeeded in so stultifying their sense for the living facts of human nature as not to perceive that every
philosopher, or man of science either, whose initiative
counts for anything in the evolution of thought, has
taken his stand on a sort of dumb conviction that the
truth must lie in one direction rather than another,
and a sort of preliminary assurance that his notion
can be made to work; and has borne his best fruit
in trying to make it work? These mental instincts
in different men are the spontaneous variations upon
which the intellectual struggle for existence is based.
The fittest conceptions survive, and with them the
names of their champions shining to all futurity.

The coil is about us, struggle as we may. The
only escape from faith is mental nullity. What we
enjoy most in a Huxley or a Clifford is not the professor with his learning, but the human personality
ready to go in for what it feels to be right, in spite of
all appearances. The concrete man has but one interest — to be right. That for him is the art of all arts,
and all means are fair which help him to it. Naked
he is flung into the world, and between him and nature there are no rules of civilized warfare. The rules
of the scientific game, burdens of proof, presumptions,
experimenta crucis, complete inductions, and the like,
are only binding on those who enter that game. As a
matter of fact we all more or less do enter it, because
it helps us to our end. But if the means presume to
frustrate the end and call us cheats for being right in

advance of their slow aid, by guesswork or by hook or crook, what shall we say of them? Were all of Clifford's works, except the Ethics of Belief, forgotten, he might well figure in future treatises on psychology in place of the somewhat threadbare instance of the miser who has been led by the association of ideas to prefer his gold to all the goods he might buy therewith.

In short, if I am born with such a superior general reaction to evidence that I can guess right and act accordingly, and gain all that comes of right action, while my less gifted neighbor (paralyzed by his scruples and waiting for more evidence which he dares not anticipate, much as he longs to) still stands shivering on the brink, by what law shall I be forbidden to reap the advantages of my superior native sensitiveness? Of course I yield to my belief in such a case as this or distrust it, alike at my peril, just as I do in any of the great practical decisions of life. If my inborn faculties are good, I am a prophet; if poor, I am a failure: nature spews me out of her mouth, and there is an end to me. In the total game of life we stake our persons all the while; and if in its theoretic part our persons will help us to a conclusion, surely we should also stake them here, however inarticulate they may be.*

---

* At most, the command laid upon us by science to believe nothing not yet verified by the senses is a prudential rule intended to maximize our right thinking and minimize our errors *in the long run*. In the particular instance we must frequently lose truth by obeying it; but on the whole we are safer if we follow it consistently, for we are sure to cover our losses with our gains. It is like those gambling and insurance rules based on probability, in which we secure ourselves against losses in detail by hedging on the total run. But this hedging philosophy requires that long run should be there; and this makes it inap-

But in being myself so very articulate in proving what to all readers with a sense for reality will seem a platitude, am I not wasting words? We cannot live or think at all without some degree of faith. Faith is synonymous with working hypothesis. The only difference is that while some hypotheses can be refuted in five minutes, others may defy ages. A chemist who conjectures that a certain wall-paper contains arsenic, and has faith enough to lead him to take the trouble to put some of it into a hydrogen bottle, finds out by the results of his action whether he was right or wrong. But theories like that of Darwin, or that of the kinetic constitution of matter, may exhaust the labors of generations in their corroboration, each tester of their truth proceeding in this simple way, — that he acts as if it were true, and expects the result to disappoint him if his assumption is false. The longer disappointment is delayed, the stronger grows his faith in his theory.

Now, in such questions as God, immortality, absolute morality, and free-will, no non-papal believer at the present day pretends his faith to be of an essentially different complexion; he can always doubt his creed. But his intimate persuasion is that the odds in its favor are strong enough to warrant him in acting all along on the assumption of its truth. His corroboration or repudiation by the nature of things may be deferred until the day of judgment. The

plicable to the question of religious faith as the latter comes home to the individual man. He plays the game of life not to escape losses, for he brings nothing with him to lose; he plays it for gains; and it is now or never with him, for the long run which exists indeed for humanity, is not there for him. Let him doubt, believe, or deny, he runs his risk, and has the natural right to choose which one it shall be.

uttermost he now means is something like this: " I *expect* then to triumph with tenfold glory; but if it should turn out, as indeed it may, that I have spent my days in a fool's paradise, why, better have been the dupe of *such* a dreamland than the cunning reader of a world like that which then beyond all doubt unmasks itself to view." In short, we *go in* against materialism very much as we should *go in,* had we a chance, against the second French empire or the Church of Rome, or any other system of things toward which our repugnance is vast enough to determine energetic action, but too vague to issue in distinct argumentation. Our reasons are ludicrously incommensurate with the volume of our feeling, yet on the latter we unhesitatingly act.

Now, I wish to show what to my knowledge has never been clearly pointed out, that belief (as measured by action) not only does and must continually outstrip scientific evidence, but that there is a certain class of truths of whose reality belief is a factor as well as a confessor; and that as regards this class of truths faith is not only licit and pertinent, but essential and indispensable. The truths cannot become true till our faith has made them so.

Suppose, for example, that I am climbing in the Alps, and have had the ill-luck to work myself into a position from which the only escape is by a terrible leap. Being without similar experience, I have no evidence of my ability to perform it successfully; but hope and confidence in myself make me sure I shall not miss my aim, and nerve my feet to execute what without those subjective emotions would perhaps have been impossible. But suppose that, on the contrary, the emotions of fear and mistrust preponderate; or suppose that, having just read the Ethics of Belief, I feel it would be sinful to act upon an assumption unverified by previous experience, — why, then I shall hesitate so long that at last, exhausted and trembling, and launching myself in a moment of despair, I miss my foothold and roll into the abyss. In this case (and it is one of an immense class) the part of wisdom clearly is to believe what one desires; for the belief is one of the indispensable preliminary conditions of the realization of its object. *There are then cases where faith creates its own verification.* Believe, and you shall be right, for you shall save yourself; doubt, and you shall again be right, for you shall perish. The only difference is that to believe is greatly to your advantage.

The future movements of the stars or the facts of past history are determined now once for all, whether I like them or not. They are given irrespective of my wishes, and in all that concerns truths like these subjective preference should have no part; it can only obscure the judgment. But in every fact into which there enters an element of personal contribution on my part, as soon as this personal contribution demands a certain degree of subjective energy which, in its turn, calls for a certain amount of faith in the result, — so that, after all, the future fact is conditioned by my present faith in it, — how trebly asinine would it be for me to deny myself the use of the subjective method, the method of belief based on desire!

In every proposition whose bearing is universal (and such are all the propositions of philosophy), the acts of the subject and their consequences throughout eternity should be included in the formula. If *M* represent the entire world *minus* the reaction of the thinker upon it, and if $M + x$ represent the absolutely total matter of philosophic propositions (x standing for the thinker's reaction and its results), — what would be a universal truth if the term x were of one complexion, might become egregious error if x altered its character. Let it not be said that x is too infinitesimal a component to change the character of the immense whole in which it lies imbedded. Everything depends on the point of view of the philosophic proposition in question. If we have to define the universe from the point of view of sensibility, the critical material for our judgment lies in the animal kingdom, insignificant as that is, quantitatively considered. The moral definition of the world may depend on phenomena more restricted still in range. In short, many a long phrase may have its sense reversed by the addition of three letters, *n-o-t;* many a monstrous mass have its unstable equilibrium discharged one way or the other by a feather weight that falls.

Let us make this clear by a few examples. The philosophy of evolution offers us to-day a new criterion to serve as an ethical test between right and wrong. Previous criteria, it says, being subjective, have left us still floundering in variations of opinion and the *status belli.* Here is a criterion which is objective and fixed: *That is to be called good which is destined to prevail or survive.* But we immediately see that this standard can only remain objective by leaving myself and my conduct out. If what prevails and survives does so by my help, and cannot do so without that help; if something else will prevail in case I alter my conduct, — how can I possibly now, conscious of alternative courses of action open before me, either of which I may suppose capable of altering the path of events, decide which course to take by asking what path events will follow? If they follow my direction, evidently my direction cannot wait on them. The only possible manner in which an evolutionist can use his standard is the obsequious method of forecasting the course society would take *but for him,* and then putting an extinguisher on all personal idiosyncrasies of desire and interest, and with bated breath and tiptoe tread following as straight as may be at the tail, and bringing up the rear of everything. Some pious creatures may find a pleasure in this; but not only does it violate our general wish to lead and not to follow (a wish which is surely not immoral if we but lead aright), but if it be treated as every ethical principle must be treated, — namely, as a rule good for all men alike, — its general observance would lead to its practical refutation by bringing about a general deadlock. Each good man hanging back and waiting for orders from the rest, absolute stagnation would ensue. Happy, then, if a few unrighteous ones contribute an initiative which sets things moving again!

All this is no caricature. That the course of destiny may be altered by individuals no wise evolutionist ought to doubt. Everything for him has small beginnings, has a bud which may be 'nipped,' and nipped by a feeble force. Human races and tendencies follow the law, and have also small beginnings. The best, according to evolution, is that which has the biggest endings. Now, if a present race of men, enlightened in the evolutionary philosophy, and able to forecast the future, were able to discern in a tribe arising near them the potentiality of future supremacy; were able to see that their own

race would eventually be wiped out of existence by
the new-comers if the expansion of these were left
unmolested, — these present sages would have two
courses open to them, either perfectly in harmony
with the evolutionary test: Strangle the new race
now, and ours survives; help the new race, and *it*
survives.   In both cases the action is right as measured by the evolutionary standard, — it is action for
the winning side.

Thus the evolutionist foundation of ethics is purely
objective only to the herd of nullities whose votes
count for zero in the march of events.   But for others,
leaders of opinion or potentates, and in general those
to whose actions position or genius gives a far-reaching
import, and to the rest of us, each in his measure, —
whenever we espouse a cause we contribute to the determination of the evolutionary standard of right.
The truly wise disciple of this school will then admit
faith as an ultimate ethical factor.   Any philosophy
which makes such questions as, What is the ideal type
of humanity?   What shall be reckoned virtues?   What
conduct is good? depend on the question, What is
going to succeed? — must needs fall back on personal
belief as one of the ultimate conditions of the truth.
For again and again success depends on energy of
act; energy again depends on faith that we shall not
fail; and that faith in turn on the faith that we are
right, — which faith thus verifies itself.

Take as an example the question of optimism or
pessimism, which makes so much noise just now in
Germany.   Every human being must sometime decide for himself whether life is worth living.   Suppose that in looking at the world and seeing how
full it is of misery, of old age, of wickedness and

pain, and how unsafe is his own future, he yields to
the pessimistic conclusion, cultivates disgust and
dread, ceases striving, and finally commits suicide. He
thus adds to the mass M of mundane phenomena, independent of his subjectivity, the subjective complement x, which makes of the whole an utterly black
picture illumined by no gleam of good. Pessimism
completed, verified by his moral reaction and the deed
in which this ends, is true beyond a doubt. $M + x$
expresses a state of things totally bad. The man's
belief supplied all that was lacking to make it so, and
now that it is made so the belief was right.

But now suppose that with the same evil facts M,
the man's reaction x is exactly reversed; suppose
that instead of giving way to the evil he braves it,
and finds a sterner, more wonderful joy than any
passive pleasure can yield in triumphing over pain and
defying fear; suppose he does this successfully, and
however thickly evils crowd upon him proves his
dauntless subjectivity to be more than their match, —
will not every one confess that the bad character of
the M is here the *conditio sine qua non* of the good
character of the x? Will not every one instantly declare a world fitted only for fair-weather human beings susceptible of every passive enjoyment, but without independence, courage, or fortitude, to be from
a moral point of view incommensurably inferior to a
world framed to elicit from the man every form of
triumphant endurance and conquering moral energy?
As James Hinton says, —

" Little inconveniences, exertions, pains, — these are
the only things in which we rightly feel our life at all.
If these be not there, existence becomes worthless, or
worse; success in putting them all away is fatal. So it

is men engage in athletic sports, spend their holidays in climbing up mountains, find nothing so enjoyable as that which taxes their endurance and their energy. This is the way we are made, I say. It may or may not be a mystery or a paradox; it is a fact. Now, this enjoyment in endurance is just according to the intensity of life: the more physical vigor and balance, the more endurance can be made an element of satisfaction. A sick man cannot stand it. The line of enjoyable suffering is not a fixed one; it fluctuates with the perfectness of the life. That our pains are, as they are, unendurable, awful, overwhelming, crushing, not to be borne save in misery and dumb impatience, which utter exhaustion alone makes patient, — that our pains are thus unendurable, means not that they are too great, but that *we are sick*. We have not got our proper life. So you perceive pain is no more necessarily an evil, but an essential element of the highest good." *

But the highest good can be achieved only by our getting our proper life; and that can come about only by help of a moral energy born of the faith that in some way or other we shall succeed in getting it if we try pertinaciously enough. This world *is* good, we must say, since it is what we make it, — and we shall make it good. How can we exclude from the cognition of a truth of faith which is involved in the creation of the truth? *M* has its character indeterminate, susceptible of forming part of a thoroughgoing pessimism on the one hand, or of a meliorism, a moral (as distinguished from a sensual) optimism on the other. All depends on the character of the

* Life of James Hinton, pp. 172, 173. See also the excellent chapter on Faith and Sight in the Mystery of Matter, by J. Allanson Picton. Hinton's Mystery of Pain will undoubtedly always remain the classical utterance on this subject.

personal contribution *x*. Wherever the facts to be formulated contain such a contribution, we may logically, legitimately, and inexpugnably believe what we desire. The belief creates its verification. The thought becomes literally father to the fact, as the wish was father to the thought.*

Let us now turn to the radical question of life, — the question whether this be at bottom a moral or an unmoral universe, — and see whether the method of faith may legitimately have a place there. It is really the question of materialism. Is the world a simple brute actuality, an existence *de facto* about which the deepest thing that can be said is that it happens so to be; or is the judgment of *better* or *worse*, of *ought*, as intimately pertinent to phenomena as the simple judgment *is* or *is not?* The materialistic theorists say that judgments of worth are themselves mere matters of fact; that the words ' good ' and ' bad ' have no sense apart from subjective passions and interests which we may, if we please, play fast and loose with at will, so far as any duty of ours to the non-human universe is concerned. Thus, when a materialist says it is better for him to suffer great inconvenience than to break a promise, he only means that his social interests have become so knit up with keeping faith that, those interests once being granted,

* Observe that in all this not a word has been said of free-will. It all applies as well to a predetermined as to an indeterminate universe. If $M + x$ is fixed in advance, the belief which leads to x and the desire which prompts the belief are also fixed. But fixed or not, these subjective states form a phenomenal condition necessarily preceding the facts; necessarily constitutive, therefore, of the truth $M + x$ which we seek. If, however, free acts be possible, a faith in their possibility, by augmenting the moral energy which gives them birth, will increase their frequency in a given individual.

it *is* better for him to keep the promise in spite of everything. But the interests themselves are neither right nor wrong, except possibly with reference to some ulterior order of interests which themselves again are mere subjective data without character, either good or bad.

For the absolute moralists, on the contrary, the interests are not there merely to be felt, — they are to be believed in and obeyed. Not only is it best for my social interests to keep my promise, but best for me to have those interests, and best for the cosmos to have this me. Like the old woman in the story who described the world as resting on a rock, and then explained that rock to be supported by another rock, and finally when pushed with questions said it was rocks all the way down, — he who believes this to be a radically moral universe must hold the moral order to rest either on an absolute and ultimate *should,* or on a series of *shoulds* all the way down.*

The practical difference between this objective sort of moralist and the other one is enormous. The subjectivist in morals, when his moral feelings are at war with the facts about him, is always free to seek harmony by toning down the sensitiveness of the feelings. Being mere data, neither good nor evil in themselves, he may pervert them or lull them to sleep by any means at his command. Truckling, compromise, time-serving, capitulations of conscience, are conventionally opprobrious names for what, if successfully carried

---

* In either case, as a later essay explains (see p. 193), the *should* which the moralist regards as binding upon *him* must be rooted in the feeling of some other thinker, or collection of thinkers, to whose demands he individually bows.

out, would be on his principles by far the easiest and most praiseworthy mode of bringing about that harmony between inner and outer relations which is all that he means by good. The absolute moralist, on the other hand, when his interests clash with the world, is not free to gain harmony by sacrificing the ideal interests. According to him, these latter should be as they are and not otherwise. Resistance then, poverty, martyrdom if need be, tragedy in a word, — such are the solemn feasts of his inward faith. Not that the contradiction between the two men occurs every day; in commonplace matters all moral schools agree. It is only in the lonely emergencies of life that our creed is tested: then routine maxims fail, and we fall back on our gods. It cannot then be said that the question, Is this a moral world? is a meaningless and unverifiable question because it deals with something non-phenomenal. Any question is full of meaning to which, as here, contrary answers lead to contrary behavior. And it seems as if in answering such a question as this we might proceed exactly as does the physical philosopher in testing an hypothesis. He deduces from the hypothesis an experimental action, x; this he adds to the facts M already existing. It fits them if the hypothesis be true; if not, there is discord. The results of the action corroborate or refute the idea from which it flowed. So here: the verification of the theory which you may hold as to the objectively moral character of the world can consist only in this, — that if you proceed to act upon your theory it will be reversed by nothing that later turns up as your action's fruit; it will harmonize so well with the entire drift of experience that the latter will, as it were, adopt it, or at most give it an ampler interpretation, without obliging you in any way to change the essence of its formulation. If this be an objectively moral universe, all acts that I make on that assumption, all expectations that I ground on it, will tend more and more completely to interdigitate with the phenomena already existing. $M + x$ will be in accord; and the more I live, and the more the fruits of my activity come to light, the more satisfactory the consensus will grow. While if it be not such a moral universe, and I mistakenly assume that it is, the course of experience will throw ever new impediments in the way of my belief, and become more and more difficult to express in its language. Epicycle upon epicycle of subsidiary hypothesis will have to be invoked to give to the discrepant terms a temporary appearance of squaring with each other; but at last even this resource will fail.

If, on the other hand, I rightly assume the universe to be not moral, in what does my verification consist? It is that by letting moral interests sit lightly, by disbelieving that there is any duty about *them* (since duty obtains only as *between* them and other phenomena) , and so throwing them over if I find it hard to get them satisfied, — it is that by refusing to take up a tragic attitude, I deal in the long-run most satisfactorily with the facts of life. " All is vanity " is here the last word of wisdom. Even though in certain limited series there may be a great appearance of seriousness, he who in the main treats things with a degree of good-natured scepticism and radical levity will find that the practical fruits of his epicurean hypothesis verify it more and more, and not only save him from pain but do honor to his sagacity. While, on the other hand, he who contrary to reality stiffens himself in the notion that certain things absolutely should be, and rejects the truth that at bottom it makes no difference what is, will find himself evermore thwarted and perplexed and be-muddled by the facts of the world, and his tragic disappointment will, as experience accumulates, seem to drift farther and farther away from that final atonement or reconciliation which certain partial tragedies often get.

Anæsthesia is the watchword of the moral sceptic brought to bay and put to his trumps. *Energy* is that of the moralist. Act on my creed, cries the latter, and the results of your action will prove the creed true, and that the nature of things is earnest infinitely. Act on mine, says the epicurean, and the results will prove that seriousness is but a superficial glaze upon a world of fundamentally trivial import. You and your acts and the nature of things will be alike enveloped in a single formula, a universal *vanitas vanitatum*.

For the sake of simplicity I have written as if the verification might occur in the life of a single philosopher, — which is manifestly untrue, since the theories still face each other, and the facts of the world give countenance to both. Rather should we expect, that, in a question of this scope, the experience of the entire human race must make the verification, and that all the evidence will not be ' in ' till the final integration of things, when the last man has had his say and contributed his share to the still unfinished x. Then the proof will be complete; then it will appear without doubt whether the moralistic x has filled up the gap which alone kept the M of the world from forming an even and harmonious unity, or whether the non-moralistic *x* has given the finishing touches which were alone needed to make the *M* appear outwardly as vain as it inwardly was.

But if this be so, is it not clear that the facts *M*, taken *per se*, are inadequate to justify a conclusion either way in advance of my action? My action is the complement which, by proving congruous or not, reveals the latent nature of the mass to which it is applied. The world may in fact be likened unto a lock, whose inward nature, moral or unmoral, will never reveal itself to our simply expectant gaze. The positivists, forbidding us to make any assumptions regarding it, condemn us to eternal ignorance, for the 'evidence' which they wait for can never come so long as we are passive. But nature has put into our hands two keys, by which we may test the lock. If we try the moral key *and it fits,* it is a moral lock. If we try the unmoral key and *it* fits, it is an unmoral lock. I cannot possibly conceive of any other sort of 'evidence' or 'proof' than this. It is quite true that the co-operation of generations is needed to educe it. But in these matters the solidarity (so called) of the human race is a patent fact. The essential thing to notice is that our active preference is a legitimate part of the game, — that it is our plain business as men to try one of the keys, and the one in which we most confide. If then the proof exist not till I have acted, and I must needs in acting run the risk of being wrong, how can the popular science professors be right in objurgating in me as infamous a 'credulity' which the strict logic of the situation requires? If this really be a moral universe; if by my acts I be a factor of its destinies; if to believe where I may doubt be itself a moral act

analogous to voting for a side not yet sure to win,
— by what right shall they close in upon me and
steadily negate the deepest conceivable function of
my being by their preposterous command that I
shall stir neither hand nor foot, but remain balancing
myself in eternal and insoluble doubt? Why, doubt
itself is a decision of the widest practical reach, if
only because we may miss by doubting what goods
we might be gaining by espousing the winning side.
But more than that! it is often practically impossible
to distinguish doubt from dogmatic negation. If I
refuse to stop a murder because I am in doubt
whether it be not justifiable homicide, I am virtually
abetting the crime. If I refuse to bale out a boat
because I am in doubt whether my efforts will keep
her afloat, I am really helping to sink her. If in the
mountain precipice I doubt my right to risk a leap,
I actively connive at my destruction. He who commands himself not to be credulous of God, of duty,
of freedom, of immortality, may again and again be
indistinguishable from him who dogmatically denies
them. Scepticism in moral matters is an active ally
of immorality. Who is not for is against. The universe will have no neutrals in these questions. In
theory as in practice, dodge or hedge, or talk as we
like about a wise scepticism, we are really doing vol-
unteer military service for one side or the other.

Yet obvious as this necessity practically is, thousands of innocent magazine readers lie paralyzed and
terrified in the network of shallow negations which
the leaders of opinion have thrown over their souls.
All they need to be free and hearty again in the
exercise of their birthright is that these fastidious
vetoes should be swept away. All that the human

heart wants is its chance. It will willingly forego certainty in universal matters if only it can be allowed to feel that in them it has that same inalienable right to run risks, which no one dreams of refusing to it in the pettiest practical affairs. And if I, in these last pages, like the mouse in the fable, have gnawed a few of the strings of the sophistical net that has been binding down its lion-strength, I shall be more than rewarded for my pains.

To sum up: No philosophy will permanently be deemed rational by all men which (in addition to meeting logical demands) does not to some degree pretend to determine expectancy, and in a still greater degree make a direct appeal to all those powers of our nature which we hold in highest esteem. Faith, being one of these powers, will always remain a factor not to be banished from philosophic constructions, the more so since in many ways it brings forth its own verification. In these points, then, it is hopeless to look for literal agreement among mankind.

The ultimate philosophy, we may therefore conclude, must not be too strait-laced in form, must not in all its parts divide heresy from orthodoxy by too sharp a line. There must be left over and above the propositions to be subscribed, *ubique, semper, et ab omnibus,* another realm into which the stifled soul may escape from pedantic scruples and indulge its own faith at its own risks; and all that can here be done will be to mark out distinctly the questions which fall within faith's sphere.

REFLEX ACTION AND THEISM *

MEMBERS OF THE MINISTERS' INSTITUTE:

LET me confess to the diffidence with which I find myself standing here to-day. When the invitation of your committee reached me last fall, the simple truth is that I accepted it as most men accept a challenge, — not because they wish to fight, but because they are ashamed to say no. Pretending in my small sphere to be a teacher, I felt it would be cowardly to shrink from the keenest ordeal to which a teacher can be exposed, — the ordeal of teaching other teachers. Fortunately, the trial will last but one short hour; and I have the consolation of remembering Goethe's verses, —

> " Vor den Wissenden sich stellen,
> Sicher ist's in allen Fällen," —

for if experts are the hardest people to satisfy, they have at any rate the liveliest sense of the difficulties of one's task, and they know quickest when one hits the mark.

Since it was as a teacher of physiology that I was most unworthily officiating when your committee's in-

---

* Address delivered to the Unitarian Ministers' Institute at Princeton, Mass., 1881, and printed in the Unitarian Review for October of that year.

vitation reached me, I must suppose it to be for the sake of bringing a puff of the latest winds of doctrine which blow over that somewhat restless sea that my presence is desired. Among all the healthy symptoms that characterize this age, I know no sounder one than the eagerness which theologians show to assimilate results of science, and to hearken to the conclusions of men of sciénce about universal matters. One runs a better chance of being listened to to-day if one can quote Darwin and Helmholtz than if one can only quote Schleiermacher or Coleridge. I almost feel myself this moment that were I to produce a frog and put him through his physiological performances in a masterly manner before your eyes, I should gain more reverential ears for what I have to say during the remainder of the hour. I will not ask whether there be not something of mere fashion in this prestige which the words of the physiologists enjoy just now. If it be a fashion, it is certainly a beneficial one upon the whole; and to challenge it would come with a poor grace from one who at the moment he speaks is so conspicuously profiting by its favors.

I will therefore only say this: that the *latest* breeze from the physiological horizon need not necessarily be the most important one. Of the immense amount of work which the laboratories of Europe and America, and one may add of Asia and Australia, are producing every year, much is destined to speedy refutation; and of more it may be said that its interest is purely technical, and not in any degree philosophical or universal.

This being the case, I know you will justify me if I fall back on a doctrine which is fundamental and well established rather than novel, and ask you whether

by taking counsel together we may not trace some
new consequences from it which shall interest us all
alike as men.   I refer to the doctrine of reflex action,
especially as extended to the brain.   This is, of course,
so familiar to you that I hardly need define it.   In a
general way, all educated people know what reflex
action means.

It means that the acts we perform are always the
result of outward discharges from the nervous centres, and that these outward discharges are themselves
the result of impressions from the external world, carried in along one or another of our sensory nerves.
Applied at first to only a portion of our acts, this
conception has ended by being generalized more
and more, so that now most physiologists tell us
that every action whatever, even the most deliberately
weighed and calculated, does, so far as its organic
conditions go, follow the reflex type.   There is not
one which cannot be remotely, if not immediately,
traced to an origin in some incoming impression of
sense.   There is no impression of sense which, unless
inhibited by some other stronger one, does not immediately or remotely express itself in action of some
kind.   There is no one of those complicated performances in the convolutions of the brain to which our
trains of thought correspond, which is not a mere
middle term interposed between an incoming sensation that arouses it and an outgoing discharge of some
sort, inhibitory if not exciting, to which itself gives
rise.   The structural unit of the nervous system is in
fact a triad, neither of whose elements has any independent existence.   The sensory impression exists
only for the sake of awaking the central process of
reflection, and the central process of reflection exists

only for the sake of calling forth the final act. All action is thus *re*-action upon the outer world; and the middle stage of consideration or contemplation or thinking is only a place of transit, the bottom of a loop, both whose ends have their point of application in the outer world. If it should ever have no roots in the outer world, if it should ever happen that it led to no active measures, it would fail of its essential function, and would have to be considered either pathological or abortive. The current of life which runs in at our eyes or ears is meant to run out at our hands, feet, or lips. The only use of the thoughts it occasions while inside is to determine its direction to whichever of these organs shall, on the whole, under the circumstances actually present, act in the way most propitious to our welfare.

The willing department of our nature, in short, dominates both the conceiving department and the feeling department; or, in plainer English, perception and thinking are only there for behavior's sake.

I am sure I am not wrong in stating this result as one of the fundamental conclusions to which the entire drift of modern physiological investigation sweeps us. If asked what great contribution physiology has made to psychology of late years, I am sure every competent authority will reply that her influence has in no way been so weighty as in the copious illustration, verification, and consolidation of this broad, general point of view.

I invite you, then, to consider what may be the possible speculative consequences involved in this great achievement of our generation. Already, it dominates all the new work done in psychology; but

what I wish to ask is whether its influence may not
extend far beyond the limits of psychology, even into
those of theology herself. The relations of the doctrine of reflex action with no less a matter than the
doctrine of theism is, in fact, the topic to which I now
invite your attention.

We are not the first in the field. There have not
been wanting writers enough to say that reflex action
and all that follows from it give the *coup de grâce* to
the superstition of a God.

If you open, for instance, such a book on comparative psychology, as der Thierische Wille of G. H.
Schneider, you will find, sandwiched in among the
admirable dealings of the author with his proper subject, and popping out upon us in unexpected places,
the most delightfully *naïf* German onslaughts on the
degradation of theologians, and the utter incompatibility of so many reflex adaptations to the environment with the existence of a creative intelligence.
There was a time, remembered by many of us here,
when the existence of reflex action and all the other
harmonies between the organism and the world were
held to prove a God. Now, they are held to disprove
him. The next turn of the whirligig may bring back
proof of him again.

Into this debate about his existence, I will not pretend to enter. I must take up humbler ground, and
limit my ambition to showing that a God, whether
existent or not, is at all events the kind of being
which, if he did exist, would form *the most adequate
possible object* for minds framed like our own to conceive as lying at the root of the universe. My thesis,
in other words, is this: that *some* outward reality of

a nature defined as God's nature must be defined, is the only ultimate object that is at the same time rational and possible for the human mind's contemplation. *Anything short of God is not rational, anything more than God is not possible,* if the human mind be in truth the triadic structure of impression, reflection, and reaction which we at the outset allowed.

Theism, whatever its objective warrant, would thus be seen to have a subjective anchorage in its congruity with our nature as thinkers; and, however it may fare with its truth, to derive from this subjective adequacy the strongest possible guaranty of its permanence. It is and will be the classic mean of rational opinion, the centre of gravity of all attempts to solve the riddle of life, — some falling below it by defect, some flying above it by excess, itself alone satisfying every mental need in strictly normal measure. Our gain will thus in the first instance be psychological. We shall merely have investigated a chapter in the natural history of the mind, and found that, as a matter of such natural history, God may be called the normal object of the mind's belief. Whether over and above this he be really the living truth is another question. If he is, it will show the structure of our mind to be in accordance with the nature of reality. Whether it be or not in such accordance is, it seems to me, one of those questions that belong to the province of personal faith to decide. I will not touch upon the question here, for I prefer to keep to the strictly natural-history point of view. I will only remind you that each one of us is entitled either to doubt or to believe in the harmony between his faculties and the truth; and that, whether he doubt or believe, he does it alike on his personal responsibility and risk.

> " Du musst glauben, du musst wagen,
>   Denn die Götter leihn kein Pfand,
>   Nur ein Wunder kann dich tragen
>   In das schöne Wunderland."

I will presently define exactly what I mean by God and by Theism, and explain what theories I referred to when I spoke just now of attempts to fly beyond the one and to outbid the other.

But, first of all, let me ask you to linger a moment longer over what I have called the reflex theory of mind, so as to be sure that we understand it absolutely before going on to consider those of its consequences of which I am more particularly to speak. I am not quite sure that its full scope is grasped even by those who have most zealously promulgated it. I am not sure, for example, that all physiologists see that it commits them to regarding the mind as an essentially teleological mechanism. I mean by this that the conceiving or theorizing faculty — the mind's middle department — functions *exclusively for the sake of ends* that do not exist at all in the world of impressions we receive by way of our senses, but are set by our emotional and practical subjectivity altogether.* It is a transformer of the world of our impressions into a totally different world, — the world of our conception; and the transformation is effected in the interests of our volitional nature, and for no other purpose whatsoever. Destroy the volitional nature, the definite subjective purposes, preferences, fond-

* See some Remarks on Spencer's Definition of Mind, in the *Journal of Speculative Philosophy* for January, 1878.

nesses for certain effects, forms, orders, and not the slightest motive would remain for the brute order of our experience to be remodelled at all. But, as we have the elaborate volitional constitution we do have, the remodelling must be effected; there is no escape. The world's contents are *given* to each of us in an order so foreign to our subjective interests that we can hardly by an effort of the imagination picture to ourselves what it is like. We have to break that order altogether, — and by picking out from it the items which concern us, and connecting them with others far away, which we say ' belong ' with them, we are able to make out definite threads of sequence and tendency; to foresee particular liabilities and get ready for them; and to enjoy simplicity and harmony in place of what was chaos. Is not the sum of your actual experience taken at this moment and impartially added together an utter chaos? The strains of my voice, the lights and shades inside the room and out, the murmur of the wind, the ticking of the clock, the various organic feelings you may happen individually to possess, do these make a whole at all? Is it not the only condition of your mental sanity in the midst of them that most of them should become non-existent for you, and that a few others — the sounds, I hope, which I am uttering — should evoke from places in your memory that have nothing to do with this scene associates fitted to combine with them in what we call a rational train of thought, — rational, because it leads to a conclusion which we have some organ to appreciate? We have no organ or faculty to appreciate the simply given order. The real world as it is given objectively at this moment is the sum total of all its beings and

events now. But can we think of such a sum? Can
we realize for an instant what a cross-section of all
existence at a definite point of time would be? While
I talk and the flies buzz, a sea-gull catches a fish at
the mouth of the Amazon, a tree falls in the Adirondack wilderness, a man sneezes in Germany, a horse
dies in Tartary, and twins are born in France. What
does that mean? Does the contemporaneity of these
events with one another and with a million others as
disjointed, form a rational bond between them, and
unite them into anything that means for us a world?
Yet just such a collateral contemporaneity, and nothing else, is the real order of the world. It is an order
with which we have nothing to do but to get away
from it as fast as possible. As I said, we break it:
we break it into histories, and we break it into arts,
and we break it into sciences; and then we begin to
feel at home. We make ten thousand separate serial
orders of it, and on any one of these we react as
though the others did not exist. We discover among
its various parts relations that were never given to
sense at all (mathematical relations, tangents, squares,
and roots and logarithmic functions) , and out of an
infinite number of these we call certain ones essential
and lawgiving, and ignore the rest. Essential these
relations are, but only *for our purpose,* the other relations being just as real and present as they; and our
purpose is to *conceive simply* and to *foresee.* Are not
simple conception and prevision subjective ends pure
and simple? They are the ends of what we call
science; and the miracle of miracles, a miracle not
yet exhaustively cleared up by any philosophy, is
that the given order lends itself to the remodelling.
It shows itself plastic to many of our scientific, to

many of our æsthetic, to many of our practical purposes and ends.

When the man of affairs, the artist, or the man of science fails, he is not rebutted. He tries again. He says the impressions of sense *must* give way, *must* be reduced to the desiderated form.* They all postulate in the interests of their volitional nature a harmony between the latter and the nature of things. The theologian does no more. And the reflex doctrine of the mind's structure, though all theology should as yet have failed of its endeavor, could but confess that the endeavor itself at least obeyed in form the mind's most necessary law.†

Now for the question I asked above: What kind of a being would God be if he did exist? The word ' God ' has come to mean many things in the history

---

* "No amount of failure in the attempt to subject the world of sensible experience to a thorough-going system of conceptions, and to bring all happenings back to cases of immutably valid law, is able to shake our faith in the rightness of our principles. We hold fast to our demand that even the greatest apparent confusion must sooner or later solve itself in transparent formulas. We begin the work ever afresh; and, refusing to believe that nature will permanently withhold the reward of our exertions, think rather that we have hitherto only failed to push them in the right direction. And all this pertinacity flows from a conviction that we *have no right* to renounce the fulfilment of our task. What, in short sustains the courage of investigators is the force of obligation of an ethical idea." (Sigwart: Logik, bd. ii., p. 23.)

This is a true account of the spirit of science. Does it essentially differ from the spirit of religion? And is any one entitled to say in advance, that, while the one form of faith shall be crowned with success, the other is certainly doomed to fail?

† Concerning the transformation of the given order into the order of conception, see S. H. Hodgson, The Philosophy of Reflection, chap. v.; H. Lotze, Logik, sects. 342–351; C. Sigwart, Logik, sects. 60–63, 105.

of human thought, from Venus and Jupiter to the
'Idee' which figures in the pages of Hegel. Even
the laws of physical nature have, in these positivis-
tic times, been held worthy of divine honor and presented as the only fitting object of our reverence.*
Of course, if our discussion is to bear any fruit, we
must mean something more definite than this. We
must not call any object of our loyalty a ' God ' without more ado, simply because to awaken our loyalty
happens to be one of God's functions. He must have
some intrinsic characteristics of his own besides;
and theism must mean the faith of that man who
believes that the object of *his* loyalty has those other
attributes, negative or positive, as the case may be.

Now, as regards a great many of the attributes
of God, and their amounts and mutual relations, the
world has been delivered over to disputes. All
such may for our present purpose be considered
as quite inessential. Not only such matters as his
mode of revealing himself, the precise extent of his
providence and power and their connection with our
free-will, the proportion of his mercy to his justice,
and the amount of his responsibility for evil; but
also his metaphysical relation to the phenomenal
world, whether causal, substantial, ideal, or what not,
— are affairs of purely sectarian opinion that need not
concern us at all. Whoso debates them presup-
poses the essential features of theism to be granted
already; and it is with these essential features, the
bare poles of the subject, that our business exclusively lies.

* Haeckel has recently (Der Monismus, 1893, p. 37) proposed the
Cosmic Ether as a divinity fitted to reconcile science with theistic
faith.

Now, what are these essential features? First, it is essential that God be conceived as the deepest power in the universe; and, second, he must be conceived under the form of a mental personality. The personality need not be determined intrinsically any further than is involved in the holding of certain things dear, and in the recognition of our dispositions toward those things, the things themselves being all good and righteous things. But, extrinsically considered, so to speak, God's personality is to be regarded, like any other personality, as something lying outside of my own and other than me, and whose existence I simply come upon and find. A power not ourselves, then, which not only makes for righteousness, but means it, and which recognizes us, — such is the definition which I think nobody will be inclined to dispute. Various are the attempts to shadow forth the other lineaments of so supreme a personality to our human imagination; various the ways of conceiving in what mode the recognition, the hearkening to our cry, can come. Some are gross and idolatrous; some are the most sustained efforts man's intellect has ever made to keep still living on that subtle edge of things where speech and thought expire. But, with all these differences, the essence remains unchanged. In whatever other respects the divine personality may differ from ours or may resemble it, the two are consanguineous at least in this, — that both have purposes for which they care, and each can hear the other's call.

Meanwhile, we can already see one consequence and one point of connection with the reflex-action theory of mind. Any mind, constructed on the

triadic-reflex pattern, must first get its impression
from the object which it confronts; then define what
that object is, and decide what active measures its
presence demands; and finally react. The stage of
reaction depends on the stage of definition, and these,
of course, on the nature of the impressing object.
When the objects are concrete, particular, and familiar, our reactions are firm and certain enough,
— often instinctive. I see the desk, and lean on it;
I see your quiet faces, and I continue to talk. But
the objects will not stay concrete and particular:
they fuse themselves into general essences, and they
sum themselves into a whole, — the universe. And
then the object that confronts us, that knocks on
our mental door and asks to be let in, and fixed and
decided upon and actively met, is just this whole
universe itself and its essence.

What are *they*, and how shall I meet *them?*

The whole flood of faiths and systems here rush in.
Philosophies and denials of philosophy, religions and
atheisms, scepticisms and mysticisms, confirmed emotional moods and habitual practical biases, jostle
one another; for all are alike trials, hasty, prolix,
or of seemly length, to answer this momentous question. And the function of them all, long or short,
that which the moods and the systems alike sub-
serve and pass into, is the third stage, — the stage
of action. For no one of them itself is final. They
form but the middle segment of the mental curve,
and not its termination. As the last theoretic pulse
dies away, it does not leave the mental process complete: it is but the forerunner of the practical moment, in which alone the cycle of mentality finds its
rhythmic pause.

We easily delude ourselves about this middle stage. Sometimes we think it final, and sometimes we fail to see, amid the monstrous diversity in the length and complication of the cogitations which may fill it, that it can have but one essential function, and that the one we have pointed out, — the function of defining the direction which our activity, immediate or remote, shall take.

If I simply say, "Vanitas vanitatum, omnia vanitas!" I am defining the total nature of things in a way that carries practical consequences with it as decidedly as if I write a treatise De Natura Rerum in twenty volumes. The treatise may trace its consequences more minutely than the saying; but the only worth of either treatise or saying is that the consequences are there. The long definition can do no more than draw them; the short definition does no less. Indeed, it may be said that if two apparently different definitions of the reality before us should have identical consequences, those two definitions would really be identical definitions, made delusively to appear different merely by the different verbiage in which they are expressed.*

My time is unfortunately too short to stay and give to this truth the development it deserves; but I will assume that you grant it without further parley, and pass to the next step in my argument. And here, too, I shall have to bespeak your close attention for a moment, while I pass over the subject far more

* See the admirably original "Illustrations of the Logic of Science," by C. S. Peirce, especially the second paper, "How to make our Thoughts clear," in the Popular Science Monthly for January, 1878.

rapidly than it deserves. Whether true or false, any view of the universe which shall completely satisfy the mind must obey conditions of the mind's own imposing, must at least let the mind be the umpire to decide whether it be fit to be called a rational universe or not. Not any nature of things which may seem to *be* will also seem to be *ipso facto* rational; and if it do not seem rational, it will afflict the mind with a ceaseless uneasiness, till it be formulated or interpreted in some other and more congenial way. The study of what the mind's criteria of rationality are, the definition of its exactions in this respect, form an intensely interesting subject into which I cannot enter now with any detail.* But so much I think you will grant me without argument, — that all three departments of the mind alike have a vote in the matter, and that no conception will pass muster which violates any of their essential modes of activity, or which leaves them without a chance to work. By what title is it that every would-be universal formula, every system of philosophy which rears its head, receives the inevitable critical volley from one half of mankind, and falls to the rear, to become at the very best the creed of some partial sect? Either it has dropped out of its net some of our impressions of sense, — what we call the facts of nature, — or it has left the theoretic and defining department with a lot of inconsistencies and unmediated transitions on its hands; or else, finally, it has left some one or more of our fundamental active and emotional powers with no object outside of themselves to react-on or to live for. Any one of these defects is fatal to its complete success. Some one

* On this subject, see the preceding Essay.

will be sure to discover the flaw, to scout the system, and to seek another in its stead.

I need not go far to collect examples to illustrate to an audience of theologians what I mean. Nor will you in particular, as champions of the Unitarianism of New England, be slow to furnish, from the motives which led to your departure from our orthodox ancestral Calvinism, instances enough under the third or practical head. A God who gives so little scope to love, a predestination which takes from endeavor all its zest with all its fruit, are irrational conceptions, because they say to our most cherished powers, There is no object for you.

Well, just as within the limits of theism some kinds are surviving others by reason of their greater practical rationality, so theism itself, by reason of its practical rationality, is certain to survive all lower creeds. Materialism and agnosticism, even were they true, could never gain universal and popular acceptance; for they both, alike, give a solution of things which is irrational to the practical third of our nature, and in which we can never volitionally feel at home. Each comes out of the second or theoretic stage of mental functioning, with its definition of the essential nature of things, its formula of formulas prepared. The whole array of active forces of our nature stands waiting, impatient for the word which shall tell them how to discharge themselves most deeply and worthily upon life. "Well!" cry they, "what shall we do?" "Ignoramus, ignorabimus!" says agnosticism. "React upon atoms and their concussions!" says materialism. What a collapse! The mental train misses fire, the middle fails to ignite the end, the cycle breaks down half-way to its conclusion; and the active powers left alone, with no proper object on which to vent their energy, must either atrophy, sicken, and die, or else by their pent-up convulsions and excitement keep the whole machinery in a fever until some less incommensurable solution, some more practically rational formula, shall provide a normal issue for the currents of the soul.

Now, theism always stands ready with the most practically rational solution it is possible to conceive. Not an energy of our active nature to which it does not authoritatively appeal, not an emotion of which it does not normally and naturally release the springs. At a single stroke, it changes the dead blank *it* of the world into a living *thou*, with whom the whole man may have dealings. To you, at any rate, I need waste no words in trying to prove its supreme commensurateness with all the demands that department Number Three of the mind has the power to impose on department Number Two.

Our volitional nature must then, until the end of time, exert a constant pressure upon the other departments of the mind to induce them to function to theistic conclusions. No contrary formulas can be more than provisionally held. Infra-theistic theories must be always in unstable equilibrium; for department Number Three ever lurks in ambush, ready to assert its rights; and on the slightest show of justification it makes its fatal spring, and converts them into the other form in which alone mental peace and order can permanently reign.

The question is, then, *Can* departments One and Two, *can* the facts of nature and the theoretic elaboration of them, always lead to theistic conclusions?

The future history of philosophy is the only author-

ity capable of answering that question. I, at all
events, must not enter into it to-day, as that would
be to abandon the purely natural-history point of
view I mean to keep.

This only is certain, that the theoretic faculty lives
between two fires which never give her rest, and
make her incessantly revise her formulations. If she
sink into a premature, short-sighted, and idolatrous
theism, in comes department Number One with its
battery of facts of sense, and dislodges her from her
dogmatic repose. If she lazily subside into equilibrium with the same facts of sense viewed in their simple mechanical outwardness, up starts the practical
reason with its demands, and makes *that* couch a
bed of thorns. From generation to generation thus it
goes, — now a movement of reception from without,
now one of expansion from within; department Number Two always worked to death, yet never excused
from taking the most responsible part in the arrange-
ments. To-day, a crop of new facts; to-morrow, a
flowering of new motives, — the theoretic faculty always having to effect the transition, and life growing
withal so complex and subtle and immense that her
powers of conceiving are almost ruptured with the
strain. See how, in France, the mummy-cloths of
the academic and official theistic philosophy are rent
by the facts of evolution, and how the young thinkers
are at work! See, in Great Britain, how the dryness
of the strict associationist school, which under the
ministration of Mill, Bain, and Spencer dominated us
but yesterday, gives way to more generous idealisms,
born of more urgent emotional needs and wrapping
the same facts in far more massive intellectual harmonies! These are but tackings to the common

port, to that ultimate *Weltanschauung* of maximum subjective as well as objective richness, which, whatever its other properties may be, will at any rate wear the theistic form.

Here let me say one word about a remark we often hear coming from the anti-theistic wing: It is base, it is vile, it is the lowest depth of immorality, to allow department Number Three to interpose its demands, and have any vote in the question of what is true and what is false; the mind must be a passive, reactionless sheet of white paper, on which reality will simply come and register its own philosophic definition, as the pen registers the curve on the sheet of a chronograph. " Of all the cants that are canted in this canting age " this has always seemed to me the most wretched, especially when it comes from professed psychologists. As if the mind could, consistently with its definition, be a reactionless sheet at all! As if conception could possibly occur except for a teleological purpose, except to show us the way from a state of things our senses cognize to another state of things our will desires! As if 'science' itself were anything else than such an end of desire, and a most peculiar one at that! And as if the ' truths ' of bare physics in particular, which these sticklers for intellectual purity contend to be the only uncontaminated form, were not as great an alteration and falsification of the simple 'given' order of the world, into an order conceived solely for the mind's convenience and delight, as any theistic doctrine possibly can be!

Physics is but one chapter in the great jugglery which our conceiving faculty is forever playing with the order of being as it presents itself to our reception. It transforms the unutterable dead level and continuum of the ' given ' world into an utterly unlike world of sharp differences and hierarchic subordinations for no other reason than to satisfy certain subjective passions we possess.*

And, so far as we can see, the given world is there only for the sake of the operation. At any rate, to operate upon it is our only chance of approaching it; for never can we get a glimpse of it in the unimaginable insipidity of its virgin estate. To bid the man's subjective interests be passive till truth express itself from out the environment, is to bid the sculptor's chisel be passive till the statue express itself from out the stone. Operate we must! and the only choice left us is that between operating to poor or to rich results. The only possible duty there can be in the matter is the duty of getting the richest results that the material given will allow. The richness lies, of course, in the energy of all three departments of the mental cycle. Not a sensible ' fact ' of department One must be left in the cold, not a faculty of department Three be paralyzed; and department Two must form an indestructible bridge. It is natural that the habitual neglect of department One by theologians should arouse indignation; but it is most *un*natural that the indignation should take the form of a wholesale denunciation of department Three. It is the story of Kant's dove over again, denouncing the pres-

* "As soon as it is recognized that our thought, as logic deals with it, reposes on our *will to think*, the primacy of the will, even in the theoretical sphere, must be conceded; and the last of presuppositions is not merely [Kant's] that ' I think' must accompany all my representations, but also that ' I will' must dominate all my thinking." (Sigwart: Logik, ii. 25.)

sure of the air. Certain of our positivists keep chiming to us, that, amid the wreck of every other god and idol, one divinity still stands upright, — that his name is Scientific Truth, and that he has but one commandment, but that one supreme, saying, *Thou shalt not be a theist,* for that would be to satisfy thy subjective propensities, and the satisfaction of those is intellectual damnation. These most conscientious gentlemen think they have jumped off their own feet, — emancipated their mental operations from the control of their subjective propensities at large and *in toto.* But they are deluded. They have simply chosen from among the entire set of propensities at their command those that were certain to construct, out of the materials given, the leanest, lowest, aridest result, — namely, the bare molecular world, — and they have sacrificed all the rest.*

Man's chief difference from the brutes lies in the exuberant excess of his subjective propensities, — his pre-eminence over them simply and solely in the number and in the fantastic and unnecessary character of his wants, physical, moral, æsthetic, and intellectual. Had his whole life not been a quest for the superfluous, he would never have established himself as inexpugnably as he has done in the necessary. And from the consciousness of this he should draw the lesson that his wants are to be trusted; that even

---

* As our ancestors said, *Fiat justitia, pereat mundus,* so we, who do not believe in justice or any absolute good, must, according to these prophets, be willing to see the world perish, in order that *scientia fiat.* Was there ever a more exquisite idol of the den, or rather of the *shop?* In the clean sweep to be made of superstitions, let the idol of stern obligation to be scientific go with the rest, and people will have a fair chance to understand one another. But this blowing of hot and of cold makes nothing but confusion.

when their gratification seems farthest off, the uneasiness they occasion is still the best guide of his life, and will lead him to issues entirely beyond his present powers of reckoning. Prune down his extravagance, sober him, and you undo him. The appetite for immediate consistency at any cost, or what the logicians call the ' law of parsimony,' — which is nothing but the passion for conceiving the universe in the most labor-saving way, — will, if made the exclusive law of the mind, end by blighting the development of the intellect itself quite as much as that of the feelings or the will. The scientific conception of the world as an army of molecules gratifies this appetite after its fashion most exquisitely. But if the religion of exclusive scientificism should ever succeed in suffocating all other appetites out of a nation's mind, and imbuing a whole race with the persuasion that simplicity and consistency demand a *tabula rasa* to be made of every notion that does not form part of the *soi-disant* scientific synthesis, that nation, that race, will just as surely go to ruin, and fall a prey to their more richly constituted neighbors, as the beasts of the field, as a whole, have fallen a prey to man.

I have myself little fear for our Anglo-Saxon race. Its moral, æsthetic, and practical wants form too dense a stubble to be mown by any scientific Occam's razor that has yet been forged. The knights of the razor will never form among us more than a sect; but when I see their fraternity increasing in numbers, and, what is worse, when I see their negations acquiring almost as much prestige and authority as their affirmations legitimately claim over the minds of the docile public, I feel as if the influences working in the direction of our mental barbarization were be-

ginning to be rather strong, and needed some positive counteraction. And when I ask myself from
what quarter the invasion may best be checked, I
can find no answer as good as the one suggested by
casting my eyes around this room. For this needful
task, no fitter body of men than the Unitarian clergy
exists. Who can uphold the rights of department
Three of the mind with better grace than those who
long since showed how they could fight and suffer for
department One? As, then, you burst the bonds of
a narrow ecclesiastical tradition, by insisting that no
fact of sense or result of science must be left out of
account in the religious synthesis, so may you still be
the champions of mental completeness and all-sided-
ness. May you, with equal success, avert the forma-
tion of a narrow scientific tradition, and burst the
bonds of any synthesis which would pretend to leave
out of account those forms of being, those relations
of reality, to which at present our active and emotional tendencies are our only avenues of approach.
I hear it said that Unitarianism is not growing in
these days. I know nothing of the truth of the statement; but if it be true, it is surely because the great
ship of Orthodoxy is nearing the port and the pilot
is being taken on board. If you will only lead in
a theistic science, as successfully as you have led in
a scientific theology, your separate name as Unita-
rians may perish from the mouths of men; for your
task will have been done, and your function at an end.
Until that distant day, you have work enough in both
directions awaiting you.

Meanwhile, let me pass to the next division of our
subject. I said that we are forced to regard God as

the normal object of the mind's belief, inasmuch as
any conception that falls short of God is irrational,
if the word 'rational' be taken in its fullest sense;
while any conception that goes beyond God is impossible, if the human mind be constructed after the
triadic-reflex pattern we have discussed at such
length. The first half of the thesis has been disposed
of. Infra-theistic conceptions, materialisms and ag-
nosticisms, are irrational because they are inadequate stimuli to man's practical nature. I have now
to justify the latter half of the thesis.

I dare say it may for an instant have perplexed
some of you that I should speak of conceptions that
aimed at going beyond God, and of attempts to fly
above him or outbid him; so I will now explain
exactly what I mean. In defining the essential attributes of God, I said he was a personality lying
outside our own and other than us, — a power not
ourselves. Now, the attempts to fly beyond theism,
of which I speak, are attempts to get over this ultimate duality of God and his believer, and to transform it into some sort or other of identity. If infra-
theistic ways of looking on the world leave it in the
third person, a mere *it;* and if theism turns the *it*
into a *thou,* — so we may say that these other theories
try to cover it with the mantle of the first person, and
to make it a part of *me.*

I am well aware that I begin here to tread on
ground in which trenchant distinctions may easily
seem to mutilate the facts.

That sense of emotional reconciliation with God
which characterizes the highest moments of the
theistic consciousness may be described as 'oneness'
with him, and so from the very bosom of theism a

monistic doctrine seem to arise. But this consciousness of self-surrender, of absolute practical union
between one's self and the divine object of one's contemplation, is a totally different thing from any sort
of substantial identity. Still the object God and the
subject I are two. Still I simply come upon him, and
find his existence given to me; and the climax of my
practical union with what is given, forms at the same
time the climax of my perception that as a numerical
fact of existence I am something radically other than
the Divinity with whose effulgence I am filled.

Now, it seems to me that the only sort of union of
creature with creator with which theism, properly so
called, comports, is of this emotional and practical
kind; and it is based unchangeably on the empirical
fact that the thinking subject and the object thought
are numerically two. How my mind and will, which
are not God, can yet cognize and leap to meet him,
how I ever came to be so separate from him, and how
God himself came to be at all, are problems that for
the theist can remain unsolved and insoluble forever.
It is sufficient for him to know that he himself simply
is, and needs God; and that behind this universe God
simply is and will be forever, and will in some way
hear his call. In the practical assurance of these
empirical facts, without ' Erkentnisstheorie ' or philosophical ontology, without metaphysics of emanation
or creation to justify or make them more intelligible,
in the blessedness of their mere acknowledgment as
given, lie all the peace and power he craves. The
floodgates of the religious life are opened, and the full
currents can pour through.

It is this empirical and practical side of the theistic
position, its theoretic chastity and modesty, which I

wish to accentuate here. The highest flights of theistic mysticism, far from pretending to penetrate the
secrets of the *me* and the *thou* in worship, and to
transcend the dualism by an act of intelligence, simply turn their backs on such attempts. The problem
for them has simply vanished, — vanished from the
sight of an attitude which refuses to notice such futile
theoretic difficulties. Get but that "peace of God
which passeth understanding," and the questions of
the understanding will cease from puzzling and pedantic scruples be at rest. In other words, theistic mysticism, that form of theism which at first sight seems
most to have transcended the fundamental otherness
of God from man, has done it least of all in the theoretic way. The pattern of its procedure is precisely
that of the simplest man dealing with the simplest
fact of his environment. Both he and the theist tarry
in department Two of their minds only so long as is
necessary to define what is the presence that confronts them. The theist decides that its character is
such as to be fitly responded to on his part by a
religious reaction; and into that reaction he forth-
with pours his soul. His insight into the *what* of life
leads to results so immediately and intimately rational
that the *why*, the *how*, and the *whence* of it are questions that lose all urgency. 'Gefühl ist Alles,' Faust
says. The channels of department Three have drained
those of department Two of their contents; and happiness over the fact that being has made itself what
it is, evacuates all speculation as to how it could make
itself at all.

But now, although to most human minds such a
position as this will be the position of rational equilibrium, it is not difficult to bring forward certain

considerations, in the light of which so simple and practical a mental movement begins to seem rather short-winded and second-rate and devoid of intellectual style. This easy acceptance of an opaque limit to our speculative insight; this satisfaction with a Being whose character we simply apprehend without comprehending anything more about him, and with whom after a certain point our dealings can be only of a volitional and emotional sort; above all, this sitting down contented with a blank unmediated dualism, — are they not the very picture of unfaithfulness to the rights and duties of our theoretic reason?

Surely, if the universe is reasonable (and we must believe that it is so), it must be susceptible, potentially at least, of being reasoned *out* to the last drop without residuum. Is it not rather an insult to the very word 'rational' to say that the rational character of the universe and its creator means no more than that we practically feel at home in their presence, and that our powers are a match for their demands? Do they not in fact demand to be *understood* by us still more than to be reacted on? Is not the unparalleled development of department Two of the mind in man his crowning glory and his very essence; and may not the *knowing of the truth* be his absolute vocation? And if it is, ought he flatly to acquiesce in a spiritual life of 'reflex type,' whose form is no higher than that of the life that animates his spinal cord, — nay, indeed, that animates the writhing segments of any mutilated worm?

It is easy to see how such arguments and queries may result in the erection of an ideal of our mental destiny, far different from the simple and practical religious one we have described. We may well begin

to ask whether such things as practical reactions can
be the final upshot and purpose of all our cognitive
energy. Mere outward acts, changes in the position of parts of matter (for they are nothing else),
can they possibly be the culmination and consummation of our relations with the nature of things? Can
they possibly form a result to which our godlike
powers of insight shall be judged merely subservient?
Such an idea, if we scan it closely, soon begins to
seem rather absurd. Whence this piece of matter
comes and whither that one goes, what difference
ought that to make to the nature of things, except
so far as with the comings and the goings our wonderful inward conscious harvest may be reaped?

And so, very naturally and gradually, one may be
led from the theistic and practical point of view to
what I shall call the *gnostical* one. We may think
that department Three of the mind, with its doings of
right and its doings of wrong, must be there only to
serve department Two; and we may suspect that the
sphere of our activity exists for no other purpose than
to illumine our cognitive consciousness by the experience of its results. Are not all sense and all emotion at bottom but turbid and perplexed modes of
what in its clarified shape is intelligent cognition? Is
not all experience just the eating of the fruit of the
tree of *knowledge* of good and evil, and nothing more?

These questions fan the fire of an unassuageable
gnostic thirst, which is as far removed from theism in
one direction as agnosticism was removed from it in
the other; and which aspires to nothing less than an
absolute unity of knowledge with its object, and refuses to be satisfied short of a fusion and solution and
saturation of both impression and action with reason,

and an absorption of all three departments of the
mind into one. Time would fail us to-day (even had
I the learning, which I have not) to speak of gnostic
systems in detail. The aim of all of them is to shadow
forth a sort of process by which spirit, emerging from
its beginnings and exhausting the whole circle of finite
experience in its sweep, shall at last return and possess itself as its own object at the climax of its career.
This climax is the religious consciousness. At the
giddy height of this conception, whose latest and
best known form is the Hegelian philosophy, definite
words fail to serve their purpose; and the ultimate
goal, — where object and subject, worshipped and wor-
shipper, facts and the knowledge of them, fall into
one, and where no other is left outstanding beyond this
one that alone is, and that we may call indifferently
act or fact, reality or idea, God or creation, — this
goal, I say, has to be adumbrated to our halting and
gasping intelligence by coarse physical metaphors,
' positings ' and ' self-returnings ' and ' removals ' and
' settings free,' which hardly help to make the matter
clear.

But from the midst of the curdling and the circling
of it all we seem dimly to catch a glimpse of a state
in which the reality to be known and the power of
knowing shall have become so mutually adequate
that each exhaustively is absorbed by the other and
the twain become one flesh, and in which the light
shall somehow have soaked up all the outer darkness
into its own ubiquitous beams. Like all headlong
ideals, this apotheosis of the bare conceiving faculty
has its depth and wildness, its pang and its charm.
To many it sings a truly siren strain; and so long
as it is held only as a postulate, as a mere vanishing

point to give perspective to our intellectual aim, it is hard to see any empirical title by which we may deny the legitimacy of gnosticism's claims. That we are not as yet near the goal it prefigures can never be a reason why we might not continue indefinitely to approach it; and to all sceptical arguments, drawn from our reason's actual finiteness, gnosticism can still oppose its indomitable faith in the infinite character of its potential destiny.

Now, here it is that the physiologist's generalization, as it seems to me, may fairly come in, and by ruling any such extravagant faith out of court help to legitimate our personal mistrust of its pretensions. I confess that I myself have always had a great mistrust of the pretensions of the gnostic faith. Not only do I utterly fail to understand what a cognitive faculty erected into the absolute of being, with itself as its object, can mean; but even if we grant it a being other than itself for object, I cannot reason myself out of the belief that however familiar and at home we might become with the character of that being, the bare being of it, the fact that it is there at all, must always be something blankly given and presupposed in order that conception may begin its work; must in short lie beyond speculation, and not be enveloped in its sphere.

Accordingly, it is with no small pleasure that as a student of physiology and psychology I find the only lesson I can learn from these sciences to be one that corroborates these convictions. From its first dawn to its highest actual attainment, we find that the cognitive faculty, where it appears to exist at all, appears but as one element in an organic mental whole, and as a minister to higher mental powers, — the powers

of will. Such a thing as its emancipation and abso-
lution from these organic relations receives no faintest color of plausibility from any fact we can discern.
Arising as a part, in a mental and objective world
which are both larger than itself, it must, whatever its
powers of growth may be (and I am far from wishing
to disparage them), remain a part to the end. This
is the character of the cognitive element in all the
mental life we know, and we have no reason to suppose that that character will ever change. On the
contrary, it is more than probable that to the end of
time our power of moral and volitional response to
the nature of things will be the deepest organ of communication therewith we shall ever possess. In every
being that is real there is something external to, and
sacred from, the grasp of every other. God's being
is sacred from ours. To co-operate with his creation
by the best and rightest response seems all he wants
of us. In such co-operation with his purposes, not in
any chimerical speculative conquest of him, not in
any theoretic drinking of him up, must lie the real
meaning of our destiny.

This is nothing new. All men know it at those rare
moments when the soul sobers herself, and leaves off
her chattering and protesting and insisting about this
formula or that. In the silence of our theories we
then seem to listen, and to hear something like the
pulse of Being beat; and it is borne in upon us that
the mere turning of the character, the dumb willingness to suffer and to serve this universe, is more than
all theories about it put together. The most any
theory about it can do is to bring us to that. Certain it is that the acutest theories, the greatest intellectual power, the most elaborate education, are a

sheer mockery when, as too often happens, they feed
mean motives and a nerveless will. And it is equally
certain that a resolute moral energy, no matter how
inarticulate or unequipped with learning its owner
may be, extorts from us a respect we should never pay
were we not satisfied that the essential root of human
personality lay there.

I have sketched my subject in the briefest outlines;
but still I hope you will agree that I have established
my point, and that the physiological view of mentality, so far from invalidating, can but give aid and comfort to the theistic attitude of mind. Between agnosticism and gnosticism, theism stands midway, and
holds to what is true in each. With agnosticism, it
goes so far as to confess that we cannot know how
Being made itself or us. With gnosticism, it goes
so far as to insist that we can know Being's character
when made, and how it asks us to behave.

If any one fear that in insisting so strongly that behavior is the aim and end of every sound philosophy
I have curtailed the dignity and scope of the speculative function in us, I can only reply that in this ascertainment of the *character* of Being lies an almost
infinite speculative task. Let the voluminous considerations by which all modern thought converges
toward idealistic or pan-psychic conclusions speak for
me. Let the pages of a Hodgson, of a Lotze, of a Renouvier, reply whether within the limits drawn by
purely empirical theism the speculative faculty finds
not, and shall not always find, enough to do. But do
it little or much, its *place* in a philosophy is always
the same, and is set by the structural form of the
mind. Philosophies, whether expressed in sonnets or

Reflex Action and Theism   143

systems, all must wear this form. The thinker starts
from some experience of the practical world, and asks
its meaning. He launches himself upon the speculative sea, and makes a voyage long or short. He as-
cends into the empyrean, and communes ·with the
eternal essences. But whatever his achievements and
discoveries be while gone, the utmost result they can
issue in is some new practical maxim or resolve, or
the denial of some old one, with which inevitably he
is sooner or later washed ashore on the *terra firma* of
concrete life again.

Whatever thought takes this voyage is a philosophy.
We have seen how theism takes it. And in the philosophy of a thinker who, though long neglected, is
doing much to renovate the spiritual life of his native
France to-day (I mean Charles Renouvier, whose
writings ought to be better known among us than they
are), we have an instructive example of the way in
which this very empirical element in theism, its confession of an ultimate opacity in things, of a dimension of being which escapes our theoretic control, may
suggest a most definite practical conclusion, — this
one, namely, that ' our wills are free.' I will say nothing of Renouvier's line of reasoning; it is contained
in many volumes which I earnestly recommend to
your attention.* But to enforce my doctrine that the
number of volumes is not what makes the philosophy,
let me conclude by recalling to you the little poem of
Tennyson, published last year, in which the speculative voyage is made, and the same conclusion reached
in a few lines: —

* Especially the Essais de Critique Générale, 2me Edition, 6 vols.,
12mo, Paris, 1875; and the Esquisse d'une Classification Systématique
des Doctrines Philosophiques, 2 vols., 8vo, Paris, 1885.

" Out of the deep, my child, out of the deep,
From that great deep before our world begins,
Whereon the Spirit of God moves as he will, —
Out of the deep, my child, out of the deep,
From that true world within the world we see,
Whereof our world is but the bounding shore, —
Out of the deep, Spirit, out of the deep,
With this ninth moon that sends the hidden sun
Down yon dark sea, thou comest, darling boy.
For in the world which is not ours, they said,
'Let us make man,' and that which should be man,
From that one light no man can look upon,
Drew to this shore lit by the suns and moons
And all the shadows. O dear Spirit, half-lost
In thine own shadow and this fleshly sign
That thou art thou, — who wailest being born
And banish'd into mystery, . . .
                    . . . our mortal veil
And shattered phantom of that Infinite One,
Who made thee unconceivably thyself
Out of his whole world-self and all in all, —
Live thou, and of the grain and husk, the grape
And ivyberry, choose; and still depart
From death to death through life and life, and find
Nearer and ever nearer Him who wrought
Not matter, nor the finite-infinite,
But this main miracle, that thou art thou,
With power on thine own act and on the world."

THE DILEMMA OF DETERMINISM *

A COMMON opinion prevails that the juice has ages ago been pressed out of the free-will controversy, and that no new champion can do more than warm up stale arguments which every one has heard. This is a radical mistake. I know of no subject less worn out, or in which inventive genius has a better chance of breaking open new ground, — not, perhaps, of forcing a conclusion or of coercing assent, but of deepening our sense of what the issue between the two parties really is, of what the ideas of fate and of free-will imply. At our very side almost, in the past few years, we have seen falling in rapid succession from the press works that present the alternative in entirely novel lights. Not to speak of the English disciples of Hegel, such as Green and Bradley; not to speak of Hinton and Hodgson, nor of Hazard here, — we see in the writings of Renouvier, Fouillée, and Delbœuf † how completely changed and refreshed is the form of all the old disputes. I cannot pretend to vie in originality with any of the masters I have named, and my ambition limits itself to just one little point. If I can make two of the necessarily implied corol-

* An Address to the Harvard Divinity Students, published in the Unitarian Review for September, 1884.

† And I may now say Charles S. Peirce, — see the Monist, for 1892–93.

laries of determinism clearer to you than they have
been made before, I shall have made it possible for you
to decide for or against that doctrine with a better understanding of what you are about. And if you prefer
not to decide at all, but to remain doubters, you will
at least see more plainly what the subject of your
hesitation is. I thus disclaim openly on the threshold
all pretension to prove to you that the freedom of the
will is true. The most I hope is to induce some of
you to follow my own example in assuming it true,
and acting as if it were true. If it be true, it seems to
me that this is involved in the strict logic of the case.
Its truth ought not to be forced willy-nilly down our
indifferent throats. It ought to be freely espoused by
men who can equally well turn their backs upon it.
In other words, our first act of freedom, if we are free,
ought in all inward propriety to be to affirm that we
are free. This should exclude, it seems to me, from
the free-will side of the question all hope of a coercive
demonstration, — a demonstration which I, for one,
am perfectly contented to go without.

With thus much understood at the outset, we can
advance. But not without one more point understood as well. The arguments I am about to urge
all proceed on two suppositions: first, when we make
theories about the world and discuss them with one
another, we do so in order to attain a conception of
things which shall give us subjective satisfaction; and,
second, if there be two conceptions, and the one
seems to us, on the whole, more rational than the
other, we are entitled to suppose that the more rational one is the truer of the two. I hope that you
are all willing to make these suppositions with me;

for I am afraid that if there be any of you here who
are not, they will find little edification in the rest of
what I have to say.   I cannot stop to argue the
point; but I myself believe that all the magnificent
achievements of mathematical and physical science —
our doctrines of evolution, of uniformity of law, and
the rest — proceed from our indomitable desire to cast
the world into a more rational shape in our minds
than the shape into which it is thrown there by the
crude order of our experience.   The world has shown
itself, to a great extent, plastic to this demand of ours
for rationality.   How much farther it will show itself
plastic no one can say.   Our only means of finding out
is to try; and I, for one, feel as free to try conceptions
of moral as of mechanical or of logical rationality.
If a certain formula for expressing the nature of the
world violates my moral demand, I shall feel as free
to throw it overboard, or at least to doubt it, as if it
disappointed my demand for uniformity of sequence,
for example; the one demand being, so far as I can
see, quite as subjective and emotional as the other is.
The principle of causality, for example, — what is it
but a postulate, an empty name covering simply a
demand that the sequence of events shall some day
manifest a deeper kind of belonging of one thing with
another than the mere arbitrary juxtaposition which
now phenomenally appears?   It is as much an altar
to an unknown god as the one that Saint Paul found
at Athens.   All our scientific and philosophic ideals
are altars to unknown gods.   Uniformity is as much
so as is free-will.   If this be admitted, we can debate
on even terms.   But if any one pretends that while
freedom and variety are, in the first instance, subjective demands, necessity and uniformity are something

altogether different, I do not see how we can debate at all.*

To begin, then, I must suppose you acquainted with all the usual arguments on the subject. I cannot stop to take up the old proofs from causation, from statistics, from the certainty with which we can foretell one another's conduct, from the fixity of character, and all the rest. But there are two *words* wh'ch usually encumber these classical arguments,

* " The whole history of popular beliefs about Nature refutes the notion that the thought of a universal physical order can possibly have arisen from the purely passive reception and association of particular perceptions. Indubitable as it is that men infer from known cases to unknown, it is equally certain that this procedure, if restricted to the phenomenal materials that spontaneously offer themselves, would never have led to the belief in a general uniformity, but only to the belief that law and lawlessness rule the world in motley alternation. From the point of view of strict experience, nothing exists but the sum of particular perceptions, with their coincidences on the one hand, their contradictions on the other.

" That,there is more order in the world than appears at first sight is not discovered *till the order is looked for.* The first impulse to look for it proceeds from practical needs: where ends must be attained, we must know trustworthy means which infallibly possess a property, or produce a result. But the practical need is only the first occasion for our reflection on the conditions of true knowledge; and even were there no such need, motives would still be present for carrying us beyond the stage of mere association. For not with an equal interest, or rather with an equal lack of interest, does man contemplate those natural processes in which a thing is linked with its former mate, and those in which it is linked to something else. *The former processes harmonize with the conditions of his own thinking:* the latter do not. In the former, his *concepts, general judgments,* and *inferences* apply to reality: in the latter, they have no such application. And thus the intellectual satisfaction which at first comes to him without reflection, at last excites in him the conscious wish to find realized throughout the entire phenomenal world those rational continuities, uniformities, and necessities which are the fundamental element and guiding principle of his own thought." (Sigwart, Logik, bd. 2, s. 382.)

and which we must immediately dispose of if we are to make any progress. One is the eulogistic word *freedom,* and the other is the opprobrious word *chance.* The word ' chance ' I wish to keep, but I wish to get rid of the word ' freedom.' Its eulogistic associations have so far overshadowed all the rest of its meaning that both parties claim the sole right to use it, and determinists to-day insist that they alone are freedom's champions. Old-fashioned determinism was what we may call *hard* determinism. It did not shrink from such words as fatality, bondage of the will, necessitation, and the like. Nowadays, we have a *soft* determinism which abhors harsh words, and, repudiating fatality, necessity, and even predetermination, says that its real name is freedom; for freedom is only necessity understood, and bondage to the highest is identical with true freedom. Even a writer as little used to making capital out of soft words as Mr. Hodgson hesitates not to call himself a ' free-will determinist.'

Now, all this is a quagmire of evasion under which the real issue of fact has been entirely smothered. Freedom in all these senses presents simply no problem at all. No matter what the soft determinist mean by it, — whether he mean the acting without external constraint; whether he mean the acting rightly, or whether he mean the acquiescing in the law of the whole, — who cannot answer him that sometimes we are free and sometimes we are not? But there *is* a problem, an issue of fact and not of words, an issue of the most momentous importance, which is often decided without discussion in one sentence, — nay, in one clause of a sentence, — by those very writers who spin out whole chapters in their efforts to show what ' true ' freedom is; and that is the question of determinism, about which we are to talk to-night.

Fortunately, no ambiguities hang about this word or about its opposite, indeterminism. Both designate an outward way in which things may happen, and their cold and mathematical sound has no sentimental associations that can bribe our partiality either way in advance. Now, evidence of an external kind to decide between determinism and indeterminism is, as I intimated a while back, strictly impossible to find. Let us look at the difference between them and see for ourselves. What does determinism profess?

It professes that those parts of the universe already laid down absolutely appoint and decree what the other parts shall be. The future has no ambiguous possibilities hidden in its womb: the part we call the present is compatible with only one totality. Any other future complement than the one fixed from eternity is impossible. The whole is in each and every part, and welds it with the rest into an absolute unity, an iron block, in which there can be no equivocation or shadow of turning.

" With earth's first clay they did the last man knead,
And there of the last harvest sowed the seed.
And the first morning of creation wrote
What the last dawn of reckoning shall read."

Indeterminism, on the contrary, says that the parts have a certain amount of loose play on one another, so that the laying down of one of them does not necessarily determine what the others shall be. It admits that possibilities may be in excess of actualities, and that things not yet revealed to our knowledge may really in themselves be ambiguous. Of two alternative futures which we conceive, both may now be really possible; and the one become impossible only at the very moment when the other excludes it by becoming real itself. Indeterminism thus denies the world to be one unbending unit of fact. It says there is a certain ultimate pluralism in it; and, so saying, it corroborates our ordinary unsophisticated view of things. To that view, actualities seem to float in a wider sea of possibilities from out of which they are chosen; and, *somewhere,* indeterminism says, such possibilities exist, and form a part of truth.

Determinism, on the contrary, says they exist *nowhere,* and that necessity on the one hand and impossibility on the other are the sole categories of the real. Possibilities that fail to get realized are, for determinism, pure illusions: they never were possibilities at all. There is nothing inchoate, it says, about this universe of ours, all that was or is or shall be actual in it having been from eternity virtually there. The cloud of alternatives our minds escort this mass of actuality withal is a cloud of sheer deceptions, to which ' impossibilities ' is the only name that rightfully belongs.

The issue, it will be seen, is a perfectly sharp one, which no eulogistic terminology can smear over or wipe out. The truth *must* lie with one side or the other, and its lying with one side makes the other false.

The question relates solely to the existence of possibilities, in the strict sense of the term, as things that may, but need not, be. Both sides admit that a volition, for instance, has occurred. The indeterminists say another volition might have occurred in its place: the determinists swear that nothing could possibly have occurred in its place. Now, can science be called in to tell us which of these two point-blank contradicters of each other is right? Science professes to draw no conclusions but such as are based on matters of fact, things that have actually happened; but how can any amount of assurance that something actually happened give us the least grain of information as to whether another thing might or might not have happened in its place? Only facts can be proved by other facts. With things that are possibilities and not facts, facts have no concern. If we have no other evidence than the evidence of existing facts, the possibility-question must remain a mystery never to be cleared up.

And the truth is that facts practically have hardly anything to do with making us either determinists or indeterminists. Sure enough, we make a flourish of quoting facts this way or that; and if we are determinists, we talk about the infallibility with which we can predict one another's conduct; while if we are indeterminists, we lay great stress on the fact that it is just because we cannot foretell one another's conduct, either in war or statecraft or in any of the great and small intrigues and businesses of men, that life is so intensely anxious and hazardous a game. But who does not see the wretched insufficiency of this so-called objective testimony on both sides? What fills up the gaps in our minds is something not objective, not external. What divides us into possibility men and anti-possibility men is different faiths or postulates, — postulates of rationality. To this man the world seems more rational with possibilities in it, — to that man more rational with possibilities excluded; and talk as we will about having to yield to evidence, what makes us monists or pluralists, deter-

minists or indeterminists, is at bottom always some
sentiment like this.

The stronghold of the deterministic sentiment is
the antipathy to the idea of chance. As soon as we
begin to talk indeterminism to our friends, we find a
number of them shaking their heads. This notion of
alternative possibility, they say, this admission that
any one of several things may come to pass, is, after
all, only a roundabout name for chance; and chance
is something the notion of which no sane mind can for
an instant tolerate in the world. What is it, they ask,
but barefaced crazy unreason, the negation of in-
telligibility and law? And if the slightest particle
of it exist anywhere, what is to prevent the whole
fabric from falling together, the stars from going
out, and chaos from recommencing her topsy-turvy
reign?

Remarks of this sort about chance will put an end
to discussion as quickly as anything one can find.
I have already told you that ' chance ' was a word I
wished to keep and use. Let us then examine exactly
what it means, and see whether it ought to be such a
terrible bugbear to us. I fancy that squeezing the
thistle boldly will rob it of its sting.

The sting of the word ' chance ' seems to lie in the
assumption that it means something positive, and
that if anything happens by chance, it must needs be
something of an intrinsically irrational and preposterous sort. Now, chance means nothing of the kind.
It is a purely negative and relative term,* giving us

* Speaking technically, it is a word with a positive denotation, but
a connotation that is negative. Other things must be silent about
what it is: it alone can decide that point at the moment in which
it reveals itself.

no information about that of which it is predicated, except that it happens to be disconnected with something else, — not controlled, secured, or necessitated by other things in advance of its own actual presence. As this point is the most subtile one of the whole lecture, and at the same time the point on which all the rest hinges, I beg you to pay particular attention to it. What I say is that it tells us nothing about what a thing may be in itself to call it 'chance.' It may be a bad thing, it may be a good thing. It may be lucidity, transparency, fitness incarnate, matching the whole system of other things, when it has once befallen, in an unimaginably perfect way. All you mean by calling it 'chance' is that this is not guaranteed, that it may also fall out otherwise. For the system of other things has no positive hold on the chance-thing. Its origin is in a certain fashion negative: it escapes, and says, Hands off! coming, when it comes, as a free gift, or not at all.

This negativeness, however, and this opacity of the chance-thing when thus considered *ab extra*, or from the point of view of previous things or distant things, do not preclude its having any amount of positiveness and luminosity from within, and at its own place and moment. All that its chance-character asserts about it is that there is something in it really of its own, something that is not the unconditional property of the whole. If the whole wants this property, the whole must wait till it can get it, if it be a matter of chance. That the universe may actually be a sort of joint-stock society of this sort, in which the sharers have both limited liabilities and limited powers, is of course a simple and conceivable notion.

Nevertheless, many persons talk as if the minutest

dose of disconnectedness of one part with another, the smallest modicum of independence, the faintest tremor of ambiguity about the future, for example, would ruin everything, and turn this goodly universe into a sort of insane sand-heap or nulliverse, no universe at all. Since future human volitions are as a matter of fact the only ambiguous things we are tempted to believe in, let us stop for a moment to make ourselves sure whether their independent and accidental character need be fraught with such direful consequences to the universe as these.

What is meant by saying that my choice of which way to walk home after the lecture is ambiguous and matter of chance as far as the present moment is concerned? It means that both Divinity Avenue and Oxford Street are called; but that only one, and that one *either* one, shall be chosen. Now, I ask you seriously to suppose that this ambiguity of my choice is real; and then to make the impossible hypothesis that the choice is made twice over, and each time falls on a different street. In other words, imagine that I first walk through Divinity Avenue, and then imagine that the powers governing the universe annihilate ten minutes of time with all that it contained, and set me back at the door of this hall just as I was before the choice was made. Imagine then that, everything else being the same, I now make a different choice and traverse Oxford Street. You, as passive spectators, look on and see the two alternative universes, — one of them with me walking through Divinity Avenue in it, the other with the same me walking through Oxford Street. Now, if you are determinists you believe one of these universes to have been from eternity impossible: you believe it to have been impossible because of the intrinsic irrationality or accidentality somewhere involved in it. But looking outwardly at these universes, can you say which is the impossible and accidental one, and which the rational and necessary one? I doubt if the most iron-clad determinist among you could have the slightest glimmer of light on this point. In other words, either universe *after the fact* and once there would, to our means of observation and understanding, appear just as rational as the other. There would be absolutely no criterion by which we might judge one necessary and the other matter of chance. Suppose now we relieve the gods of their hypothetical task and assume my choice, once made, to be made forever. I go through Divinity Avenue for good and all. If, as good determinists, you now begin to affirm, what all good determinists punctually do affirm, that in the nature of things I *couldn't* have gone through Oxford Street, — had I done so it would have been chance, irrationality, insanity, a horrid gap in nature, — I simply call your attention to this, that your affirmation is what the Germans call a *Machtspruch,* a mere conception fulminated as a dogma and based on no insight into details. Before my choice, either street seemed as natural to you as to me. Had I happened to take Oxford Street, Divinity Avenue would have figured in your philosophy as the gap in nature; and you would have so proclaimed it with the best deterministic conscience in the world.

But what a hollow outcry, then, is this against a chance which, if it were present to us, we could by no character whatever distinguish from a rational necessity! I have taken the most trivial of examples, but no possible example could lead to any different result. For what are the alternatives which, in point of fact, offer themselves to human volition? What are those futures that now seem matters of chance? Are they not one and all like the Divinity Avenue and Oxford Street of our example? Are they not all of them *kinds* of things already here and based in the existing frame of nature? Is any one ever tempted to produce an *absolute* accident, something utterly irrelevant to the rest of the world? Do not all the motives that assail us, all the futures that offer themselves to our choice, spring equally from the soil of the past; and would not either one of them, whether realized through chance or through necessity, the moment it was realized, seem to us to fit that past, and in the completest and most continuous manner to interdigitate with the phenomena already there? *

The more one thinks of the matter, the more one wonders that so empty and gratuitous a hubbub as this outcry against chance should have found so great an echo in the hearts of men. It is a word which tells us absolutely nothing about what chances, or about the *modus operandi* of the chancing; and the use of it as a war-cry shows only a temper of intel-

* A favorite argument against free-will is that if it be true, a man's murderer may as probably be his best friend as his worst enemy, a mother be as likely to strangle as to suckle her first-born, and all of us be as ready to jump from fourth-story windows as to go out of front doors, etc. Users of this argument should properly be excluded from debate till they learn what the real question is. 'Free-will' does not say that everything that is physically conceivable is also morally possible. It merely says that of alternatives that really *tempt* our will more than one is really possible. Of course, the alternatives that do thus tempt our will are vastly fewer than the physical possibilities we can coldly fancy. Persons really tempted often do murder their best friends, mothers do strangle their first-born, people do jump out of fourth-story windows, etc.

lectual absolutism, a demand that the world shall be a solid block, subject to one control, — which temper, which demand, the world may not be bound to gratify at all. In every outwardly verifiable and practical respect, a world in which the alternatives that now actually distract *your* choice were decided by pure chance would be by *me* absolutely undistinguished from the world in which I now live. I am, therefore, entirely willing to call it, so far as your choices go, a world of chance for me. To *yourselves,* it is true, those very acts of choice, which to me are so blind, opaque, and external, are the opposites of this, for you are within them and effect them. To you they appear as decisions; and decisions, for him who makes them, are altogether peculiar psychic facts. Self-luminous and self-justifying at the living moment at which they occur, they appeal to no outside moment to put its stamp upon them or make them continuous with the rest of nature. Themselves it is rather who seem to make nature continuous; and in their strange and intense function of granting consent to one possibility and withholding it from another, to transform an equivocal and double future into an inalterable and simple past.

But with the psychology of the matter we have no concern this evening. The quarrel which determinism has with chance fortunately has nothing to do with this or that psychological detail. It is a quarrel altogether metaphysical. Determinism denies the ambiguity of future volitions, because it affirms that nothing future can be ambiguous. But we have said enough to meet the issue. Indeterminate future volitions *do* mean chance. Let us not fear to shout it from the house-tops if need be; for we now know that the idea of chance is, at bottom, exactly the same thing as the idea of gift, — the one simply being a disparaging, and the other a eulogistic, name for anything on which we have no effective *claim*. And whether the world be the better or the worse for having either chances or gifts in it will depend altogether on *what* these uncertain and unclaimable things turn out to be.

And this at last brings us within sight of our subject. We have seen what determinism means: we have seen that indeterminism is rightly described as meaning chance; and we have seen that chance, the very name of which we are urged to shrink from as from a metaphysical pestilence, means only the negative fact that no part of the world, however big, can claim to control absolutely the destinies of the whole. But although, in discussing the word ' chance,' I may at moments have seemed to be arguing for its real existence, I have not meant to do so yet. We have not yet ascertained whether this be a world of chance or no; at most, we have agreed that it seems so. And I now repeat what I said at the outset, that, from any strict theoretical point of view, the question is insoluble. To deepen our theoretic sense of the *difference* between a world with chances in it and a deterministic world is the most I can hope to do; and this I may now at last begin upon, after all our tedious clearing of the way.

I wish first of all to show you just what the notion that this is a deterministic world implies. The implications I call your attention to are all bound up with the fact that it is a world in which we constantly have to make what I shall, with your permission, call judgments of regret. Hardly an hour passes in

which we do not wish that something might be otherwise; and happy indeed are those of us whose hearts
have never echoed the wish of Omar Khayam —

" That we might clasp, ere closed, the book of fate,
    And make the writer on a fairer leaf
Inscribe our names, or quite obliterate.

" Ah! Love, could you and I with fate conspire
To mend this sorry scheme of things entire,
    Would we not shatter it to bits, and then
Remould it nearer to the heart's desire? "

Now, it is undeniable that most of these regrets are
foolish, and quite on a par in point of philosophic
value with the criticisms on the universe of that friend
of our infancy, the hero of the fable The Atheist and
the Acorn, —

" Fool! had that bough a pumpkin bore,
Thy whimsies would have worked no more," etc.

Even from the point of view of our own ends, we
should probably make a botch of remodelling the
universe. How much more then from the point of
view of ends we cannot see! Wise men therefore
regret as little as they can. But still some regrets
are pretty obstinate and hard to stifle, — regrets
for acts of wanton cruelty or treachery, for example, whether performed by others or by ourselves.
Hardly any one can remain *entirely* optimistic after
reading the confession of the murderer at Brockton
the other day: how, to get rid of the wife whose
continued existence bored him, he inveigled her into
a desert spot, shot her four times, and then, as she
lay on the ground and said to him, " You didn't do
it on purpose, did you, dear? " replied, " No, I

didn't do it on purpose," as he raised a rock and smashed her skull. Such an occurrence, with the mild sentence and self-satisfaction of the prisoner, is a field for a crop of regrets, which one need not take up in detail. We feel that, although a perfect mechanical fit to the rest of the universe, it is a bad moral fit, and that something else would really have been better in its place.

But for the deterministic philosophy the murder, the sentence, and the prisoner's optimism were all necessary from eternity; and nothing else for a moment had a ghost of a chance of being put into their place. To admit such a chance, the determinists tell us, would be to make a suicide of reason; so we must steel our hearts against the thought. And here our plot thickens, for we see the first of those difficult implications of determinism and monism which it is my purpose to make you feel. If this Brockton murder was called for by the rest of the universe, if it had to come at its preappointed hour, and if nothing else would have been consistent with the sense of the whole, what are we to think of the universe? Are we stubbornly to stick to our judgment of regret, and say, though it *couldn't* be, yet it *would* have been a better universe with something different from this Brockton murder in it? That, of course, seems the natural and spontaneous thing for us to do; and yet it is nothing short of deliberately espousing a kind of pessimism. The judgment of regret calls the murder bad. Calling a thing bad means, if it mean anything at all, that the thing ought not to be, that something else ought to be in its stead. Determinism, in denying that anything else can be in its stead, virtually defines the universe

as a place in which what ought to be is impossible, —
in other words, as an organism whose constitution
is afflicted with an incurable taint, an irremediable
flaw. The pessimism of a Schopenhauer says no
more than this, — that the murder is a symptom;
and that it is a vicious symptom because it belongs
to a vicious whole, which can express its nature no
otherwise than by bringing forth just such a symptom as that at this particular spot. Regret for the
murder must transform itself, if we are determinists
and wise, into a larger regret. It is absurd to regret
the murder alone. Other things being what they are,
it could not be different. What we should regret is
that whole frame of things of which the murder is one
member. I see no escape whatever from this pessimistic conclusion, if, being determinists, our judgment
of regret is to be allowed to stand at all.

The only deterministic escape from pessimism is
everywhere to abandon the judgment of regret. That
this can be done, history shows to be not impossible.
The devil, *quoad existentiam,* may be good. That is,
although he be a *principle* of evil, yet the universe,
with such a principle in it, may practically be a
better universe than it could have been without. On
every hand, in a small way, we find that a certain
amount of evil is a condition by which a higher form
of good is brought. There is nothing to prevent
anybody from generalizing this view, and trusting
that if we could but see things in the largest of all
ways, even such matters as this Brockton murder
would appear to be paid for by the uses that follow
in their train. An optimism *quand même,* a systematic and infatuated optimism like that ridiculed
by Voltaire in his Candide, is one of the possible

ideal ways in which a man may train himself to look on life. Bereft of dogmatic hardness and lit up with the expression of a tender and pathetic hope, such an optimism has been the grace of some of the most religious characters that ever lived.

" Throb thine with Nature's throbbing breast,
    And all is clear from east to west."

Even cruelty and treachery may be among the absolutely blessed fruits of time, and to quarrel with any of their details may be blasphemy. The only real blasphemy, in short, may be that pessimistic temper of the soul which lets it give way to such things as regrets, remorse, and grief.

Thus, our deterministic pessimism may become a deterministic optimism at the price of extinguishing our judgments of regret.

But does not this immediately bring us into a curious logical predicament? Our determinism leads us to call our judgments of regret wrong, because they are pessimistic in implying that what is impossible yet ought to be. But how then about the judgments of regret themselves? If they are wrong, other judgments, judgments of approval presumably, ought to be in their place. But as they are necessitated, nothing else *can* be in their place; and the universe is just what it was before, — namely, a place in which what ought to be appears impossible. We have got one foot out of the pessimistic bog, but the other one sinks all the deeper. We have rescued our actions from the bonds of evil, but our judgments are now held fast. When murders and treacheries cease to be sins, regrets are theoretic absurdities and errors. The theoretic and the active life thus play a kind of see-

saw with each other on the ground of evil. The rise
of either sends the other down. Murder and treachery cannot be good without regret being bad: regret
cannot be good without treachery and murder being
bad. Both, however, are supposed to have been
foredoomed; so something must be fatally unreason-
able, absurd, and wrong in the world. It must be a
place of which either sin or error forms a necessary
part. From this dilemma there seems at first sight
no escape. Are we then so soon to fall back into the
pessimism from which we thought we had emerged?
And is there no possible way by which we may, with
good intellectual consciences, call the cruelties and
the treacheries, the reluctances and the regrets, *all*
good together?

Certainly there is such a way, and you are probably
most of you ready to formulate it yourselves. But,
before doing so, remark how inevitably the question
of determinism and indeterminism slides us into the
question of optimism and pessimism, or, as our fathers
called it, ' the question of evil.' The theological form
of all these disputes is the simplest and the deepest,
the form from which there is the least escape, — not
because, as some have sarcastically said, remorse and
regret are clung to with a morbid fondness by the
theologians as spiritual luxuries, but because they are
existing facts of the world, and as such must be taken
into account in the deterministic interpretation of all
that is fated to be. If they are fated to be error, does
not the bat's wing of irrationality still cast its shadow
over the world?

The refuge from the quandary lies, as I said, not
far off. The necessary acts we erroneously regret

may be good, and yet our error in so regretting them
may be also good, on one simple condition; and that
condition is this: The world must not be regarded as
a machine whose final purpose is the making real of
any outward good, but rather as a contrivance for
deepening the theoretic consciousness of what goodness and evil in their intrinsic natures are. Not the
doing either of good or of evil is what nature cares
for, but the knowing of them. Life is one long eating
of the fruit of the tree of *knowledge*. I am in the
habit, in thinking to myself, of calling this point of
view the *gnostical* point of view. According to it, the
world is neither an optimism nor a pessimism, but a
gnosticism. But as this term may perhaps lead to
some misunderstandings, I will use it as little as possible here, and speak rather of *subjectivism,* and the
subjectivistic point of view.

Subjectivism has three great branches, — we may
call them scientificism, sentimentalism, and sensualism, respectively. They all agree essentially about
the universe, in deeming that what happens there is
subsidiary to what we think or feel about it. Crime
justifies its criminality by awakening our intelligence
of that criminality, and eventually our remorses and
regrets; and the error included in remorses and regrets, the error of supposing that the past could have
been different, justifies itself by its use. Its use is to
quicken our sense of *what* the irretrievably lost is.
When we think of it as that which might have been
(' the saddest words of tongue or pen '), the quality
of its worth speaks to us with a wilder sweetness; and,
conversely, the dissatisfaction wherewith we think of
what seems to have driven it from its natural place
gives us the severer pang. Admirable artifice of

nature! we might be tempted to exclaim, — deceiving us in order the better to enlighten us, and leaving nothing undone to accentuate to our consciousness the yawning distance of those opposite poles of good and evil between which creation swings.

We have thus clearly revealed to our view what may be called the dilemma of determinism, so far as determinism pretends to think things out at all. A merely mechanical determinism, it is true, rather rejoices in not thinking them out. It is very sure that the universe must satisfy its postulate of a physical continuity and coherence, but it smiles at any one who comes forward with a postulate of moral coherence as well. I may suppose, however, that the number of purely mechanical or hard determinists among you this evening is small. The determinism to whose seductions you are most exposed is what I have called soft determinism, — the determinism which allows considerations of good and bad to mingle with those of cause and effect in deciding what sort of a universe this may rationally be held to be. The dilemma of this determinism is one whose left horn is pessimism and whose right horn is subjectivism. In other words, if determinism is to escape pessimism, it must leave off looking at the goods and ills of life in a simple objective way, and regard them as materials, indifferent in themselves, for the production of consciousness, scientific and ethical, in us.

To escape pessimism is, as we all know, no easy task. Your own studies have sufficiently shown you the almost desperate difficulty of making the notion that there is a single principle of things, and that principle absolute perfection, rhyme together with our daily vision of the facts of life. If perfection be the principle, how comes there any imperfection here? If God be good, how came he to create — or, if he did not create, how comes he to permit — the devil? The evil facts must be explained as seeming: the devil must be whitewashed, the universe must be disinfected, if neither God's goodness nor his unity and power are to remain impugned. And of all the various ways of operating the disinfection, and making bad seem less bad, the way of subjectivism appears by far the best.*

For, after all, is there not something rather absurd in our ordinary notion of external things being good or bad in themselves? Can murders and treacheries, considered as mere outward happenings, or motions of matter, be bad without any one to feel their badness? And could paradise properly be good in the absence of a sentient principle by which the goodness was perceived? Outward goods and evils seem practically indistinguishable except in so far as they result in getting moral judgments made about them. But then the moral judgments seem the main thing, and the outward facts mere perishing instruments for their production. This is subjectivism. Every one must at some time have wondered at that strange paradox of our moral nature, that, though the pur-

---

* To a reader who says he is satisfied with a pessimism, and has no objection to thinking the whole bad, I have no more to say: he makes fewer demands on the world than I, who, making them, wish to look a little further before I give up all hope of having them satisfied. If, however, all he means is that the badness of some parts does not prevent his acceptance of a universe whose *other* parts give him satisfaction, I welcome him as an ally. He has abandoned the notion of the *Whole*, which is the essence of deterministic monism, and views things as a pluralism, just as I do in this paper.

suit of outward good is the breath of its nostrils, the attainment of outward good would seem to be its suffocation and death. Why does the painting of any paradise or utopia, in heaven or on earth, awaken such yawnings for nirvana and escape? The white-robed harp-playing heaven of our sabbath-schools, and the ladylike tea-table elysium represented in Mr. Spencer's Data of Ethics, as the final consummation of progress, are exactly on a par in this respect, — lubberlands, pure and simple, one and all.* We look upon them from this delicious mess of insanities and realities, strivings and deadnesses, hopes and fears, agonies and exultations, which forms our present state, and *tedium vitæ* is the only sentiment they awaken in our breasts. To our crepuscular natures, born for the conflict, the Rembrandtesque moral chiaroscuro, the shifting struggle of the sunbeam in the gloom, such pictures of light upon light are vacuous and expressionless, and neither to be enjoyed nor understood. If *this* be the whole fruit of the victory, we say; if the generations of mankind suffered and laid down their lives; if prophets confessed and martyrs sang in the fire, and all the sacred tears were shed for no other end than that a race of creatures of such unexampled insipidity should succeed, and protract *in saecula saeculorum* their contented and inoffensive lives, — why, at such a rate, better lose than win the battle, or at all events better ring down the curtain before the last act of the play, so that a business that began so importantly may be saved from so singularly flat a winding-up.

* Compare Sir James Stephen's Essays by a Barrister, London, 1862, pp. 138, 318.

All this is what I should instantly say, were I called on to plead for gnosticism; and its real friends, of whom you will presently perceive I am not one, would say without difficulty a great deal more. Regarded as a stable finality, every outward good becomes a mere weariness to the flesh. It must be menaced, be occasionally lost, for its goodness to be fully felt as such. Nay, more than occasionally lost. No one knows the worth of innocence till he knows it is gone forever, and that money cannot buy it back. Not the saint, but the sinner that repenteth, is he to whom the full length and breadth, and height and depth, of life's meaning is revealed. Not the absence of vice, but vice there, and virtue holding her by the throat, seems the ideal human state. And there seems no reason to suppose it not a permanent human state. There is a deep truth in what the school of Schopenhauer insists on, — the illusoriness of the notion of moral progress. The more brutal forms of evil that go are replaced by others more subtle and more poisonous. Our moral horizon moves with us as we move, and never do we draw nearer to the far-off line where the black waves and the azure meet. The final purpose of our creation seems most plausibly to be the greatest possible enrichment of our ethical consciousness, through the intensest play of contrasts and the widest diversity of characters. This of course obliges some of us to be vessels of wrath, while it calls others to be vessels of honor. But the subjectivist point of view reduces all these outward distinctions to a common denominator. The wretch languishing in the felon's cell may be drinking draughts of the wine of truth that will never pass the lips of the so-called favorite of fortune. And the peculiar consciousness of each of them is an indispensable note in the great ethical concert which the centuries as they roll are grinding out of the living heart of man.

So much for subjectivism! If the dilemma of determinism be to choose between it and pessimism, I see little room for hesitation from the strictly theoretical point of view. Subjectivism seems the more rational scheme. And the world may, possibly, for aught I know, be nothing else. When the healthy love of life is on one, and all its forms and its appetites seem so unutterably real; when the most brutal and the most spiritual things are lit by the same sun, and each is an integral part of the total richness, — why, then it seems a grudging and sickly way of meeting so robust a universe to shrink from any of its facts and wish them not to be. Rather take the strictly dramatic point of view, and treat the whole thing as a great unending romance which the spirit of the universe, striving to realize its own content, is eternally thinking out and representing to itself.*

No one, I hope, will accuse me, after I have said all this, of underrating the reasons in favor of subjectivism. And now that I proceed to say why those reasons, strong as they are, fail to convince my own mind, I trust the presumption may be that my objections are stronger still.

I frankly confess that they are of a practical order. If we practically take up subjectivism in a sincere and radical manner and follow its consequences, we meet with some that make us pause. Let a subjectivism

* Cet univers est un spectacle que Dieu se donne à lui-même. Servons les intentions du grand chorège en contribuant à rendre le spectacle aussi brillant, aussi varié que possible. — RENAN.

begin in never so severe and intellectual a way, it is
forced by the law of its nature to develop another
side of itself and end with the corruptest curiosity.
Once dismiss the notion that certain duties are good
in themselves, and that we are here to do them, no
matter how we feel about them; once consecrate the
opposite notion that our performances and our vio-
lations of duty are for a common purpose, the attainment of subjective knowledge and feeling, and
that the deepening of these is the chief end of our
lives, — and at what point on the downward slope are
we to stop?   In theology, subjectivism develops as
its 'left wing' antinomianism.   In literature, its left
wing is romanticism.   And in practical life it is either
a nerveless sentimentality or a sensualism without
bounds.

Everywhere it fosters the fatalistic mood of mind.
It makes those who are already too inert more passive
still; it renders wholly reckless those whose energy is
already in excess.   All through history we find how
subjectivism, as soon as it has a free career, exhausts
itself in every sort of spiritual, moral, and practical
license.   Its optimism turns to an ethical indifference, which infallibly brings dissolution in its train.
It is perfectly safe to say now that if the Hegelian
gnosticism, which has begun to show itself here and
in Great Britain, were to become a popular philosophy, as it once was in Germany, it would certainly
develop its left wing here as there, and produce a reaction of disgust.   Already I have heard a graduate of
this very school express in the pulpit his willingness to
sin like David, if only he might repent like David.   You
may tell me he was only sowing his wild, or rather
his tame, oats; and perhaps he was.   But the point is

that in the subjectivistic or gnostical philosophy oat-sowing, wild or tame, becomes a systematic necessity and the chief function of life. After the pure and classic truths, the exciting and rancid ones must be experienced; and if the stupid virtues of the philistine herd do not then come in and save society from the influence of the children of light, a sort of inward putrefaction becomes its inevitable doom.

Look at the last runnings of the romantic school, as we see them in that strange contemporary Parisian literature, with which we of the less clever countries are so often driven to rinse out our minds after they have become clogged with the dulness and heaviness of our native pursuits. The romantic school began with the worship of subjective sensibility and the revolt against legality of which Rousseau was the first great prophet: and through various fluxes and refluxes, right wings and left wings, it stands to-day with two men of genius, M. Renan and M. Zola, as its principal exponents, — one speaking with its masculine, and the other with what might be called its feminine, voice. I prefer not to think now of less noble members of the school, and the Renan I have in mind is of course the Renan of latest dates. As I have used the term gnostic, both he and Zola are gnostics of the most pronounced sort. Both are athirst for the facts of life, and both think the facts of human sensibility to be of all facts the most worthy of attention. Both agree, moreover, that sensibility seems to be there for no higher purpose, — certainly not, as the Philistines say, for the sake of bringing mere outward rights to pass and frustrating outward wrongs. One dwells on the sensibilities for their energy, the other for their sweetness; one speaks with a voice of bronze, the other with that of an Æolian harp; one ruggedly ignores the distinction of good and evil, the other plays the coquette between the craven unmanliness of his Philosophic Dialogues and the butterfly optimism of his Souvenirs de Jeunesse. But under the pages of both there sounds incessantly the hoarse bass of *vanitas vanitatum, omnia vanitas,* which the reader may hear, whenever he will, between the lines. No writer of this French romantic school has a word of rescue from the hour of satiety with the things of life, — the hour in which we say, " I take no pleasure in them," — or from the hour of terror at the world's vast meaningless grinding, if perchance such hours should come. For terror and satiety are facts of sensibility like any others; and at their own hour they reign in their own right. The heart of the romantic utterances, whether poetical, critical, or historical, is this inward remedilessness, what Carlyle calls this far-off whimpering of wail and woe. And from this romantic state of mind there is absolutely no possible *theoretic* escape. Whether, like Renan, we look upon life in a more refined way, as a romance of the spirit; or whether, like the friends of M. Zola, we pique ourselves on our ' scientific ' and ' analytic ' character, and prefer to be cynical, and call the world a ' roman expérimental ' on an infinite scale, — in either case the world appears to us potentially as what the same Carlyle once called it, a vast, gloomy, solitary Golgotha and mill of death.

The only escape is by the practical way. And since I have mentioned the nowadays much-reviled name of Carlyle, let me mention it once more, and say it is the way of his teaching. No matter for Carlyle's life, no matter for a great deal of his writing. What was the most important thing he said to us? He said: "Hang your sensibilities! Stop your snivelling complaints, and your equally snivelling raptures! Leave off your general emotional tomfoolery, and get to WORK like men!" But this means a complete rupture with the subjectivist philosophy of things. It says conduct, and not sensibility, is the ultimate fact for our recognition. With the vision of certain works to be done, of certain outward changes to be wrought or resisted, it says our intellectual horizon terminates. No matter how we succeed in doing these outward duties, whether gladly and spontaneously, or heavily and unwillingly, do them we somehow must; for the leaving of them undone is perdition. No matter how we feel; if we are only faithful in the outward act and refuse to do wrong, the world will in so far be safe, and we quit of our debt toward it. Take, then, the yoke upon our shoulders; bend our neck beneath the heavy legality of its weight; regard something else than our feeling as our limit, our master, and our law; be willing to live and die in its service, — and, at a stroke, we have passed from the subjective into the objective philosophy of things, much as one awakens from some feverish dream, full of bad lights and noises, to find one's self bathed in the sacred coolness and quiet of the air of the night.

But what is the essence of this philosophy of objective conduct, so old-fashioned and finite, but so chaste and sane and strong, when compared with its romantic rival? It is the recognition of limits, foreign and opaque to our understanding. It is the willingness, after bringing about some external good, to feel at peace; for our responsibility ends with the

performance of that duty, and the burden of the rest
we may lay on higher powers.*

> " Look to thyself, O Universe,
>   Thou art better and not worse,"

we may say in that philosophy, the moment we have
done our stroke of conduct, however small. For in
the view of that philosophy the universe belongs to
a plurality of semi-independent forces, each one of
which may help or hinder, and be helped or hindered
by, the operations of the rest.

But this brings us right back, after such a long
détour, to the question of indeterminism and to the
conclusion of all I came here to say to-night. For
the only consistent way of representing a pluralism and
a world whose parts may affect one another through
their conduct being either good or bad is the inde-
terministic way. What interest, zest, or excitement
can there be in achieving the right way, unless we
are enabled to feel that the wrong way is also a possible and a natural way, — nay, more, a menacing
and an imminent way? And what sense can there
be in condemning ourselves for taking the wrong
way, unless we need have done nothing of the sort,
unless the right way was open to us as well? I cannot understand the willingness to act, no matter how
we feel, without the belief that acts are really good
and bad. I cannot understand the belief that an act
is bad, without regret at its happening. I cannot
understand regret without the admission of real,
genuine possibilities in the world. Only *then* is it

* The burden, for example, of seeing to it that the *end* of all our
righteousness be some positive universal gain.

other than a mockery to feel, after we have failed to do our best, that an irreparable opportunity is gone from the universe, the loss of which it must forever after mourn.

If you insist that this is all superstition, that possibility is in the eye of science and reason impossibility, and that if I act badly 'tis that the universe was foredoomed to suffer this defect, you fall right back into the dilemma, the labyrinth, of pessimism and subjectivism, from out of whose toils we have just wound our way.

Now, we are of course free to fall back, if we please. For my own part, though, whatever difficulties may beset the philosophy of objective right and wrong, and the indeterminism it seems to imply, determinism, with its alternative of pessimism or romanticism, contains difficulties that are greater still. But you will remember that I expressly repudiated awhile ago the pretension to offer any arguments which could be coercive in a so-called scientific fashion in this matter. And I consequently find myself, at the end of this long talk, obliged to state my conclusions in an altogether personal way. This personal method of appeal seems to be among the very conditions of the problem; and the most any one can do is to confess as candidly as he can the grounds for the faith that is in him, and leave his example to work on others as it may.

Let me, then, without circumlocution say just this. The world is enigmatical enough in all conscience, whatever theory we may take up toward it. The indeterminism I defend, the free-will theory of popular sense based on the judgment of regret, represents that world as vulnerable, and liable to be injured by certain of its parts if they act wrong. And it represents their acting wrong as a matter of possibility or accident, neither inevitable nor yet to be infallibly warded off. In all this, it is a theory devoid either of transparency or of stability. It gives us a pluralistic, restless universe, in which no single point of view can ever take in the whole scene; and to a mind possessed of the love of unity at any cost, it will, no doubt, remain forever inacceptable. A friend with such a mind once told me that the thought of my universe made him sick, like the sight of the horrible motion of a mass of maggots in their carrion bed.

But while I freely admit that the pluralism and the restlessness are repugnant and irrational in a certain way, I find that every alternative to them is irrational in a deeper way. The indeterminism with its maggots, if you please to speak so about it, offends only the native absolutism of my intellect, — an absolutism which, after all, perhaps, deserves to be snubbed and kept in check. But the determinism with its necessary carrion, to continue the figure of speech, and with no possible maggots to eat the latter up, violates my sense of moral reality through and through. When, for example, I imagine such carrion as the Brockton murder, I cannot conceive it as an act by which the universe, as a whole, logically and necessarily expresses its nature without shrinking from complicity with such a whole. And I deliberately refuse to keep on terms of loyalty with the universe by saying blankly that the murder, since it does flow from the nature of the whole, is not carrion. There are *some* instinctive reactions which

I, for one, will not tamper with. The only remaining alternative, the attitude of gnostical romanticism, wrenches my personal instincts in quite as violent a way. It falsifies the simple objectivity of their deliverance. It makes the goose-flesh the murder excites in me a sufficient reason for the perpetration of the crime. It transforms life from a tragic reality into an insincere melodramatic exhibition, as foul or as tawdry as any one's diseased curiosity pleases to carry it out. And with its consecration of the 'roman naturaliste' state of mind, and its enthronement of the baser crew of Parisian *littérateurs* among the eternally indispensable organs by which the infinite spirit of things attains to that subjective illumination which is the task of its life, it leaves me in presence of a sort of subjective carrion considerably more noisome than the objective carrion I called it in to take away.

No! better a thousand times, than such systematic corruption of our moral sanity, the plainest pessimism, so that it be straightforward; but better far than that the world of chance. Make as great an uproar about chance as you please, I know that chance means pluralism and nothing more. If some of the members of the pluralism are bad, the philosophy of pluralism, whatever broad views it may deny me, permits me, at least, to turn to the other members with a clean breast of affection and an unsophisticated moral sense. And if I still wish to think of the world as a totality, it lets me feel that a world with a *chance* in it of being altogether good, even if the chance never come to pass, is better than a world with no such chance at all. That 'chance' whose very notion I am exhorted and conjured to banish from my view of the future as the suicide of reason concerning it, that 'chance' is — what? Just this, — the chance that in moral respects the future may be other and better than the past has been. This is the only chance we have any motive for supposing to exist. Shame, rather, on its repudiation and its denial! For its presence is the vital air which lets the world live, the salt which keeps it sweet.

And here I might legitimately stop, having expressed all I care to see admitted by others to-night. But I know that if I do stop here, misapprehensions will remain in the minds of some of you, and keep all I have said from having its effect; so I judge it best to add a few more words.

In the first place, in spite of all my explanations, the word 'chance' will still be giving trouble. Though you may yourselves be adverse to the deterministic doctrine, you wish a pleasanter word than 'chance' to name the opposite doctrine by; and you very likely consider my preference for such a word a perverse sort of a partiality on my part. It certainly *is* a bad word to make converts with; and you wish I had not thrust it so butt-foremost at you, — you wish to use a milder term.

Well, I admit there may be just a dash of perversity in its choice. The spectacle of the mere word-grabbing game played by the soft determinists has perhaps driven me too violently the other way; and, rather than be found wrangling with them for the good words, I am willing to take the first bad one which comes along, provided it be unequivocal. The question is of things, not of eulogistic names for them; and the best word is the one that enables men to

know the quickest whether they disagree or not about
the things. But the word ' chance,' with its singular
negativity, is just the word for this purpose. Who-
ever uses it instead of ' freedom,' squarely and reso-
lutely gives up all pretence to control the things he
says are free. For *him,* he confesses that they are no
better than mere chance would be. It is a word of
impotence, and is therefore the only sincere word we
can use, if, in granting freedom to certain things, we
grant it honestly, and really risk the game. " Who
chooses me must give and forfeit all he hath." Any
other word permits of quibbling, and lets us, after the
fashion of the soft determinists, make a pretence of
restoring the caged bird to liberty with one hand,
while with the other we anxiously tie a string to its
leg to make sure it does not get beyond our sight.

But now you will bring up your final doubt. Does
not the admission of such an unguaranteed chance or
freedom preclude utterly the notion of a Providence
governing the world? Does it not leave the fate of
the universe at the mercy of the chance-possibilities,
and so far insecure? Does it not, in short, deny the
craving of our nature for an ultimate peace behind all
tempests, for a blue zenith above all clouds?
To this my answer must be very brief. The belief
in free-will is not in the least incompatible with the
belief in Providence, provided you do not restrict the
Providence to fulminating nothing but *fatal* decrees.
If you allow him to provide possibilities as well as
actualities to the universe, and to carry on his own
thinking in those two categories just as we do ours,
chances may be there, uncontrolled even by him,
and the course of the universe be really ambiguous;

and yet the end of all things may be just what he intended it to be from all eternity.

An analogy will make the meaning of this clear. Suppose two men before a chessboard, — the one a novice, the other an expert player of the game. The expert intends to beat. But he cannot foresee exactly what any one actual move of his adversary may be. He knows, however, all the *possible* moves of the latter; and he knows in advance how to meet each of them by a move of his own which leads in the direction of victory. And the victory infallibly arrives, after no matter how devious a course, in the one predestined form of check-mate to the novice's king.

Let now the novice stand for us finite free agents, and the expert for the infinite mind in which the universe lies. Suppose the latter to be thinking out his universe before he actually creates it. Suppose him to say, I will lead things to a certain end, but I will not *now* * decide on all the steps thereto. At various points, ambiguous possibilities shall be left

---

* This of course leaves the creative mind subject to the law of time. And to any one who insists on the timelessness of that mind I have no reply to make. A mind to whom all time is simultaneously present must see all things under the form of actuality, or under some form to us unknown. If he thinks certain moments as ambiguous in their content while future, he must simultaneously know how the ambiguity will have been decided when they are past. So that none of his mental judgments can possibly be called hypothetical, and his world is one from which chance is excluded. Is not, however, the timeless mind rather a gratuitous fiction? And is not the notion of eternity being given at a stroke to omniscience only just another way of whacking upon us the block-universe, and of denying that possibilities exist? — just the point to be proved. To say that time is an illusory appearance is only a roundabout manner of saying there is no real plurality, and that the frame of things is an absolute unit. Admit plurality, and time may be its form.

open, *either* of which, at a given instant, may become actual. But whichever branch of these bifurcations become real, I know what I shall do at the *next* bifurcation to keep things from drifting away from the final result I intend.*

The creator's plan of the universe would thus be left blank as to many of its actual details, but all possibilities would be marked down. The realization of some of these would be left absolutely to chance; that is, would only be determined when the moment of realization came. Other possibilities would be *contingently* determined; that is, their decision would have to wait till it was seen how the matters of absolute chance fell out. But the rest of the plan, including its final upshot, would be rigorously determined once for all. So the creator himself would not need to know *all* the details of actuality until they came; and at any time his own view of the world would be a view partly of facts and partly of possibilities, exactly as ours is now. Of one thing, however, he might be certain; and that is that his world was safe, and that no matter how much it might zigzag he could surely bring it home at last.

* And this of course means 'miraculous' interposition, but not necessarily of the gross sort our fathers took such delight in representing, and which has so lost its magic for us. Emerson quotes some Eastern sage as saying that if evil were really done under the sun, the sky would incontinently shrivel to a snakeskin and cast it out in spasms. But, says, Emerson, the spasms of Nature are years and centuries; and it will tax man's patience to wait so long. We may think of the reserved possibilities God keeps in his own hand, under as invisible and molecular and slowly self-summating a form as we please. We may think of them as counteracting human agencies which he inspires *ad hoc*. In short, signs and wonders and convulsions of the earth and sky are not the only neutralizers of obstruction to a god's plans of which it is possible to think.

Now, it is entirely immaterial, in this scheme, whether the creator leave the absolute chance-possibilities to be decided by himself, each when its proper moment arrives, or whether, on the contrary, he alienate this power from himself, and leave the decision out and out to finite creatures such as we men are. The great point is that the possibilities are really *here*. Whether it be we who solve them, or he working through us, at those soul-trying moments when fate's scales seem to quiver, and good snatches the victory from evil or shrinks nerveless from the fight, is of small account, so long as we admit that the issue is decided nowhere else than *here* and *now*. *That* is what gives the palpitating reality to our moral life and makes it tingle, as Mr. Mallock says, with so strange and elaborate an excitement. This reality, this excitement, are what the determinisms, hard and soft alike, suppress by their denial that *anything* is decided here and now, and their dogma that all things were foredoomed and settled long ago. If it be so, may you and I then have been foredoomed to the error of continuing to believe in liberty.* It is fortunate for the winding up of controversy that in every discussion with determinism this *argumentum ad hominem* can be its adversary's last word.

* As long as languages contain a future perfect tense, determinists, following the bent of laziness or passion, the lines of least resistance, can reply in that tense, saying, "It will have been fated," to the still small voice which urges an opposite course; and thus excuse themselves from effort in a quite unanswerable way.

THE MORAL PHILOSOPHER AND THE MORAL LIFE *

THE main purpose of this paper is to show that there is no such thing possible as an ethical philosophy dogmatically made up in advance. We all help to determine the content of ethical philosophy so far as we contribute to the race's moral life. In other words, there can be no final truth in ethics any more than in physics, until the last man has had his experience and said his say. In the one case as in the other, however, the hypotheses which we now make while waiting, and the acts to which they prompt us, are among the indispensable conditions which determine what that 'say' shall be.

First of all, what is the position of him who seeks an ethical philosophy? To begin with, he must be distinguished from all those who are satisfied to be ethical sceptics. He *will* not be a sceptic; therefore so far from ethical scepticism being one possible fruit of ethical philosophizing, it can only be regarded as that residual alternative to all philosophy which from the outset menaces every would-be philosopher who may give up the quest discouraged, and renounce his original aim. That aim is to find an account of the moral relations that obtain among things, which

* An Address to the Yale Philosophical Club, published in the International Journal of Ethics, April, 1891.

will weave them into the unity of a stable system, and make of the world what one may call a genuine universe from the ethical point of view. So far as the world resists reduction to the form of unity, so far as ethical propositions seem unstable, so far does the philosopher fail of his ideal. The subject-matter of his study is the ideals he finds existing in the world; the purpose which guides him is this ideal of his own, of getting them into a certain form. This ideal is thus a factor in ethical philosophy whose legitimate presence must never be overlooked; it is a positive contribution which the philosopher himself necessarily makes to the problem. But it is his only positive contribution. At the outset of his inquiry he ought to have no other ideals. Were he interested peculiarly in the triumph of any one kind of good, he would *pro tanto* cease to be a judicial investigator, and become an advocate for some limited element of the case.

There are three questions in ethics which must be kept apart. Let them be called respectively the *psychological* question, the *metaphysical* question, and the *casuistic* question. The psychological question asks after the historical *origin* of our moral ideas and judgments; the metaphysical question asks what the very *meaning* of the words ' good,' ' ill,' and ' obligation ' are; the casuistic question asks what is the *measure* of the various goods and ills which men recognize, so that the philosopher may settle the true order of human obligations.

I

THE psychological question is for most disputants the only question. When your ordinary doctor of divinity has proved to his own satisfaction that an altogether unique faculty called ' conscience ' must be postulated to tell us what is right and what is wrong; or when your popular-science enthusiast has proclaimed that ' apriorism ' is an exploded superstition, and that our moral judgments have gradually resulted from the teaching of the environment, each of these persons thinks that ethics is settled and nothing more is to be said.   The familiar pair of names, Intuitionist and Evolutionist, so commonly used now to connote all possible differences in ethical opinion, really refer to the psychological question alone.   The discussion of this question hinges so much upon particular details that it is impossible to enter upon it at all within the limits of this paper.   I will therefore only express dogmatically my own belief, which is this, — that the Benthams, the Mills, and the Bains have done a lasting service in taking so many of our human ideals and showing how they must have arisen from the association with acts of simple bodily pleasures and reliefs from pain.   Association with many remote pleasures will unquestionably make a thing significant of goodness in our minds; and the more vaguely the goodness is conceived of, the more mysterious will its source appear to be.   But it is surely impossible to explain all our sentiments and preferences in this simple way.   The more minutely psychology studies human nature, the more clearly it finds there traces of secondary affections, relating the impressions of the environment with one another and with our impulses in quite different ways from those mere associations of coexistence and succession which are practically all that pure empiricism can admit.   Take the love of drunkenness; take bashfulness, the terror of high places, the tendency to sea-sickness, to faint at the sight of blood, the susceptibility to musical sounds; take the emotion of the comical, the passion for poetry, for mathematics, or for metaphysics, — no one of these things can be wholly explained by either association or utility. They *go with* other things that can be so explained, no doubt; and some of them are prophetic of future utilities, since there is nothing in us for which some use may not be found. But their origin is in incidental complications to our cerebral structure, a structure whose original features arose with no reference to the perception of such discords and harmonies as these.

Well, a vast number of our moral perceptions also are certainly of this secondary and brain-born kind. They deal with directly felt fitnesses between things, and often fly in the teeth of all the prepossessions of habit and presumptions of utility. The moment you get beyond the coarser and more commonplace moral maxims, the Decalogues and Poor Richard's Almanacs, you fall into schemes and positions which to the eye of common-sense are fantastic and overstrained. The sense for abstract justice which some persons have is as excentric a variation, from the natural-history point of view, as is the passion for music or for the higher philosophical consistencies which consumes the soul of others. The feeling of the inward dignity of certain spiritual attitudes, as peace, serenity, simplicity, veracity; and of the essential vulgarity of others, as querulousness, anxiety, egoistic fussiness, etc., — are quite inexplicable except by an innate preference of the more ideal attitude for its own pure sake. The nobler thing *tastes* better, and that is all that we can say. 'Ex-

perience' of consequences may truly teach us what
things are *wicked,* but what have consequences to
do with what is *mean* and *vulgar?* If a man has
shot his wife's paramour, by reason of what subtile repugnancy in things is it that we are so disgusted when we hear that the wife and the husband
have made it up and are living comfortably together
again? Or if the hypothesis were offered us of a
world in which Messrs. Fourier's and Bellamy's and
Morris's utopias should all be outdone, and millions
kept permanently happy on the one simple condition
that a certain lost soul on the far-off edge of things
should lead a life of lonely torture, what except a
specifical and independent sort of emotion can it be
which would make us immediately feel, even though
an impulse arose within us to clutch at the happiness
so offered, how hideous a thing would be its enjoyment when deliberately accepted as the fruit of such
a bargain? To what, once more, but subtile brain-
born feelings of discord can be due all these recent
protests against the entire race-tradition of retributive
justice? — I refer to Tolstoï with his ideas of non-
resistance, to Mr. Bellamy with his substitution of
oblivion for repentance (in his novel of Dr. Heiden-
hain's Process), to M. Guyau with his radical con-
demnation of the punitive ideal. All these subtileties
of the moral sensibility go as much beyond what can
be ciphered out from the 'laws of association' as
the delicacies of sentiment possible between a pair
of young lovers go beyond such precepts of the
'etiquette to be observed during engagement' as
are printed in manuals of social form.

No! Purely inward forces are certainly at work
here. All the higher, more penetrating ideals are

revolutionary. They present themselves far less in the guise of effects of past experience than in that of probable causes of future experience, factors to which the environment and the lessons it has so far taught us must learn to bend.

This is all I can say of the psychological question now. In the last chapter of a recent work * I have sought to prove in a general way the existence, in our thought, of relations which do not merely repeat the couplings of experience. Our ideals have certainly many sources. They are not all explicable as signifying corporeal pleasures to be gained, and pains to be escaped. And for having so constantly perceived this psychological fact, we must applaud the intuitionist school. Whether or not such applause must be extended to that school's other characteristics will appear as we take up the following questions.

The next one in order is the metaphysical question, of what we mean by the words ' obligation,' ' good,' and ' ill.'

II

FIRST of all, it appears that such words can have no application or relevancy in a world in which no sentient life exists. Imagine an absolutely material world, containing only physical and chemical facts, and existing from eternity without a God, without even an interested spectator: would there be any sense in saying of that world that one of its states is better than another? Or if there were two such worlds possible, would there be any rhyme or reason in calling one good and the other bad, — good or

* The Principles of Psychology, New York, H. Holt & Co. 1890.

bad positively, I mean, and apart from the fact that
one might relate itself better than the other to the
philosopher's private interests? But we must leave
these private interests out of the account, for the
philosopher is a mental fact, and we are asking whether
goods and evils and obligations exist in physical facts
per se. Surely there is no *status* for good and evil to
exist in, in a purely insentient world. How can one
physical fact, considered simply as a physical fact, be
'better' than another? Betterness is not a physical
relation. In its mere material capacity, a thing can
no more be good or bad than it can be pleasant or
painful. Good for what? Good for the production
of another physical fact, do you say? But what in a
purely physical universe demands the production of
that other fact? Physical facts simply *are* or are
not; and neither when present or absent, can they
be supposed to make demands. If they do, they can
only do so by having desires; and then they have
ceased to be purely physical facts, and have become
facts of conscious sensibility. Goodness, badness, and
obligation must be *realized* somewhere in order really
to exist; and the first step in ethical philosophy is to
see that no merely inorganic 'nature of things' can
realize them. Neither moral relations nor the moral
law can swing *in vacuo.* Their only habitat can be a
mind which feels them; and no world composed of
merely physical facts can possibly be a world to which
ethical propositions apply.

The moment one sentient being, however, is made
a part of the universe, there is a chance for goods
and evils really to exist. Moral relations now have
their *status,* in that being's consciousness. So far as
he feels anything to be good, he *makes* it good. It

is good, for him; and being good for him, is absolutely good, for he is the sole creator of values in
that universe, and outside of his opinion things have
no moral character at all.

In such a universe as that it would of course be
absurd to raise the question of whether the solitary
thinker's judgments of good and ill are true or not.
Truth supposes a standard outside of the thinker to
which he must conform; but here the thinker is a
sort of divinity, subject to no higher judge. Let us
call the supposed universe which he inhabits a *moral
solitude*. In such a moral solitude it is clear that
there can be no outward obligation, and that the only
trouble the god-like thinker is liable to have will be
over the consistency of his own several ideals with
one another. Some of these will no doubt be more
pungent and appealing than the rest, their goodness
will have a profounder, more penetrating taste; they
will return to haunt him with more obstinate regrets
if violated. So the thinker will have to order his life
with them as its chief determinants, or else remain
inwardly discordant and unhappy. Into whatever
equilibrium he may settle, though, and however he
may straighten out his system, it will be a right system; for beyond the facts of his own subjectivity
there is nothing moral in the world.

If now we introduce a second thinker with his likes
and dislikes into the universe, the ethical situation
becomes much more complex, and several possibilities
are immediately seen to obtain.

One of these is that the thinkers may ignore each
other's attitude about good and evil altogether, and
each continue to indulge his own preferences, indifferent to what the other may feel or do. In such a

case we have a world with twice as much of the ethical quality in it as our moral solitude, only it is without ethical unity. The same object is good or bad there, according as you measure it by the view which this one or that one of the thinkers takes. Nor can you find any possible ground in such a world for saying that one thinker's opinion is more correct than the other's, or that either has the truer moral sense. Such a world, in short, is not a moral universe but a moral dualism. Not only is there no single point of view within it from which the values of things can be unequivocally judged, but there is not even a demand for such a point of view, since the two thinkers are supposed to be indifferent to each other's thoughts and acts. Multiply the thinkers into a pluralism, and we find realized for us in the ethical sphere something like that world which the antique sceptics conceived of, — in which individual minds are the measures of all things, and in which no one ' objective ' truth, but only a multitude of ' subjective ' opinions, can be found.

But this is the kind of world with which the philosopher, so long as he holds to the hope of a philosophy, will not put up. Among the various ideals represented, there must be, he thinks, some which have the more truth or authority; and to these the others *ought* to yield, so that system and subordination may reign. Here in the word ' ought ' the notion of *obligation* comes emphatically into view, and the next thing in order must be to make its meaning clear.

Since the outcome of the discussion so far has been to show us that nothing can be good or right except so far as some consciousness feels it to be good or thinks it to be right, we perceive on the very threshold that the real superiority and authority which are postulated by the philosopher to reside in some of the opinions, and the really inferior character which he supposes must belong to others, cannot be explained by any abstract moral 'nature of things' existing antecedently to the concrete thinkers themselves with their ideals. Like the positive attributes good and bad, the comparative ones better and worse must be *realized* in order to be real. If one ideal judgment be objectively better than another, that betterness must be made flesh by being lodged concretely in some one's actual perception. It cannot float in the atmosphere, for it is not a sort of meteorological phenomenon, like the aurora borealis or the zodiacal light. Its *esse* is *percipi*, like the *esse* of the ideals themselves between which it obtains. The philosopher, therefore, who seeks to know which ideal ought to have supreme weight and which one ought to be subordinated, must trace the *ought* itself to the *de facto* constitution of some existing consciousness, behind which, as one of the data of the universe, he as a purely ethical philosopher is unable to go. This consciousness must make the one ideal right by feeling it to be right, the other wrong by feeling it to be wrong. But now what particular consciousness in the universe *can* enjoy this prerogative of obliging others to conform to a rule which it lays down?

If one of the thinkers were obviously divine, while all the rest were human, there would probably be no practical dispute about the matter. The divine thought would be the model, to which the others should conform. But still the theoretic question would remain, What is the ground of the obligation, even here?

In our first essays at answering this question, there is an inevitable tendency to slip into an assumption which ordinary men follow when they are disputing with one another about questions of good and bad. They imagine an abstract moral order in which the objective truth resides; and each tries to prove that this pre-existing order is more accurately reflected in his own ideas than in those of his adversary. It is because one disputant is backed by this overarching abstract order that we think the other should submit. Even so, when it is a question no longer of two finite thinkers, but of God and ourselves, — we follow our usual habit, and imagine a sort of *de jure* relation, which antedates and overarches the mere facts, and would make it right that we should conform our thoughts to God's thoughts, even though he made no claim to that effect, and though we preferred *de facto* to go on thinking for ourselves.

But the moment we take a steady look at the question, *we see not only that without a claim actually made by some concrete person there can be no obligation, but that there is some obligation wherever there is a claim.* Claim and obligation are, in fact, coextensive terms; they cover each other exactly. Our ordinary attitude of regarding ourselves as subject to an overarching system of moral relations, true ' in themselves,' is therefore either an out-and-out superstition, or else it must be treated as a merely provisional abstraction from that real Thinker in whose actual demand upon us to think as he does our obligation must be ultimately based. In a theistic-ethical philosophy that thinker in question is, of course, the Deity to whom the existence of the universe is due.

I know well how hard it is for those who are accustomed to what I have called the superstitious view, to realize that every *de facto* claim creates in so far forth an obligation. We inveterately think that something which we call the 'validity' of the claim is what gives to it its obligatory character, and that this validity is something outside of the claim's mere existence as a matter of fact. It rains down upon the claim, we think, from some sublime dimension of being, which the moral law inhabits, much as upon the steel of the compass-needle the influence of the Pole rains down from out of the starry heavens. But again, how can such an inorganic abstract character of imperativeness, additional to the imperativeness which is in the concrete claim itself, *exist?* Take any demand, however slight, which any creature, however weak, may make. Ought it not, for its own sole sake, to be satisfied? If not, prove why not. The only possible kind of proof you could adduce would be the exhibition of another creature who should make a demand that ran the other way. The only possible reason there can be why any phenomenon ought to exist is that such a phenomenon actually is desired. Any desire is imperative to the extent of its amount; it *makes* itself valid by the fact that it exists at all. Some desires, truly enough, are small desires; they are put forward by insignificant persons, and we customarily make light of the obligations which they bring. But the fact that such personal demands as these impose small obligations does not keep the largest obligations from being personal demands.

If we must talk impersonally, to be sure we can say

that ' the universe ' requires, exacts, or makes obligatory such or such an action, whenever it expresses
itself through the desires of such or such a creature.
But it is better not to talk about the universe in this
personified way, unless we believe in a universal or
divine consciousness which actually exists. If there
be such a consciousness, then its demands carry the
most of obligation simply because they are the greatest in amount. But it is even then not *abstractly*
right that we should respect them. It is only *concretely* right, — or right after the fact, and by virtue
of the fact, that they are actually made. Suppose we
do not respect them, as seems largely to be the case
in this queer world. That ought not to be, we say;
that is wrong. But in what way is this fact of wrong-
ness made more acceptable or intelligible when we
imagine it to consist rather in the laceration of an *à
priori* ideal order than in the disappointment of a living personal God? Do we, perhaps, think that we
cover God and protect him and make his impotence
over us less ultimate, when we back him up with this *à
priori* blanket from which he may draw some warmth
of further appeal? But the only force of appeal to *us,*
which either a living God or an abstract ideal order
can wield, is found in the ' everlasting ruby vaults ' of
our own human hearts, as they happen to beat responsive and not irresponsive to the claim. So far as
they do feel it when made by a living consciousness,
is is life answering to life. A claim thus livingly acknowledged is acknowledged with a solidity and fulness which no thought of an ' ideal ' backing can
render more complete; while if, on the other hand,
the heart's response is withheld, the stubborn phenomenon is there of an impotence in the claims

which the universe embodies, which no talk about
an eternal nature of things can gloze over or dispel.
An ineffective *à priori* order is as impotent a thing
as an ineffective God; and in the eye of philosophy,
it is as hard a thing to explain.

We may now consider that what we distinguished
as the metaphysical question in ethical philosophy
is sufficiently answered, and that we have learned
what the words 'good,' 'bad,' and 'obligation' severally mean. They mean no absolute natures, independent of personal support. They are objects of
feeling and desire, which have no foothold or anchorage in Being, apart from the existence of actually
living minds.
Wherever such minds exist, with judgments of
good and ill, and demands upon one another, there
is an ethical world in its essential features. Were
all other things, gods and men and starry heavens,
blotted out from this universe, and were there left
but one rock with two loving souls upon it, that rock
would have as thoroughly moral a constitution as any
possible world which the eternities and immensities
could harbor. It would be a tragic constitution, because the rock's inhabitants would die. But while
they lived, there would be real good things and real
bad things in the universe; there would be obligations, claims, and expectations; obediences, refusals,
and disappointments; compunctions and longings for
harmony to come again, and inward peace of conscience when it was restored; there would, in short,
be a moral life, whose active energy would have no
limit but the intensity of interest in each other with
which the hero and heroine might be endowed.

We, on this terrestrial globe, so far as the visible
facts go, are just like the inhabitants of such a rock.
Whether a God exist, or whether no God exist, in
yon blue heaven above us bent, we form at any rate
an ethical republic here below. And the first reflection which this leads to is that ethics have as genuine and real a foothold in a universe where the highest
consciousness is human, as in a universe where there
is a God as well. ' The religion of humanity ' affords
a basis for ethics as well as theism does. Whether
the purely human system can gratify the philosopher's demand as well as the other is a different question, which we ourselves must answer ere we close.

III

THE last fundamental question in Ethics was, it will
be remembered, the *casuistic* question. Here we are,
in a world where the existence of a divine thinker has
been and perhaps always will be doubted by some of
the lookers-on, and where, in spite of the presence
of a large number of ideals in which human beings
agree, there are a mass of others about which no
general consensus obtains. It is hardly necessary to
present a literary picture of this, for the facts are too
well known. The wars of the flesh and the spirit in
each man, the concupiscences of different individuals
pursuing the same unshareable material or social
prizes, the ideals which contrast so according to races,
circumstances, temperaments, philosophical beliefs,
etc., — all form a maze of apparently inextricable confusion with no obvious Ariadne's thread to lead one
out. Yet the philosopher, just because he is a philosopher, adds his own peculiar ideal to the confusion

(with which if he were willing to be a sceptic he would be passably content), and insists that over all these individual opinions there is a *system of truth* which he can discover if he only takes sufficient pains.

We stand ourselves at present in the place of that philosopher, and must not fail to realize all the features that the situation comports. In the first place we will not be sceptics; we hold to it that there is a truth to be ascertained. But in the second place we have just gained the insight that that truth cannot be a self-proclaiming set of laws, or an abstract 'moral reason,' but can only exist in act, or in the shape of an opinion held by some thinker really to be found. There is, however, no visible thinker invested with authority. Shall we then simply proclaim our own ideals as the lawgiving ones? No; for if we are true philosophers we must throw our own spontaneous ideals, even the dearest, impartially in with that total mass of ideals which are fairly to be judged. But how then can we as philosophers ever find a test; how avoid complete moral scepticism on the one hand, and on the other escape bringing a wayward personal standard of our own along with us, on which we simply pin our faith?

The dilemma is a hard one, nor does it grow a bit more easy as we revolve it in our minds. The entire undertaking of the philosopher obliges him to seek an impartial test. That test, however, must be incarnated in the demand of some actually existent person; and how can he pick out the person save by an act in which his own sympathies and prepossessions are implied?

One method indeed presents itself, and has as a matter of history been taken by the more serious ethical schools. If the heap of things demanded proved on inspection less chaotic than at first they seemed, if they furnished their own relative test and measure, then the casuistic problem would be solved. If it were found that all goods *quâ* goods contained a common essence, then the amount of this essence involved in any one good would show its rank in the scale of goodness, and order could be quickly made; for this essence would be *the* good upon which all thinkers were agreed, the relatively objective and universal good that the philosopher seeks. Even his own private ideals would be measured by their share of it, and find their rightful place among the rest.

Various essences of good have thus been found and proposed as bases of the ethical system. Thus, to be a mean between two extremes; to be recognized by a special intuitive faculty; to make the agent happy for the moment; to make others as well as him happy in the long run; to add to his perfection or dignity; to harm no one; to follow from reason or flow from universal law; to be in accordance with the will of God; to promote the survival of the human species on this planet, — are so many tests, each of which has been maintained by somebody to constitute the essence of all good things or actions so far as they are good.

No one of the measures that have been actually proposed has, however, given general satisfaction. Some are obviously not universally present in all cases, — *e. g.*, the character of harming no one, or that of following a universal law; for the best course is often cruel; and many acts are reckoned good on the sole condition that they be exceptions, and serve not as examples of a universal law. Other characters, such as following the will of God, are unascertainable and vague. Others again, like survival, are quite indeterminate in their consequences, and leave us in the lurch where we most need their help: a philosopher of the Sioux Nation, for example, will be certain to use the survival-criterion in a very different way from ourselves. The best, on the whole, of these marks and measures of goodness seems to be the capacity to bring happiness. But in order not to break down fatally, this test must be taken to cover innumerable acts and impulses that never *aim* at happiness; so that, after all, in seeking for a universal principle we inevitably are carried onward to the *most* universal principle, — that *the essence of good is simply to satisfy demand.* The demand may be for anything under the sun. There is really no more ground for supposing that all our demands can be accounted for by one universal underlying kind of motive than there is ground for supposing that all physical phenomena are cases of a single law. The elementary forces in ethics are probably as plural as those of physics are. The various ideals have no common character apart from the fact that they are ideals. No single abstract principle can be so used as to yield to the philosopher anything like a scientifically accurate and genuinely useful casuistic scale.

A look at another peculiarity of the ethical universe, as we find it, will still further show us the philosopher's perplexities. As a purely theoretic problem, namely, the casuistic question would hardly ever come up at all. If the ethical philosopher were only asking after the best *imaginable* system of goods he would indeed have an easy task; for all demands as such are *primâ facie* respectable, and the best simply imaginary world would be one in which *every* demand was gratified as soon as made. Such a world would, however, have to have a physical constitution entirely different from that of the one which we inhabit. It would need not only a space, but a time, ' of *n*–dimensions, to include all the acts and experiences incompatible with one another here below, which would then go on in conjunction, — such as spending our money, yet growing rich; taking our holiday, yet getting ahead with our work; shooting and fishing, yet doing no hurt to the beasts; gaining no end of experience, yet keeping our youthful freshness of heart; and the like. There can be no question that such a system of things, however brought about, would be the absolutely ideal system; and that if a philosopher could create universes *a priori,* and provide all the mechanical conditions, that is the sort of universe which he should unhesitatingly create.

But this world of ours is made on an entirely different pattern, and the casuistic question here is most tragically practical. The actually possible in this world is vastly narrower than all that is demanded; and there is always a *pinch* between the ideal and the actual which can only be got through by leaving part of the ideal behind. There is hardly a good which we can imagine except as competing for the possession of the same bit of space and time with some other imagined good. Every end of desire that presents itself appears exclusive of some other end of desire. Shall a man drink and smoke, *or* keep his nerves in condition? — he cannot do both. Shall he follow his fancy for Amelia, *or* for Henrietta? — both cannot be the choice of his heart. Shall he have the

dear old Republican party, *or* a spirit of unsophistica-
tion in public affairs? — he cannot have both, etc.
So that the ethical philosopher's demand for the right
scale of subordination in ideals is the fruit of an altogether practical need. Some part of the ideal must
be butchered, and he needs to know which part. It
is a tragic situation, and no mere speculative conun-
drum, with which he has to deal.

Now *we* are blinded to the real difficulty of the
philosopher's task by the fact that we are born into a
society whose ideals are largely ordered already. If
we follow the ideal which is conventionally highest,
the others which we butcher either die and do not return to haunt us; or if they come back and accuse us
of murder, every one applauds us for turning to them
a deaf ear. In other words, our environment encour-
ages us not to be philosophers but partisans. The
philosopher, however, cannot, so long as he clings to
his own ideal of objectivity, rule out any ideal from
being heard. He is confident, and rightly confident,
that the simple taking counsel of his own intuitive
preferences would be certain to end in a mutilation of
the fulness of the truth. The poet Heine is said to
have written ' Bunsen ' in the place of ' Gott ' in his
copy of that author's work entitled " God in History," so as to make it read ' Bunsen in der Geschichte.'
Now, with no disrespect to the good and learned
Baron, is it not safe to say that any single philosopher, however wide his sympathies, must be just
such a Bunsen in der Geschichte of the moral world,
so soon as he attempts to put his own ideas of order
into that howling mob of desires, each struggling to
get breathing-room for the ideal to which it clings?
The very best of men must not only be insensible, but

be ludicrously and peculiarly insensible, to many goods. As a militant, fighting free-handed that the goods to which he *is* sensible may not be submerged and lost from out of life, the philosopher, like every other human being, is in a natural position. But think of Zeno and of Epicurus, think of Calvin and of Paley, think of Kant and Schopenhauer, of Herbert Spencer and John Henry Newman, no longer as one-sided champions of special ideals, but as schoolmasters deciding what all must think, — and what more grotesque topic could a satirist wish for on which to exercise his pen? The fabled attempt of Mrs. Partington to arrest the rising tide of the North Atlantic with her broom was a reasonable spectacle compared with their effort to substitute the content of their clean-shaven systems for that exuberant mass of goods with which all human nature is in travail, and groaning to bring to the light of day. Think, furthermore, of such individual moralists, no longer as mere schoolmasters, but as pontiffs armed with the temporal power, and having authority in every concrete case of conflict to order which good shall be butchered and which shall be suffered to survive, — and the notion really turns one pale. All one's slumbering revolutionary instincts waken at the thought of any single moralist wielding such powers of life and death. Better chaos forever than an order based on any closet-philosopher's rule, even though he were the most enlightened possible member of his tribe. No! if the philosopher is to keep his judicial position, he must never become one of the parties to the fray.

What can he do, then, it will now be asked, except to fall back on scepticism and give up the notion of being a philosopher at all?

But do we not already see a perfectly definite path of escape which is open to him just because he is a philosopher, and not the champion of one particular ideal? Since everything which is demanded is by that fact a good, must not the guiding principle for ethical philosophy (since all demands conjointly cannot be satisfied in this poor world) be simply to satisfy at all times *as many demands as we can?* That act must be the best act, accordingly, which makes for the *best whole,* in the sense of awakening the least sum of dissatisfactions. In the casuistic scale, therefore, those ideals must be written highest which *prevail at the least cost,* or by whose realization the least possible number of other ideals are destroyed. Since victory and defeat there must be, the victory to be philosophically prayed for is that of the more inclusive side, — of the side which even in the hour of triumph will to some degree do justice to the ideals in which the vanquished party's interests lay. The course of history is nothing but the story of men's struggles from generation to generation to find the more and more inclusive order. *Invent some manner* of realizing your own ideals which will also satisfy the alien demands, — that and that only is the path of peace! Following this path, society has shaken itself into one sort of relative equilibrium after another by a series of social discoveries quite analogous to those of science. Polyandry and polygamy and slavery, private warfare and liberty to kill, judicial torture and arbitrary royal power have slowly succumbed to actually aroused complaints; and though some one's ideals are unquestionably the worse off for each improvement, yet a vastly greater total number of them find shelter in our civilized society than in the older

savage ways. So far then, and up to date, the casuistic scale is made for the philosopher already far better than he can ever make it for himself. An experiment of the most searching kind has proved that the
laws and usages of the land are what yield the maximum of satisfaction to the thinkers taken all together.
The presumption in cases of conflict must always be
in favor of the conventionally recognized good. The
philosopher must be a conservative, and in the construction of his casuistic scale must put the things most
in accordance with the customs of the community on
top.

And yet if he be a true philosopher he must see
that there is nothing final in any actually given equilibrium of human ideals, but that, as our present
laws and customs have fought and conquered other
past ones, so they will in their turn be overthrown
by any newly discovered order which will hush up
the complaints that they still give rise to, without
producing others louder still. " Rules are made for
man, not man for rules," — that one sentence is
enough to immortalize Green's Prolegomena to
Ethics. And although a man always risks much
when he breaks away from established rules and
strives to realize a larger ideal whole than they permit, yet the philosopher must allow that it is at
all times open to any one to make the experiment,
provided he fear not to stake his life and character
upon the throw. The pinch is always here. Pent in
under every system of moral rules are innumerable
persons whom it weighs upon, and goods which it
represses; and these are always rumbling and grum-
bling in the background, and ready for any issue by
which they may get free. See the abuses which the

institution of private property covers, so that even to-day it is shamelessly asserted among us that one of the prime functions of the national government is to help the adroiter citizens to grow rich. See the unnamed and unnamable sorrows which the tyranny, on the whole so beneficent, of the marriage-institution brings to so many, both of the married and the unwed. See the wholesale loss of opportunity under our *régime* of so-called equality and industrialism, with the drummer and the counter-jumper in the saddle, for so many faculties and graces which could flourish in the feudal world. See our kindliness for the humble and the outcast, how it wars with that stern weeding out which until now has been the condition of every perfection in the breed. See everywhere the struggle and the squeeze; and everlastingly the problem how to make them less. The anarchists, nihilists, and free-lovers; the free-silverites, socialists, and single-tax men; the free-traders and civil-service reformers; the prohibitionists and anti-vivisectionists; the radical darwinians with their idea of the suppression of the weak, — these and all the conservative sentiments of society arrayed against them, are simply deciding through actual experiment by what sort of conduct the maximum amount of good can be gained and kept in this world. These experiments are to be judged, not *a priori*, but by actual finding, after the fact of their making, how much more outcry or how much appeasement comes about. What closet-solutions can possibly anticipate the result of trials made on such a scale? Or what can any superficial theorist's judgment be worth, in a world where every one of hundreds of ideals has its special champion already provided in the shape of some genius expressly born to feel it, and to fight to death in its behalf? The pure philosopher can only follow the windings of the spectacle, confident that the line of least resistance will always be towards the richer and the more inclusive arrangement, and that by one tack after another some approach to the kingdom of heaven is incessantly made.

IV

ALL this amounts to saying that, so far as the casuistic question goes, ethical science is just like physical science, and instead of being deducible all at once from abstract principles, must simply bide its time, and be ready to revise its conclusions from day to day. The presumption of course, in both sciences, always is that the vulgarly accepted opinions are true, and the right casuistic order that which public opinion believes in; and surely it would be folly quite as great, in most of us, to strike out independently and to aim at originality in ethics as in physics. Every now and then, however, some one is born with the right to be original, and his revolutionary thought or action may bear prosperous fruit. He may replace old 'laws of nature' by better ones; he may, by breaking old moral rules in a certain place, bring in a total condition of things more ideal than would have followed had the rules been kept.

On the whole, then, we must conclude that no philosophy of ethics is possible in the old-fashioned absolute sense of the term. Everywhere the ethical philosopher must wait on facts. The thinkers who create the ideals come he knows not whence, their sensibilities are evolved he knows not how; and the question as to which of two conflicting ideals will give the best universe then and there, can be answered by him only through the aid of the experience of other men. I said some time ago, in treating of the 'first' question, that the intuitional moralists deserve credit for keeping most clearly to the psychological facts. They do much to spoil this merit on the whole, however, by mixing with it that dogmatic temper which, by absolute distinctions and unconditional ' thou shalt nots,' changes a growing, elastic, and continuous life into a superstitious system of relics and dead bones. In point of fact, there are no absolute evils, and there are no non-moral goods; and the *highest* ethical life — however few may be called to bear its burdens — consists at all times in the breaking of rules which have grown too narrow for the actual case. There is but one unconditional commandment, which is that we should seek incessantly, with fear and trembling, so to vote and to act as to bring about the very largest total universe of good which we can see. Abstract rules indeed can help; but they help the less in proportion as our intuitions are more piercing, and our vocation is the stronger for the moral life. For every real dilemma is in literal strictness a unique situation; and the exact combination of ideals realized and ideals disappointed which each decision creates is always a universe without a precedent, and for which no adequate previous rule exists. The philosopher, then, *quâ* philosopher, is no better able to determine the best universe in the concrete emergency than other men. He sees, indeed, somewhat better than most men what the question always is, — not a question of this good or that good simply taken, but of the two total universes with which these goods respectively belong. He knows that he must vote always for the richer universe, for the good which seems most organizable, most fit to enter into complex combinations, most apt to be a member of a more inclusive whole. But which particular universe this is he cannot know for certain in advance; he only knows that if he makes a bad mistake the cries of the wounded will soon inform him of the fact. In all this the philosopher is just like the rest of us non-philosophers, so far as we are just and sympathetic instinctively, and so far as we are open to the voice of complaint. His function is in fact indistinguishable from that of the best kind of statesman at the present day. His books upon ethics, therefore, so far as they truly touch the moral life, must more and more ally themselves with a literature which is confessedly tentative and sugges-tive rather than dogmatic, — I mean with novels and dramas of the deeper sort, with sermons, with books on statecraft and philanthropy and social and eco-nomical reform. Treated in this way ethical treatises may be voluminous and luminous as well; but they never can be *final,* except in their abstractest and vaguest features; and they must more and more abandon the old-fashioned, clear-cut, and would-be 'scientific' form.

V

THE chief of all the reasons why concrete ethics cannot be final is that they have to wait on meta-physical and theological beliefs. I said some time back that real ethical relations existed in a purely human world. They would exist even in what we called a moral solitude if the thinker had various

ideals which took hold of him in turn. His self of
one day would make demands on his self of another;
and some of the demands might be urgent and tyrannical, while others were gentle and easily put aside.
We call the tyrannical demands *imperatives*. If we
ignore these we do not hear the last of it. The good
which we have wounded returns to plague us with
interminable crops of consequential damages, compunctions, and regrets. Obligation can thus exist
inside a single thinker's consciousness; and perfect
peace can abide with him only so far as he lives
according to some sort of a casuistic scale which
keeps his more imperative goods on top. It is the
nature of these goods to be cruel to their rivals.
Nothing shall avail when weighed in the balance
against them. They call out all the mercilessness in
our disposition, and do not easily forgive us if we are
so soft-hearted as to shrink from sacrifice in their
behalf.

The deepest difference, practically, in the moral
life of man is the difference between the easy-going
and the strenuous mood. When in the easy-going
mood the shrinking from present ill is our ruling consideration. The strenuous mood, on the contrary,
makes us quite indifferent to present ill, if only the
greater ideal be attained. The capacity for the strenuous mood probably lies slumbering in every man,
but it has more difficulty in some than in others in
waking up. It needs the wilder passions to arouse it,
the big fears, loves, and indignations; or else the
deeply penetrating appeal of some one of the higher
fidelities, like justice, truth, or freedom. Strong relief
is a necessity of its vision; and a world where all the
mountains are brought down and all the valleys are

[margin handwriting: imperatives not desires or wishes, but demands of a certain behaviour a way of acting... indeed may actually interfere to circumvent the fulfillment of a desire]

exalted is no congenial place for its habitation. This
is why in a solitary thinker this mood might slumber
on forever without waking. His various ideals, known
to him to be mere preferences of his own, are too
nearly of the same denominational value: he can
play fast or loose with them at will. This too is why,
in a merely human world without a God, the appeal
to our moral energy falls short of its maximal stim-
ulating power. Life, to be sure, is even in such a
world a genuinely ethical symphony; but it is played
in the compass of a couple of poor octaves, and the
infinite scale of values fails to open up. Many of us,
indeed, — like Sir James Stephen in those eloquent
' Essays by a Barrister,' — would openly laugh at the
very idea of the strenuous mood being awakened in
us by those claims of remote posterity which constitute the last appeal of the religion of humanity. We
do not love these men of the future keenly enough;
and we love them perhaps the less the more we hear
of their evolutionized perfection, their high average
longevity and education, their freedom from war and
crime, their relative immunity from pain and zymotic
disease, and all their other negative superiorities.
This is all too finite, we say; we see too well the
vacuum beyond. It lacks the note of infinitude and
mystery, and may all be dealt with in the don't-care
mood. No need of agonizing ourselves or making
others agonize for these good creatures just at present.

When, however, we believe that a God is there, and
that he is one of the claimants, the infinite perspective
opens out. The scale of the symphony is incalculably
prolonged. The more imperative ideals now begin
to speak with an altogether new objectivity and significance, and to utter the penetrating, shattering,

tragically challenging note of appeal. They ring out like the call of Victor Hugo's alpine eagle, "qui parle au précipice et que le gouffre entend," and the strenuous mood awakens at the sound. It saith among the trumpets, ha, ha! it smelleth the battle afar off, the thunder of the captains and the shouting. Its blood is up; and cruelty to the lesser claims, so far from being a deterrent element, does but add to the stern joy with which it leaps to answer to the greater. All through history, in the periodical conflicts of puritanism with the don't-care temper, we see the antagonism of the strenuous and genial moods, and the contrast between the ethics of infinite and mysterious obligation from on high, and those of prudence and the satisfaction of merely finite need.

The capacity of the strenuous mood lies so deep down among our natural human possibilities that even if there were no metaphysical or traditional grounds for believing in a God, men would postulate one simply as a pretext for living hard, and getting out of the game of existence its keenest possibilities of zest. Our attitude towards concrete evils is entirely different in a world where we believe there are none but finite demanders, from what it is in one where we joyously face tragedy for an infinite demander's sake. Every sort of energy and endurance, of courage and capacity for handling life's evils, is set free in those who have religious faith. For this reason the strenuous type of character will on the battle-field of human history always outwear the easy-going type, and religion will drive irreligion to the wall.

It would seem, too, — and this is my final conclusion, — that the stable and systematic moral universe for which the ethical philosopher asks is fully possible only in a world where there is a divine thinker with all-enveloping demands. If such a thinker existed, his way of subordinating the demands to one another would be the finally valid casuistic scale; his claims would be the most appealing; his ideal universe would be the most inclusive realizable whole. If he now exist, then actualized in his thought already must be that ethical philosophy which we seek as the pattern which our own must evermore approach.* In the interests of our own ideal of systematically unified moral truth, therefore, we, as would-be philosophers, must postulate a divine thinker, and pray for the victory of the religious cause. Meanwhile, exactly what the thought of the infinite thinker may be is hidden from us even were we sure of his existence; so that our postulation of him after all serves only to let loose in us the strenuous mood. But this is what it does in all men, even those who have no interest in philosophy. The ethical philosopher, therefore, whenever he ventures to say which course of action is the best, is on no essentially different level from the common man. " See, I have set before thee this day life and good, and death and evil; therefore, choose life that thou and thy seed may live," — when this challenge comes to us, it is simply our total character and personal genius that are on trial; and if we invoke any so-called philosophy, our choice and use of that also are but revelations of our personal aptitude or incapacity for moral life. From this unsparing practical ordeal no professor's lectures and no array of books

* All this is set forth with great freshness and force in the work of my colleague, Professor Josiah Royce: "The Religious Aspect of Philosophy." Boston, 1885.

can save us. The solving word, for the learned and the unlearned man alike, lies in the last resort in the dumb willingnesses and unwillingnesses of their interior characters, and nowhere else. It is not in heaven, neither is it beyond the sea; but the word is very nigh unto thee, in thy mouth and in thy heart, that thou mayest do it.

De. 30:14.

THE ENERGIES OF MEN*

EVERYONE knows what it is to start a piece of work, either intellectual or muscular, feeling stale — or *oold,* as an Adirondack guide once put it to me. And everybody knows what it is to "warm up" to his job. The process of warming up gets particularly striking in the phenomenon known as "second wind." On usual occasions we make a practice of stopping an occupation as soon as we meet the first effective layer (so to call it) of fatigue. We have then walked, played, or worked "enough," so we desist. That amount of fatigue is an efficacious obstruction on this side of which our usual life is cast. But if an unusual necessity forces us to press onward, a surprising thing occurs. The fatigue gets worse up to a certain critical point, when gradually or suddenly it passes away, and we are fresher than before. We have evidently tapped a level of new energy, masked until then by the fatigue-obstacle usually obeyed. There may be layer after layer of this experience. A third and a fourth "wind" may

* This was the title originally given to the Presidential Address delivered before the American Philosophical Association at Columbia University, December 28, 1906, and published as there delivered in the *Philosophical Review* for January, 1907. The address was later published, after slight alteration, in the *American Magazine* for October, 1907, under the title "The Powers of Men." The more popular form is here reprinted under the title which the author himself preferred.

supervene. Mental activity shows the phenomenon as well as physical, and in exceptional cases we may find, beyond the very extremity of fatigue-distress, amounts of ease and power that we never dreamed ourselves to own, — sources of strength habitually not taxed at all, because habitually we never push through the obstruction, never pass those early critical points.

For many years I have mused on the phenomenon of second wind, trying to find a physiological theory. It is evident that our organism has stored-up reserves of energy that are ordinarily not called upon, but that may be called upon: deeper and deeper strata of combustible or explosible material, discontinuously arranged, but ready for use by anyone who probes so deep, and repairing themselves by rest as well as do the superficial strata. Most of us continue living unnecessarily near our surface. Our energy-budget is like our nutritive budget. Physiologists say that a man is in "nutritive equilibrium" when day after day he neither gains nor loses weight. But the odd thing is that this condition may obtain on astonishingly different amounts of food. Take a man in nutritive equilibrium, and systematically increase or lessen his rations. In the first case he will begin to gain weight, in the second case to lose it. The change will be greatest on the first day, less on the second, less still on the third; and so on, till he has gained all that he will gain, or lost all that he will lose, on that altered diet. He is now in nutritive equilibrium again, but with a new weight; and this neither lessens nor increases because his various combustion-processes have adjusted themselves to the changed dietary. He gets rid, in one way or another, of just as much N, C, H, etc., as he takes in *per diem*.

Just so one can be in what I might call "efficiency-equilibrium" (neither gaining nor losing power when once the equilibrium is reached) on astonishingly different quantities of work, no matter in what direction the work may be measured. It may be physical work, intellectual work, moral work, or spiritual work.

Of course there are limits: the trees don't grow into the sky. But the plain fact remains that men the world over possess amounts of resource which only very exceptional individuals push to their extremes of use. But the very same individual, pushing his energies to their extreme, may in a vast number of cases keep the pace up day after day, and find no "reaction" of a bad sort, so long as decent hygienic conditions are preserved. His more active rate of energizing does not wreck him; for the organism adapts itself, and as the rate of waste augments, augments correspondingly the rate of repair.

I say the *rate* and not the *time* of repair. The busiest man needs no more hours of rest than the idler. Some years ago Professor Patrick, of the Iowa State University, kept three young men awake for four days and nights. When his observations on them were finished, the subjects were permitted to sleep themselves out. All awoke from this sleep completely refreshed, but the one who took longest to restore himself from his long vigil only slept one-third more time than was regular with him.

If my reader will put together these two conceptions, first, that few men live at their maximum of energy, and second, that anyone may be in vital equilibrium at very different rates of energizing, he will find, I think, that a very pretty practical problem of national economy, as well as of individual ethics, opens upon his view. In rough terms, we may say that a man who energizes below his normal maximum fails by just so much to profit by his chance at life; and that a nation filled with such men is inferior to a nation run at higher pressure. The problem is, then, how can men be trained up to their most useful pitch of energy? And how can nations make such training most accessible to all their sons and daughters. This, after all, is only the general problem of education, formulated in slightly different terms.

"Rough" terms, I said just now, because the words "energy" and "maximum" may easily suggest only *quantity* to the reader's mind, whereas in measuring the human energies of which I speak, qualities as well as quantities have to be taken into account. Everyone feels that his total *power* rises when he passes to a higher *qualitative* level of life.

Writing is higher than walking, thinking is higher than writing, deciding higher than thinking, deciding "no" higher than deciding "yes" — at least the man who passes from one of these activities to another will usually say that each later one involves a greater element of *inner work* than the earlier ones, even though the total heat given out or the foot-pounds expended by the organism, may be less. Just how to conceive this inner work physiologically is as yet impossible, but psychologically we all know what the word means. We need a particular spur or effort to start us upon inner work; it tires us to sustain it; and when long sustained, we know how easily we lapse. When I speak of "energizing," and its rates and levels and sources, I mean therefore our inner as well as our outer work.

Let no one think, then, that our problem of in-dividual and national economy is solely that of the

maximum of pounds raisable against gravity, the
maximum of locomotion, or of agitation of any sort,
that human beings can accomplish. That might sig-
nify little more than hurrying and jumping about in
inco-ordinated ways; whereas inner work, though it so
often reinforces outer work, quite as often means its
arrest. To relax, to say to ourselves (with the "new
thoughters") "Peace! be still!" is sometimes a great
achievement of inner work. When I speak of human
energizing in general, the reader must therefore understand that sum-total of activities, some outer and some
inner, some muscular, some emotional, some moral,
some spiritual, of whose waxing and waning in himself he is at all times so well aware. How to keep
it at an appreciable maximum? How not to let the
level lapse? That is the great problem. But the
work of men and women is of innumerable kinds,
each kind being, as we say, carried on by a particular
faculty; so the great problem splits into two sub-prob-
lems thus:

(1). What are the limits of human faculty in various
directions?

(2). By what diversity of means, in the differing
types of human beings, may the faculties be stimulated
to their best results?

Read in one way, these two questions sound both
trivial and familiar: there is a sense in which we have
all asked them ever since we were born. Yet *as a
methodical programme of scientific inquiry,* I doubt
whether they have ever been seriously taken up. If
answered fully, almost the whole of mental science and
of the science of conduct would find a place under
them. I propose, in what follows, to press them on
the reader's attention in an informal way.

The first point to agree upon in this enterprise is that *as a rule men habitually use only a small part of the powers which they actually possess and which they might use under appropriate conditions.* Every one is familiar with the phenomenon of feeling more or less alive on different days. Every one knows on any given day that there are energies slumbering in him which the incitements of that day do not call forth, but which he might display if these were greater. Most of us feel as if a sort of cloud weighed upon us, keeping us below our highest notch of clearness in discernment, sureness in reasoning, or firmness in deciding. Compared with what we ought to be, we are only half awake. Our fires are damped, our drafts are checked. We are making use of only a small part of our possible mental and physical resources. In some persons this sense of being cut off from their rightful resources is extreme, and we then get the formidable neurasthenic and psychasthenic conditions, with life grown into one tissue of impossibilities, that so many medical books describe.

Stating the thing broadly, the human individual thus lives usually far within his limits; he possesses powers of various sorts which he habitually fails to use. He energizes below his *maximum*, and he behaves below his *optimum*. In elementary faculty, in co-ordination, in power of *inhibition* and control, in every conceivable way, his life is contracted like the field of vision of an hysteric subject — but with less excuse, for the poor hysteric is diseased, while in the rest of us it is only an inveterate *habit* — the habit of inferiority to our full self — that is bad.

Admit so much, then, and admit also that the charge of being inferior to their full self is far truer of some men than of others; then the practical question ensues: *to what do the better men owe their escape? and, in the fluctuations which all men feel in their own degree of energizing, to what are the improvements due, when they occur?*

In general terms the answer is plain:

Either some unusual stimulus fills them with emotional excitement, or some unusual idea of necessity induces them to make an extra effort of will. *Excitements, ideas, and efforts,* in a word, are what carry us over the dam.

In those "hyperesthetic" conditions which chronic invalidism so often brings in its train, the dam has changed its normal place. The slightest functional exercise gives a distress which the patient yields to and stops. In such cases of "habit-neurosis" a new range of power often comes in consequence of the "bullying-treatment," of efforts which the doctor obliges the patient, much against his will, to make. First comes the very extremity of distress, then follows unexpected relief. There seems no doubt that *we are each and all of us to some extent victims of habit-neurosis.* We have to admit the wider potential range and the habitually narrow actual use. We live subject to arrest by degrees of fatigue which we have come only from habit to obey. Most of us may learn to push the barrier farther off, and to live in perfect comfort on much higher levels of power.

Country people and city people, as a class, illustrate this difference. The rapid rate of life, the number of decisions in an hour, the many things to keep account of, in a busy city man's or woman's life, seem monstrous to a country brother. He doesn't see how we live at all. A day in New York or Chicago fills him with terror. The danger and noise make it appear like a permanent earthquake. But *settle* him there, and in a year or two he will have caught the pulse-beat. He will vibrate to the city's rhythms; and if he only succeeds in his avocation, whatever that may be, he will find a joy in all the hurry and the tension, he will keep the pace as well as any of us, and get as much out of himself in any week as he ever did in ten weeks in the country.

The stimuli of those who successfully respond and undergo the transformation here, are duty, the example of others, and crowd-pressure and contagion. The transformation, moreover, is a chronic one: the new level of energy becomes permanent. The duties of new offices of trust are constantly producing this effect on the human beings appointed to them. The physiologists call a stimulus "dynamogenic" when it increases the muscular contractions of men to whom it is applied; but appeals can be dynamogenic morally as well as muscularly. We are witnessing here in America today the dynamogenic effect of a very exalted political office upon the energies of an individual who had already manifested a healthy amount of energy before the office came.

Humbler examples show perhaps still better what chronic effects duty's appeal may produce in chosen individuals. John Stuart Mill somewhere says that women excel men in the power of keeping up sustained moral excitement. Every case of illness nursed by wife or mother is a proof of this; and where can one find greater examples of sustained endurance than in those thousands of poor homes, where the woman successfully holds the family together and keeps it going by taking all the thought and doing all the work —

nursing, teaching, cooking, washing, sewing, scrub-
bing, saving, helping neighbors, "choring" outside —
where does the catalogue end? If she does a bit of
scolding now and then who can blame her? But often
she does just the reverse; keeping the children clean
and the man good tempered, and soothing and
smoothing the whole neighborhood into finer shape.

Eighty years ago a certain Montyon left to the
Académie Française a sum of money to be given in
small prizes, to the best examples of "virtue" of the
year. The academy's committees, with great good
sense, have shown a partiality to virtues simple and
chronic, rather than to her spasmodic and dramatic
flights; and the exemplary housewives reported on
have been wonderful and admirable enough. In Paul
Bourget's report for this year we find numerous cases,
of which this is a type; Jeanne Chaix, eldest of six
children; mother insane, father chronically ill. Jeanne,
with no money but her wages at a pasteboard-box
factory, directs the household, brings up the children,
and successfully maintains the family of eight, which
thus subsists, morally as well as materially, by the
sole force of her valiant will. In some of these French
cases charity to outsiders is added to the inner family burden; or helpless relatives, young or old, are
adopted, as if the strength were inexhaustible and
ample for every appeal. Details are too long to quote
here; but human nature, responding to the call of
duty, appears nowhere sublimer than in the person
of these humble heroines of family life.

Turning from more chronic to acuter proofs of
human nature's reserves of power, we find that the
stimuli that carry us over the usually effective dam are
most often the classic emotional ones, love, anger,

crowd-contagion or despair. Despair lames most people, but it wakes others fully up. Every siege or shipwreck or polar expedition brings out some hero who keeps the whole company in heart. Last year there was a terrible colliery explosion at Courrières in France. Two hundred corpses, if I remember rightly, were exhumed. After twenty days of excavation, the rescuers heard a voice. *"Me voici,"* said the first man unearthed. He proved to be a collier named Nemy, who had taken command of thirteen others in the darkness, disciplined them and cheered them, and brought them out alive. Hardly any of them could see or speak or walk when brought into the day. Five days later, a different type of vital endurance was unexpectedly unburied in the person of one Berton who, isolated from any but dead companions, had been able to sleep away most of his time.

A new position of responsibility will usually show a man to be a far stronger creature than was supposed. Cromwell's and Grant's careers are the stock examples of how war will wake a man up. I owe to Professor C. E. Norton, my colleague, the permission to print part of a private letter from Colonel Baird-Smith written shortly after the six weeks' siege of Delhi, in 1857, for the victorious issue of which that excellent officer was chiefly to be thanked. He writes as follows:

" . . . My poor wife had some reason to think that war and disease between them had left very little of a husband to take under nursing when she got him again. An attack of camp-scurvy had filled my mouth with sores, shaken every joint in my body, and covered me all over with sores and livid spots, so that I was marvellously unlovely to look upon. A smart knock

on the ankle-joint from the splinter of a shell that
burst in my face, in itself a mere *bagatelle* of a wound,
had been of necessity neglected under the pressing
and incessant calls upon me, and had grown worse and
worse till the whole foot below the ankle became a
black mass and seemed to threaten mortification. I
insisted, however, on being allowed to use it till the
place was taken, mortification or no; and though the
pain was sometimes horrible, I carried my point and
kept up to the last. On the day after the assault I had
an unlucky fall on some bad ground, and it was an
open question for a day or two whether I hadn't
broken my arm at the elbow. Fortunately it turned
out to be only a severe sprain, but I am still conscious
of the wrench it gave me. To crown the whole pleasant catalogue, I was worn to a shadow by a constant
diarrhœa, and consumed as much opium as would
have done credit to my father-in-law (Thomas De
Quincey). However, thank God, I have a good share
of Tapleyism in me and come out strong under difficulties. I think I may confidently say that no man
ever saw me out of heart, or ever heard one croaking
word from me even when our prospects were gloom-
iest. We were sadly scourged by the cholera, and it
was almost appalling to me to find that out of twenty-
seven officers present, I could only muster fifteen for
the operations of the attack. However, it was done,
and after it was done came the collapse. Don't be
horrified when I tell you that for the whole of the
actual siege, and in truth for some little time before,
I almost lived on brandy. Appetite for food I had
none, but I forced myself to eat just sufficient to sustain life, and I had an incessant craving for brandy as
the strongest stimulant I could get. Strange to say,

I was quite unconscious of its affecting me in the slightest degree. *The excitement of the work was so great that no lesser one seemed to have any chance against it, and I certainly never found my intellect clearer or my nerves stronger in my life.* It was only my wretched body that was weak, and the moment the real work was done by our becoming complete masters of Delhi, I broke down without delay and discovered that if I wished to live I must continue no longer the system that had kept me up until the crisis was passed. With it passed away as if in a moment all desire to stimulate, and a perfect loathing of my late staff of life took possession of me."

Such experiences show how profound is the alteration in the manner in which, under excitement, our organism will sometimes perform its physiological work. The processes of repair become different when the reserves have to be used, and for weeks and months the deeper use may go on.

Morbid cases, here as elsewhere, lay the normal machinery bare. In the first number of Dr. Morton Prince's *Journal of Abnormal Psychology,* Dr. Janet has discussed five cases of morbid impulse, with an explanation that is precious for my present point of view. One is a girl who eats, eats, eats, all day. Another walks, walks, walks, and gets her food from an automobile that escorts her. Another is a dipsomaniac. A fourth pulls out her hair. A fifth wounds her flesh and burns her skin. Hitherto such freaks of impulse have received Greek names (as bulimia, dromomania, etc.) and been scientifically disposed of as "episodic syndromata of hereditary degeneration." But it turns out that Janet's cases are all what he calls psychasthenics, or victims of a chronic sense of weak-

ness, torpor, lethargy, fatigue, insufficiency, impossibility, unreality and powerlessness of will; and that
in each and all of them the particular activity pursued, deleterious though it be, has the temporary result of raising the sense of vitality and making the
patient feel alive again.   These things reanimate:
they would reanimate *us*, but it happens that in each
patient the particular freak-activity chosen is the only
thing that does reanimate; and therein lies the morbid
state.   The way to treat such persons is to discover to
them more usual and useful ways of throwing their
stores of vital energy into gear.

Colonel Baird-Smith, needing to draw on altogether
extraordinary stores of energy, found that brandy and
opium were ways of throwing them into gear.

Such cases are humanly typical.   We are all to some
degree oppressed, unfree.   We don't come to our own.
It is there, but we don't get at it.   The threshold must be
made to shift.   Then many of us find that an eccentric
activity — a "spree," say — relieves.   There is no doubt
that to some men sprees and excesses of almost any
kind are medicinal, temporarily at any rate, in spite
of what the moralists and doctors say.

But when the normal tasks and stimulations of life
don't put a man's deeper levels of energy on tap, and
he requires distinctly deleterious excitements, his constitution verges on the abnormal.   The normal opener
of deeper and deeper levels of energy is the will.   The
difficulty is to use it, to make the effort which the
word volition implies.   But if we *do* make it (or if a
god, though he were only the god Chance, makes it
through us) , it will act dynamogenically on us for a
month.   It is notorious that a single successful effort
of moral volition, such as saying "no" to some habitual

temptation, or performing some courageous act, will launch a man on a higher level of energy for days and weeks, will give him a new range of power. "In the act of uncorking a whiskey bottle which I had brought home to get drunk upon," said a man to me, "I suddenly found myself running out into the garden, where I smashed it on the ground. I felt so happy and uplifted after this act, that for two months I wasn't tempted to touch a drop."

The emotions and excitements due to usual situations are the usual inciters of the will. But these act discontinuously; and in the intervals the shallower levels of life tend to close in and shut us off. Accordingly the best practical knowers of the human soul have invented the thing known as methodical ascetic discipline to keep the deeper levels constantly in reach. Beginning with easy tasks, passing to harder ones, and exercising day by day, it is, I believe, admitted that disciples of asceticism can reach very high levels of freedom and power of will.

Ignatius Loyola's spiritual exercises must have produced this result in innumerable devotees. But the most venerable ascetic system, and the one whose results have the most voluminous experimental corroboration is undoubtedly the Yoga system in Hindustan. From time immemorial, by Hatha Yoga, Raja Yoga, Karma Yoga, or whatever code of practice it might be, Hindu aspirants to perfection have trained themselves, month in and out, for years. The result claimed, and certainly in many cases accorded by impartial judges, is strength of character, personal power, unshakability of soul. In an article in the *Philosophical Review*,* from which I am largely copying

* "The Energies of Men." *Philosophical Review*, vol. xvi, No. 1, January, 1907. Compare note on p. 216.

here, I have quoted at great length the experience with "Hatha Yoga" of a very gifted European friend of mine who, by persistently carrying out for several months its methods of fasting from food and sleep, its exercises in breathing and thought-concentration, and its fantastic posture-gymnastics, seems to have succeeded in waking up deeper and deeper levels of will and moral and intellectual power in himself, and to have escaped from a decidedly menacing brain-condition of the "circular" type, from which he had suffered for years.

Judging by my friend's letters, of which the last I have is written fourteen months after the Yoga training began, there can be no doubt of his relative regeneration. He has undergone material trials with indifference, travelled third-class on Mediterranean steamers, and fourth-class on African trains, living with the poorest Arabs and sharing their unaccustomed food, all with equanimity. His devotion to certain interests has been put to heavy strain, and nothing is more remarkable to me than the changed moral tone with which he reports the situation. A profound modification has unquestionably occurred in the running of his mental machinery. The gearing has changed, and his will is available otherwise than it was.

My friend is a man of very peculiar temperament. Few of us would have had the will to start upon the Yoga training, which, once started, seemed to conjure the further willpower needed out of itself. And not all of those who could launch themselves would have reached the same results. The Hindus themselves admit that in some men the results may come without call or bell. My friend writes to me: "You are quite

right in thinking that religious crises, love-crises, in-
dignation-crises may awaken in a very short time
powers similar to those reached by years of patient
Yoga-practice."

Probably most medical men would treat this individual's case as one of what it is fashionable now to
call by the name of "self-suggestion," or "expectant
attention" — as if those phrases were explanatory, or
meant more than the fact that certain men can be
influenced, while others cannot be influenced, by certain sorts of *ideas*. This leads me to say a word about
ideas considered as dynamogenic agents, or stimuli for
unlocking what would otherwise be unused reservoirs
of individual power.

One thing that ideas do is to contradict other ideas
and keep us from believing them. An idea that thus
negates a first idea may itself in turn be negated by a
third idea, and the first idea may thus regain its
natural influence over our belief and determine our
behavior. Our philosophic and religious development
proceeds thus by credulities, negations, and the negat-
ing of negations.

But whether for arousing or for stopping belief,
ideas may fail to be efficacious, just as a wire at one
time alive with electricity, may at another time be
dead. Here our insight into causes fails us, and we
can only note results in general terms. In general,
whether a given idea shall be a live idea depends
more on the person into whose mind it is injected
than on the idea itself. Which is the suggestive idea
for this person, and which for that one? Mr. Fletcher's
disciples regenerate themselves by the idea (and the
fact) that they are chewing, and re-chewing, and
super-chewing their food. Dr. Dewey's pupils regen-

erate themselves by going without their breakfast — a fact, but also an ascetic idea. Not every one can use *these* ideas with the same success.

But apart from such individually varying suscep- tibilities, there are common lines along which men simply as men tend to be inflammable by ideas. As certain objects naturally awaken love, anger, or cupid- ity, so certain ideas naturally awaken the energies of loyalty, courage, endurance, or devotion. When these ideas are effective in an individual's life, their effect is often very great indeed. They may transfigure it, unlocking innumerable powers which, but for the idea, would never have come into play. "Fatherland," "the Flag," "the Union," "Holy Church," "the Monroe Doctrine," "Truth," "Science," "Liberty," Garibaldi's phrase, "Rome or Death," etc., are so many examples of energy-releasing ideas. The social nature of such phrases is an essential factor of their dynamic power. They are forces of detent in situations in which no other force produces equivalent effects, and each is a force of detent only in a specific group of men.

The memory that an oath or vow has been made will nerve one to abstinences and efforts otherwise im- possible; witness the "pledge" in the history of the temperance movement. A mere promise to his sweet- heart will clean up a youth's life all over — at any rate for a time. For such effects an educated susceptibility is required. The idea of one's "honor," for example, unlocks energy only in those of us who have had the education of a "gentleman," so called.

That delightful being, Prince Pueckler-Muskau, writes to his wife from England that he has invented "a sort of artificial resolution respecting things that are difficult of performance. My device," he continues, "is this: *I give my word of honor most solemnly to myself* to do or to leave undone this or that. I am of course extremely cautious in the use of this expedient, but when once the word is given, even though I afterwards think I have been precipitate or mistaken, I hold it to be perfectly irrevocable, whatever inconveniences I foresee likely to result. If I were capable of breaking my word after such mature consideration, I should lose all respect for myself, — and what man of sense would not prefer death to such an alternative? . . . When the mysterious formula is pronounced, no alteration in my own view, nothing short of physical impossibilities, must, for the welfare of my soul, alter my will. . . . I find something very satisfactory in the thought that man has the power of framing such props and weapons out of the most trivial materials, indeed out of nothing, merely by the force of his will, which thereby truly deserves the name of omnipotent." *

Conversions, whether they be political, scientific, philosophic, or religious, form another way in which bound energies are let loose. They unify us, and put a stop to ancient mental interferences. The result is freedom, and often a great enlargement of power. A belief that thus settles upon an individual always acts as a challenge to his will. But, for the particular challenge to operate, he must be the right challeng*ee*. In religious conversions we have so fine an adjustment that the idea may be in the mind of the challengee for years before it exerts effects; and why it should do so then is often so far from obvious that the event is taken for a miracle of grace, and not a natural occur-

* "Tour in England, Ireland, and France," Philadelphia, 1833, p. 435.

rence. Whatever it is, it may be a highwater mark of energy, in which "noes," once impossible, are easy, and in which a new range of "yeses" gains the right of way.

We are just now witnessing a very copious unlocking of energies by ideas in the persons of those converts to "New Thought," "Christian Science," "Metaphysical Healing," or other forms of spiritual philosophy, who are so numerous among us today. The ideas here are healthy-minded and optimistic; and it is quite obvious that a wave of religious activity, analogous in some respects to the spread of early Christianity, Buddhism, and Mohammedanism, is passing over our American world. The common feature of these optimistic faiths is that they all tend to the suppression of what Mr. Horace Fletcher calls "fearthought." Fearthought he defines as the "self-suggestion of inferiority"; so that one may say that these systems all operate by the suggestion of power. And the power, small or great, comes in various shapes to the individual, — power, as he will tell you, not to "mind" things that used to vex him, power to concentrate his mind, good cheer, good temper — in short, to put it mildly, a firmer, more elastic moral tone.

The most genuinely saintly person I have ever known is a friend of mine now suffering from cancer of the breast — I hope that she may pardon my citing her here as an example of what ideas can do. Her ideas have kept her a practically well woman for months after she should have given up and gone to bed. They have annulled all pain and weakness and given her a cheerful active life, unusually beneficent to others to whom she has afforded help. Her doctors, acquiescing in results they could not under-

stand, have had the good sense to let her go her own
way.

How far the mind-cure movement is destined to
extend its influence, or what intellectual modifica-
tions it may yet undergo, no one can foretell. It is
essentially a religious movement, and to academically
nurtured minds its utterances are tasteless and often
grotesque enough. It also incurs the natural enmity
of medical politicians, and of the whole trades-union
wing of that profession. But no unprejudiced observer can fail to recognize its importance as a social
phenomenon today, and the higher medical minds are
already trying to interpret it fairly, and make its power
available for their own therapeutic ends.

Dr. Thomas Hyslop, of the great West Riding
Asylum in England, said last year to the British Medical Association that the best sleep-producing agent
which his practice had revealed to him, was *prayer*.
I say this, he added (I am sorry here that I must quote
from memory), purely as a medical man. The exercise of prayer, in those who habitually exert it, must
be regarded by us doctors as the most adequate and
normal of all the pacifiers of the mind and calmers
of the nerves.

But in few of us are functions not tied up by the
exercise of other functions. Relatively few medical
men and scientific men, I fancy, can pray. Few can
carry on any living commerce with "God." Yet many
of us are well aware of how much freer and abler our
lives would be, were such important forms of energizing not sealed up by the critical atmosphere in
which we have been reared. There are in every one
potential forms of activity that actually are shunted
out from use. Part of the imperfect vitality under

which we labor can thus be easily explained. One part of our mind dams up — even *damns* up! — the other parts.

Conscience makes cowards of us all. Social conventions prevent us from telling the truth after the fashion of the heroes and heroines of Bernard Shaw. We all know persons who are models of excellence, but who belong to the extreme philistine type of mind. So deadly is their intellectual respectability that we can't converse about certain subjects at all, can't let our minds play over them, can't even mention them in their presence. I have numbered among my dearest friends persons thus inhibited intellectually, with whom I would gladly have been able to talk freely about certain interests of mine, certain authors, say, as Bernard Shaw, Chesterton, Edward Carpenter, H. G. Wells, but it wouldn't do, it made them too uncomfortable, they wouldn't play, I had to be silent. An intellect thus tied down by literality and decorum makes on one the same sort of an impression that an able-bodied man would who should habituate himself to do his work with only one of his fingers, locking up the rest of his organism and leaving it unused.

I trust that by this time I have said enough to convince the reader both of the truth and of the importance of my thesis. The two questions, first, that of the possible extent of our powers; and, second, that of the various avenues of approach to them, the various keys for unlocking them in diverse individuals, dominate the whole problem of individual and national education. We need a topography of the limits of human power, similar to the chart which oculists use of the field of human vision. We need also a study of the various types of human being with reference to the different ways in which their energy-reserves may be appealed to and set loose. Biographies and individual experiences of every kind may be drawn upon for evidence here. *

* "This would be an absolutely concrete study . . . The limits of power must be limits that have been realized in actual persons, and the various ways of unlocking the reserves of power must have been exemplified in individual lives . . . So here is a program of concrete individual psychology . . . It is replete with interesting facts, and points to practical issues superior in importance to anything we know." *From the address as originally delivered before the Philosophical Association; see xvi, Philosophical Review, 1, 19.*

THE GOSPEL OF RELAXATION

I WISH in the following hour to take certain
psychological doctrines and show their practical
applications to mental hygiene — to the hygiene of
our American life more particularly. Our people,
especially in academic circles, are turning towards
psychology nowadays with great expectations; and, if
psychology is to justify them, it must be by showing
fruits in the pedagogic and therapeutic lines.

The reader may possibly have heard of a peculiar
theory of the emotions, commonly referred to in
psychological literature as the Lange-James theory.
According to this theory, our emotions are mainly due
to those organic stirrings that are aroused in us in a
reflex way by the stimulus of the exciting object or
situation. An emotion of fear, for example, or surprise, is not a direct effect of the object's presence on the
mind, but an effect of that still earlier effect, the
bodily commotion which the object suddenly excites;
so that, were this bodily commotion suppressed, we
should not so much *feel* fear as call the situation
fearful; we should not feel surprise, but coldly recognize that the object was indeed astonishing. One enthusiast has even gone so far as to say that when we
feel sorry it is because we weep, when we feel afraid
it is because we run away, and not conversely. Some
of you may perhaps be acquainted with the paradoxical formula. Now, whatever exaggeration may

possibly lurk in this account of our emotions (and I doubt myself whether the exaggeration be very great), it is certain that the main core of it is true, and that the mere giving way to tears, for example, or to the outward expression of an anger-fit, will result for the moment in making the inner grief or anger more acutely felt. There is, accordingly, no better known or more generally useful precept in the moral training of youth, or in one's personal self-discipline, than that which bids us pay primary attention to what we do and express, and not to care too much for what we feel. If we only check a cowardly impulse in time, for example, or if we only *don't* strike the blow or rip out with the complaining or insulting word that we shall regret as long as we live, our feelings themselves will presently be the calmer and better, with no particular guidance from us on their own account. Action seems to follow feeling, but really action and feeling go together; and by regulating the action, which is under the more direct control of the will, we can indirectly regulate the feeling, which is not.

Thus the sovereign voluntary path to cheerfulness, if our spontaneous cheerfulness be lost, is to sit up cheerfully, to look round cheerfully, and to act and speak as if cheerfulness were already there. If such conduct does not make you soon feel cheerful, nothing else on that occasion can. So to feel brave, act as if we *were* brave, use all our will to that end, and a courage-fit will very likely replace the fit of fear. Again, in order to feel kindly toward a person to whom we have been inimical, the only way is more or less deliberately to smile, to make sympathetic inquiries, and to force ourselves to say genial things. One hearty laugh together will bring enemies into a closer communion of heart than hours spent on both sides in inward wrestling with the mental demon of uncharitable feeling. To wrestle with a bad feeling only pins our attention on it, and keeps it still fastened in the mind: whereas, if we act as if from some better feeling, the old bad feeling soon folds its tent like an Arab, and silently steals away.

The best manuals of religious devotion accordingly reiterate the maxim that we must let our feelings go, and pay no regard to them whatever. In an admirable and widely successful little book called "The Christian's Secret of a Happy Life," by Mrs. Hannah Whitall Smith, I find this lesson on almost every page. *Act* faithfully, and you really have faith, no matter how cold and even how dubious you may feel. "It is your purpose God looks at," writes Mrs. Smith, "not your feelings about that purpose; and your purpose, or will, is therefore the only thing you need attend to. . . . Let your emotions come or let them go, just as God pleases, and make no account of them either way. . . . They really have nothing to do with the matter. They are not the indicators of your spiritual state, but are merely the indicators of your temperament or of your present physical condition."

But you all know these facts already, so I need no longer press them on your attention. From our acts and from our attitudes ceaseless inpouring currents of sensation come, which help to determine from moment to moment what our inner states shall be: that is a fundamental law of psychology which I will therefore proceed to assume.

A Viennese neurologist of considerable reputation has recently written about the *Binnenleben,* as he terms it, or buried life of human beings. No doctor, this writer says, can get into really profitable relations with a nervous patient until he gets some sense of what the patient's *Binnenleben* is, of the sort of unuttered inner atmosphere in which his consciousness dwells alone with the secrets of its prison-house. This inner personal tone is what we can't communicate or describe articulately to others; but the wraith and ghost of it, so to speak, are often what our friends and intimates feel as our most characteristic quality. In the unhealthy-minded, apart from all sorts of old regrets, ambitions checked by shames and aspirations obstructed by timidities, it consists mainly of bodily discomforts not distinctly localized by the sufferer, but breeding a general self-mistrust and sense that things are not as they should be with him. Half the thirst for alchohol that exists in the world exists simply because alchohol acts as a temporary anæsthetic and effacer to all these morbid feelings that never ought to be in a human being at all. In the healthy-minded, on the contrary, there are no fears or shames to discover; and the sensations that pour in from the organism only help to swell the general vital sense of security and readiness for anything that may turn up.

Consider, for example, the effects of a well-toned *motor-apparatus,* nervous and muscular, on our general personal self-consciousness, the sense of elasticity and efficiency that results. They tell us that in Norway the life of the women has lately been entirely revolutionized by the new order of muscular feelings with which the use of the *ski,* or long snow-shoes, as a sport for both sexes, has made the women acquainted. Fifteen years ago the Norwegian women were even more than the women of other lands vo-

taries of the old-fashioned ideal of femininity, 'the
domestic angel,' the 'gentle and refining influence'
sort of thing. Now these sedentary fireside tabby-
cats of Norway have been trained, they say, by the
snow-shoes into lithe and audacious creatures, for
whom no night is too dark or height too giddy, and
who are not only saying good-bye to the traditional
feminine pallor and delicacy of constitution, but actually taking the lead in every educational and social
reform. I cannot but think that the tennis and
tramping and skating habits and the bicycle-craze
which are so rapidly extending among our dear sisters
and daughters in this country are going also to lead
to a sounder and heartier moral tone, which will send
its tonic breath through all our American life.

I hope that here in America more and more the
ideal of the well-trained and vigorous body will be
maintained neck by neck with that of the well-trained
and vigorous mind as the two coequal halves of the
higher education for men and women alike. The
strength of the British Empire lies in the strength of
character of the individual Englishman, taken all
alone by himself. And that strength, I am persuaded,
is perennially nourished and kept up by nothing so
much as by the national worship, in which all classes
meet, of athletic outdoor life and sport.

I recollect, years ago, reading a certain work by an
American doctor on hygiene and the laws of life and
the type of future humanity. I have forgotten its author's name and its title, but I remember well an
awful prophecy that it contained about the future
of our muscular system. Human perfection, the writer
said, means ability to cope with the environment; but
the environment will more and more require mental

power from us, and less and less will ask for bare brute strength. Wars will cease, machines will do all our heavy work, man will become more and more a mere director of nature's energies, and less and less an exerter of energy on his own account. So that, if the *homo sapiens* of the future can only digest his food and think, what need will he have of well-developed muscles at all? And why, pursued this writer, should we not even now be satisfied with a more delicate and intellectual type of beauty than that which pleased our ancestors? Nay, I have heard a fanciful friend make a still further advance in this 'new-man' direction. With our future food, he says, itself prepared in liquid form from the chemical elements of the atmosphere, pepsinated or half-digested in advance, and sucked up through a glass tube from a tin can, what need shall we have of teeth, or stomachs even? They may go, along with our muscles and our physical courage, while, challenging ever more and more our proper admiration, will grow the gigantic domes of our crania, arching over our spectacled eyes, and animating our flexible little lips to those floods of learned and ingenious talk which will constitute our most congenial occupation.

I am sure that your flesh creeps at this apocalyptic vision. Mine certainly did so; and I cannot believe that our muscular vigor will ever be a superfluity. Even if the day ever dawns in which it will not be needed for fighting the old heavy battles against Nature, it will still always be needed to furnish the background of sanity, serenity, and cheerfulness to life, to give moral elasticity to our disposition, to round off the wiry edge of our fretfulness, and make us good-humored and easy of approach. Weakness is too apt to be what the doctors call irritable weakness. And that blessed internal peace and confidence, that *acquiescentia in seipso,* as Spinoza used to call it, that wells up from every part of the body of a muscularly well-trained human being, and soaks the indwelling soul of him with satisfaction, is, quite apart from every consideration of its mechanical utility, an element of spiritual hygiene of supreme significance.

And now let me go a step deeper into mental hygiene, and try to enlist your insight and sympathy in a cause which I believe is one of paramount patriotic importance to us Yankees. Many years ago a Scottish medical man, Dr. Clouston, a mad-doctor as they call him there, or what we should call an asylum physician (the most eminent one in Scotland), visited this country, and said something that has remained in my memory ever since. "You Americans," he said, "wear too much expression on your faces. You are living like an army with all its reserves engaged in action. The duller countenances of the British population betoken a better scheme of life. They suggest stores of reserved nervous force to fall back upon, if any occasion should arise that requires it. This inexcitability, this presence at all times of power not used, I regard," continued Dr. Clouston, "as the great safeguard of our British people. The other thing in you gives me a sense of insecurity, and you ought somehow to tone yourselves down. You really do carry too much expression, you take too intensely the trivial moments of life."

Now Dr. Clouston is a trained reader of the secrets of the soul as expressed upon the countenance, and the observation of his which I quote seems to me to mean a great deal. And all Americans who stay in

Europe long enough to get accustomed to the spirit that reigns and expresses itself there, so unexcitable as compared with ours, make a similar observation when they return to their native shores. They find a wild-eyed look upon their compatriots' faces, either of too desperate eagerness and anxiety or of too intense responsiveness and good-will. It is hard to say whether the men or the women show it most. It is true that we do not all feel about it as Dr. Clouston felt. Many of us, far from deploring it, admire it. We say: "What intelligence it shows! How different from the stolid cheeks, the codfish eyes, the slow, inanimate demeanor we have been seeing in the British Isles!" Intensity, rapidity, vivacity of appearance, are indeed with us something of a nationally accepted ideal; and the medical notion of 'irritable weakness' is not the first thing suggested by them to our mind, as it was to Dr. Clouston's. In a weekly paper not very long ago I remember reading a story in which, after describing the beauty and interest of the heroine's personality, the author summed up her charms by saying that to all who looked upon her an impression as of 'bottled lightning' was irresistibly conveyed.

Bottled lightning, in truth, is one of our American ideals, even of a young girl's character! Now it is most ungracious, and it may seem to some persons unpatriotic, to criticise in public the physical peculiarities of one's own people, of one's own family, so to speak. Besides, it may be said, and said with justice, that there are plenty of bottled-lightning temperaments in other countries, and plenty of phlegmatic temperaments here; and that, when all is said and done, the more or less of tension about which I am making such a fuss is a very small item in the sum

total of a nation's life, and not worth solemn treat-
ment at a time when agreeable rather than disagreeable things should be talked about. Well, in one
sense the more or less of tension in our faces and in our
unused muscles *is* a small thing: not much mechanical
work is done by these contractions. But it is not
always the material size of a thing that measures its
importance: often it is its place and function. One
of the most philosophical remarks I ever heard made
was by an unlettered workman who was doing some
repairs at my house many years ago. "There is very
little difference between one man and another," he
said, "when you go to the bottom of it. But what
little there is, is very important." And the remark
certainly applies to this case. The general over-con-
traction may be small when estimated in foot-pounds,
but its importance is immense on account of its *effects
on the over-contracted person's spiritual life.* This
follows as a necessary consequence from the theory of
our emotions to which I made reference at the beginning of this article. For by the sensations that so
incessantly pour in from the over-tense excited body
the over-tense and excited habit of mind is kept up;
and the sultry, threatening, exhausting, thunderous
inner atmosphere never quite clears away. If you
never wholly give yourself up to the chair you sit in,
but always keep your leg- and body-muscles half contracted for a rise; if you breathe eighteen or nineteen
instead of sixteen times a minute, and never quite
breathe out at that, — what mental mood *can* you be
in but one of inner panting and expectancy, and how
can the future and its worries possibly forsake your
mind? On the other hand, how can they gain admission to your mind if your brow be unruffled, your

respiration calm and complete, and your muscles all relaxed?

Now what is the cause of this absence of repose, this bottled-lightning quality in us Americans? The explanation of it that is usually given is that it comes from the extreme dryness of our climate and the acrobatic performances of our thermometer, coupled with the extraordinary progressiveness of our life, the hard work, the railroad speed, the rapid success, and all the other things we know so well by heart. Well, our climate is certainly exciting, but hardly more so than that of many parts of Europe, where nevertheless no bottled-lightning girls are found. And the work done and the pace of life are as extreme in every great capital of Europe as they are here. To me both of these pretended causes are utterly insufficient to ex plain the facts.

To explain them, we must go not to physical geography, but to psychology and sociology. The latest chapter both in sociology and in psychology to be developed in a manner that approaches adequacy is the chapter on the imitative impulse. First Bagehot, then Tarde, then Royce and Baldwin here, have shown that invention and imitation, taken together, form, one may say, the entire warp and woof of human life, in so far as it is social. The American over-tension and jerkiness and breathlessness and intensity and agony of expression are primarily social, and only secondarily physiological, phenomena. They are *bad habits,* nothing more or less, bred of custom and example, born of the imitation of bad models and the cultivation of false personal ideals. How are idioms acquired, how do local peculiarities of phrase and accent come about? Through an accidental example set by some one, which struck the ears of others, and was quoted and copied till at last every one in the locality chimed in. Just so it is with national tricks of vocalization or intonation, with national manners, fashions of movement and gesture, and habitual expressions of face. We, here in America, through following a succession of pattern-setters whom it is now impossible to trace, and through influencing each other in a bad direction, have at last settled down collectively into what, for better or worse, is our own characteristic national type, — a type with the production of which, so far as these habits go, the climate and conditions have had practically nothing at all to do.

This type, which we have thus reached by our imitativeness, we now have fixed upon us, for better or worse. Now no type can be *wholly* disadvantageous; but, so far as our type follows the bottled-lightning fashion, it cannot be wholly good. Dr. Clouston was certainly right in thinking that eagerness, breathlessness, and anxiety are not signs of strength: they are signs of weakness and of bad coordination. The even forehead, the slab-like cheek, the codfish eye, may be less interesting for the moment; but they are more promising signs than intense expression is of what we may expect of their possessor in the long run. Your dull, unhurried worker gets over a great deal of ground, because he never goes backward or breaks down. Your intense, convulsive worker breaks down and has bad moods so often that you never know where he may be when you most need his help, — he may be having one of his 'bad days.' We say that so many of our fellow-countrymen collapse, and have to be sent abroad to rest their nerves, because they work so hard. I suspect that this is an immense mistake. I suspect that neither the nature nor the amount of our work is accountable for the frequency and severity of our breakdowns, but that their cause lies rather in those absurd feelings of hurry and having no time, in that breathlessness and tension, that anxiety of feature and that solicitude for results, that lack of inner harmony and ease, in short, by which with us the work is so apt to be accompanied, and from which a European who should do the same work would nine times out of ten be free. These perfectly wanton and unnecessary tricks of inner attitude and outer manner in us, caught from the social atmosphere, kept up by tradition, and idealized by many as the admirable way of life, are the last straws that break the American camel's back, the final overflowers of our measure of wear and tear and fatigue.

The voice, for example, in a surprisingly large number of us has a tired and plaintive sound. Some of us are really tired (for I do not mean absolutely to deny that our climate has a tiring quality) ; but far more of us are not tired at all, or would not be tired at all unless we had got into a wretched trick of feeling tired, by following the prevalent habits of vocalization and expression. And if talking high and tired, and living excitedly and hurriedly, would only enable us to *do* more by the way, even while breaking us down in the end, it would be different. There would be some compensation, some excuse, for going on so. But the exact reverse is the case. It is your relaxed and easy worker, who is in no hurry, and quite thoughtless most of the while of consequences, who is your efficient worker; and tension and anxiety, and present and future, all mixed up to-

gether in our mind at once, are the surest drags upon
steady progress and hindrances to our success.   My
colleague, Professor Münsterberg, an excellent observer, who came here recently, has written some notes
on America to German papers.   He says in substance
that the appearance of unusual energy in America is
superficial and illusory, being really due to nothing
but the habits of jerkiness and bad co-ordination for
which we have to thank the defective training of our
people.   I think myself that it is high time for old
legends and traditional opinions to be changed; and
that, if any one should begin to write about Yankee
inefficiency and feebleness, and inability to do anything with time except to waste it, he would have a
very pretty paradoxical little thesis to sustain, with a
great many facts to quote, and a great deal of experience to appeal to in its proof.

Well, my friends, if our dear American character is
weakened by all this over-tension, — and I think, whatever reserves you may make, that you will agree as to
the main facts, — where does the remedy lie?   It lies,
of course, where lay the origins of the disease.   If a
vicious fashion and taste are to blame for the thing,
the fashion and taste must be changed.   And, though
it is no small thing to inoculate seventy millions of
people with new standards, yet, if there is to be any
relief, that will have to be done.   We must change
ourselves from a race that admires jerk and snap for
their own sakes, and looks down upon low voices and
quiet ways as dull, to one that, on the contrary, has
calm for its ideal, and for their own sakes loves harmony, dignity, and ease.

So we go back to the psychology of imitation again.
There is only one way to improve ourselves, and that

is by some of us setting an example which the others
may pick up and imitate till the new fashion spreads
from east to west. Some of us are in more favorable
positions than others to set new fashions. Some are
much more striking personally and imitable, so to
speak. But no living person is sunk so low as not to
be imitated by somebody. Thackeray somewhere says
of the Irish nation that there never was an Irishman
so poor that he didn't have a still poorer Irishman
living at his expense; and, surely, there is no human
being whose example doesn't work contagiously in
some particular. The very idiots at our public insti-
tutions imitate each other's peculiarities. And, if you
should individually achieve calmness and harmony in
your own person, you may depend upon it that a wave
of imitation will spread from you, as surely as the
circles spread outward when a stone is dropped into
a lake.

Fortunately, we shall not have to be absolute
pioneers. Even now in New York they have formed
a society for the improvement of our national vocalization, and one perceives its machinations already in
the shape of various newspaper paragraphs intended
to stir up dissatisfaction with the awful thing that it is.
And, better still than that, because more radical and
general, is the gospel of relaxation, as one may call it,
preached by Miss Annie Payson Call, of Boston, in
her admirable little volume called 'Power through
Repose,' a book that ought to be in the hands of every
teacher and student in America of either sex. You
need only be followers, then, on a path already opened
up by others. But of one thing be confident: others
still will follow you.

And this brings me to one more application of

psychology to practical life, to which I will call attention briefly, and then close. If one's example of easy and calm ways is to be effectively contagious, one feels by instinct that the less voluntarily one aims at getting imitated, the more unconscious one keeps in the matter, the more likely one is to succeed. *Become the imitable thing,* and you may then discharge your minds of all responsibility for the imitation. The laws of social nature will take care of that result. Now the psychological principle on which this precept reposes is a law of very deep and wide-spread importance in the conduct of our lives, and at the same time a law which we Americans most grievously neglect. Stated technically, the law is this: that *strong feeling about one's self tends to arrest the free association of one's objective ideas and motor processes.* We get the extreme example of this in the mental disease called melancholia.

A melancholic patient is filled through and through with intensely painful emotion about himself. He is threatened, he is guilty, he is doomed, he is annihilated, he is lost. His mind is fixed as if in a cramp on these feelings of his own situation, and in all the books on insanity you may read that the usual varied flow of his thoughts has ceased. His associative processes, to use the technical phrase, are inhibited; and his ideas stand stock-still, shut up to their one monotonous function of reiterating inwardly the fact of the man's desperate estate. And this inhibitive influence is not due to the mere fact that his emotion is *painful.* Joyous emotions about the self also stop the association of our ideas. A saint in ecstasy is as motionless and irresponsive and one-idea'd as a melancholiac. And, without going as far as ecstatic saints, we know how in every one a great or sudden pleasure may paralyze the flow of thought. Ask young people returning from a party or a spectacle, and all excited about it, what it was. "Oh, it was *fine!* it was *fine!* it was *fine!*" is all the information you are likely to receive until the excitement has calmed down. Probably every one of my hearers has been made temporarily half-idiotic by some great success or piece of good fortune. "*Good!* GOOD! GOOD!" is all we can at such times say to ourselves until we smile at our own very foolishness.

Now from all this we can draw an extremely practical conclusion. If, namely, we wish our trains of ideation and volition to be copious and varied and effective, we must form the habit of freeing them from the inhibitive influence of reflection upon them, of egoistic preoccupation about their results. Such a habit, like other habits, can be formed. Prudence and duty and self-regard, emotions of ambition and emotions of anxiety, have, of course, a needful part to play in our lives. But confine them as far as possible to the occasions when you are making your general resolutions and deciding on your plans of campaign, and keep them out of the details. When once a decision is reached and execution is the order of the day, dismiss absolutely all responsibility and care about the outcome. *Unclamp,* in a word, your intellectual and practical machinery, and let it run free; and the service it will do you will be twice as good. Who are the scholars who get 'rattled' in the recitation-room? Those who think of the possibilities of failure and feel the great importance of the act. Who are those who do recite well? Often those who are most indifferent. *Their* ideas reel themselves out of their memory of their own accord. Why do we hear the complaint so often that social life in New England is either less rich and expressive or more fatiguing than it is in some other parts of the world? To what is the fact, if fact it be, due unless to the over-active conscience of the people, afraid of either saying something too trivial and·obvious, or something insincere, or something unworthy of one's interlocutor, or something in some way or other not adequate to the occasion? How can conversation possibly steer itself through such a sea of responsibilities and inhibitions as this? On the other hand, conversation does flourish and society is refreshing, and neither dull on the one hand nor exhausting from its effort on the other, wherever people forget their scruples and take the brakes off their hearts, and let their tongues wag as automatically and irresponsibly as they will.

They talk much in pedagogic circles today about the duty of the teacher to prepare for every lesson in advance. To some extent this is useful. But we Yankees are assuredly not those to whom such a general doctrine should be preached. We are only too careful as it is. The advice I should give to most teachers would be in the words of one who is herself an admirable teacher. Prepare yourself in the *subject so well that it shall be always on tap:* then in the class-room trust your spontaneity and fling away all further care.

My advice to students, especially to girl-students, would be somewhat similar. Just as a bicycle-chain may be too tight, so may one's carefulness and conscientiousness be so tense as to hinder the running of one's mind. Take, for example, periods when there are many successive days of examination impending.

One ounce of good nervous tone in an examination is worth many pounds of anxious study for it in advance. If you want really to do your best in an examination, fling away the book the day before, say to yourself, "I won't waste another minute on this miserable thing, and I don't care an iota whether I succeed or not." Say this sincerely, and feel it; and go out and play, or go to bed and sleep, and I am sure the results next day will encourage you to use the method permanently. I have heard this advice given to a student by Miss Call, whose book on muscular relaxation I quoted a moment ago. In her later book, entitled 'As a Matter of Course,' the gospel of moral relaxation, of dropping things from the mind, and not 'caring' is preached with equal success. Not only our preachers, but our friends the theosophists and mind-curers of various religious sects are also harping on this string. And with the doctors, the Delsarteans, the various mind-curing sects, and such writers as Mr. Dresser, Prentice Mulford, Mr. Horace Fletcher, and Mr. Trine to help, and the whole band of school-teachers and magazine-readers chiming in, it really looks as if a good start might be made in the direction of changing our American mental habit into something more .indifferent and strong.

Worry means always and invariably inhibition of associations and loss of effective power. Of course, the sovereign cure for worry is religious faith; and this, of course, you also know. The turbulent billows of the fretful surface leave the deep parts of the ocean undisturbed, and to him who has a hold on vaster and more permanent realities the hourly vicissitudes of his personal destiny seem relatively insignificant things. The really religious person is accordingly unshakable

and full of equanimity, and calmly ready for any duty
that the day may bring forth. This is charmingly
illustrated by a little work with which I recently became acquainted, "The Practice of the Presence of
God, the Best Ruler of a Holy Life, by Brother Lawrence, being Conversations and Letters of Nicholas
Herman of Lorraine, Translated from the French." *
I extract a few passages, the conversations being given
in indirect discourse. Brother Lawrence was a Car-
melite friar, converted at Paris in 1666. "He said that
he had been footman to M. Fieubert, the Treasurer,
and that he was a great awkward fellow, who broke
everything. That he had desired to be received into
a monastery, thinking that he would there be made
to smart for his awkwardness and the faults he should
commit, and so he should sacrifice to God his life, with
its pleasures; but that God had disappointed him, he
having met with nothing but satisfaction in that
state. . . .

"That he had long been troubled in mind from a
certain belief that he should be damned; that all the
men in the world could not have persuaded him to
the contrary; but that he had thus reasoned with himself about it: *I engaged in a religious life only for the
love of God, and I have endeavored to act only for
Him; whatever becomes of me, whether I be lost or
saved, I will always continue to act purely for the love
of God. I shall have this good at least, that till death
I shall have done all that is in me to love Him.* . . .
That since then he had passed his life in perfect
liberty and continual joy.

"That when an occasion of practising some virtue

* Fleming H. Revell Company, New York.

offered, he addressed himself to God, saying, 'Lord, I cannot do this unless thou enablest me'; and that then he received strength more than sufficient. That, when he had failed in his duty, he only confessed his fault, saying to God, 'I shall never do otherwise, if You leave me to myself; it is You who must hinder my failing, and mend what is amiss.' That after this he gave himself no further uneasiness about it.

"That he had been lately sent into Burgundy to buy the provision of wine for the society, which was a very unwelcome task for him, because he had no turn for business, and because he was lame, and could not go about the boat but by rolling himself over the casks. That, however, he gave himself no uneasiness about it, nor about the purchase of the wine. That he said to God, 'It was his business he was about,' and that he afterward found it well performed. That he had been sent into Auvergne, the year before, upon the same account; that he could not tell how the matter passed, but that it proved very well.

"So, likewise, in his business in the kitchen (to which he had naturally a great aversion), having accustomed himself to do everything there for the love of God, and with prayer upon all occasions, for his grace to do his work well, he had found everything easy during fifteen years that he had been employed there.

"That he was very well pleased with the post he was now in, but that he was as ready to quit that as the former, since he was always pleasing himself in every condition, by doing little things for the love of God.

"That the goodness of God assured him he would not forsake him utterly, and that he would give him strength to bear whatever evil he permitted to happen

to him; and, therefore, that he feared nothing, and
had no occasion to consult with anybody about his
state. That, when he had attempted to do it, he had
always come away more perplexed."

The simple-heartedness of the good Brother Lawrence, and the relaxation of all unnecessary solicitudes
and anxieties in him, is a refreshing spectacle.

The need of feeling responsible all the livelong
day has been preached long enough in our New England. Long enough exclusively, at any rate, — and
long enough to the female sex. What our girl-students
and woman-teachers most need nowadays is not the
exacerbation, but rather the toning-down of their
moral tensions. Even now I fear that some one of
my fair hearers may be making an undying resolve to
become strenuously relaxed, cost what it will, for the
remainder of her life. It is needless to say that that
is not the way to do it. The way to do it, paradoxical
as it may seem, is genuinely not to care whether you
are doing it or not. Then, possibly, by the grace of
God, you may all at once find that you *are* doing it,
and, having learned what the trick feels like, you may
(again by the grace of God) be enabled to go on.

And that something like this may be the happy
experience of all my hearers is, in closing, my most
earnest wish.

ON A CERTAIN BLINDNESS IN
HUMAN BEINGS

OUR judgments concerning the worth of things, big or little, depend on the *feelings* the things arouse in us. Where we judge a thing to be precious in consequence of the *idea* we frame of it, this is only because the idea is itself associated already with a feeling. If we were radically feelingless, and if ideas were the only things our mind could entertain, we should lose all our likes and dislikes at a stroke, and be unable to point to any one situation or experience in life more valuable or significant than any other.

Now the blindness in human beings, of which this discourse will treat, is the blindness with which we all are afflicted in regard to the feelings of creatures and people different from ourselves.

We are practical beings, each of us with limited functions and duties to perform. Each is bound to feel intensely the importance of his own duties and the significance of the situations that call these forth. But this feeling is in each of us a vital secret, for sympathy with which we vainly look to others. The others are too much absorbed in their own vital secrets to take an interest in ours. Hence the stupidity and injustice of our opinions, so far as they deal with the significance of alien lives. Hence the falsity of our judgments, so far as they presume to decide in an absolute way on the value of other persons' conditions or ideals.

Take our dogs and ourselves, connected as we are by a tie more intimate than most ties in this world; and yet, outside of that tie of friendly fondness, how insensible, each of us, to all that makes life significant for the other! — we to the rapture of bones under hedges, or smells of trees and lamp-posts, they to the delights of literature and art. As you sit reading the most moving romance you ever fell upon, what sort of a judge is your fox-terrier of your behavior? With all his good will toward you, the nature of your conduct is absolutely excluded from his comprehension. To sit there like a senseless statue, when you might be taking him to walk and throwing sticks for him to catch! What queer disease is this that comes over you every day, of holding things and staring at them like that for hours together, paralyzed of motion and vacant of all conscious life? The African savages came nearer the truth; but they, too, missed it, when they gathered wonderingly round one of our American travellers who, in the interior, had just come into possession of a stray copy of the New York *Commercial Advertiser,* and was devouring it column by column. When he got through, they offered him a high price for the mysterious object; and, being asked for what they wanted it, they said: "For an eye medicine," — that being the only reason they could conceive of for the protracted bath which he had given his eyes upon its surface.

The spectator's judgment is sure to miss the root of the matter, and to possess no truth. The subject judged knows a part of the world of reality which the judging spectator fails to see, knows more while the spectator knows less; and, wherever there is conflict of opinion and difference of vision, we are bound to believe that the truer side is the side that feels the more, and not the side that feels the less.

Let me take a personal example of the kind that befalls each one of us daily:

Some years ago, while journeying in the mountains of North Carolina, I passed by a large number of 'coves,' as they call them there, or heads of small valleys between the hills, which had been newly cleared and planted. The impression on my mind was one of unmitigated squalor. The settler had in every case cut down the more manageable trees, and left their charred stumps standing. The larger trees he had girdled and killed, in order that their foliage should not cast a shade. He had then built a log cabin, plastering its chinks with clay, and had set up a tall zigzag rail fence around the scene of his havoc, to keep the pigs and cattle out. Finally, he had irregularly planted the intervals between the stumps and trees with Indian corn, which grew among the chips; and there he dwelt with his wife and babes — an axe, a gun, a few utensils, and some pigs and chickens feeding in the woods, being the sum total of his possessions.

The forest had been destroyed; and what had 'improved' it out of existence was hideous, a sort of ulcer, without a single element of artificial grace to make up for the loss of Nature's beauty. Ugly, indeed, seemed the life of the squatter, scudding, as the sailors say, under bare poles, beginning again away back where our first ancestors started, and by hardly a single item the better off for all the achievements of the intervening generations.

Talk about going back to nature! — I said to myself, oppressed by the dreariness, as I drove by. Talk of a

country life for one's old age and for one's children!
Never thus, with nothing but the bare ground and
one's bare hands to fight the battle! Never, without
the best spoils of culture woven in! The beauties and
commodities gained by the centuries are sacred. They
are our heritage and birthright. No modern person
ought to be willing to live a day in such a state of
rudimentariness and denudation.

Then I said to the mountaineer who was driving
me, "What sort of people are they who have to make
these new clearings?" "All of us," he replied. "Why,
we ain't happy here, unless we are getting one of these
coves under cultivation." I instantly felt that I had
been losing the whole inward significance of the situation. Because to me the clearings spoke of naught but
denudation, I thought that to those whose sturdy arms
and obedient axes had made them they could tell no
other story. But, when *they* looked on the hideous
stumps, what they thought of was personal victory.
The chips, the girdled trees, and the vile split rails
spoke of honest sweat, persistent toil and final reward.
The cabin was a warrant of safety for self and wife
and babes. In short, the clearing, which to me was
a mere ugly picture on the retina, was to them a sym-
bol redolent with moral memories and sang a very
pæan of duty, struggle, and success.

I had been as blind to the peculiar ideality of their
conditions as they certainly would also have been to
the ideality of mine, had they had a peep at my
strange indoor academic ways of life at Cambridge.

Wherever a process of life communicates an eagerness to him who lives it, there the life becomes genuinely significant. Sometimes the eagerness is more

knit up with the motor activities, sometimes with the
perceptions, sometimes with the imagination, sometimes with reflective thought. But, wherever it is
found, there is the zest, the tingle, the excitement of
reality; and there *is* 'importance' in the only real and
positive sense in which importance ever anywhere
can be.

Robert Louis Stevenson has illustrated this by a
case, drawn from the sphere of the imagination, in an
essay which I really think deserves to become immortal, both for the truth of its matter and the excellence of its form.

"Toward the end of September," Stevenson writes,
"when school-time was drawing near, and the nights
were already black, we would begin to sally from our
respective villas, each equipped with a tin bull's-eye
lantern. The thing was so well known that it had
worn a rut in the commerce of Great Britain; and the
grocers, about the due time, began to garnish their
windows with our particular brand of luminary. We
wore them buckled to the waist upon a cricket belt,
and over them, such was the rigor of the game, a buttoned top-coat. They smelled noisomely of blistered
tin. They never burned aright, though they would
always burn our fingers. Their use was naught, the
pleasure of them merely fanciful, and yet a boy with
a bull's-eye under his top-coat asked for nothing more.
The fishermen used lanterns about their boats, and it
was from them, I suppose, that we had got the hint;
but theirs were not bull's-eyes, nor did we ever play
at being fishermen. The police carried them at their
belts, and we had plainly copied them in that; yet
we did not pretend to be policemen. Burglars, indeed, we may have had some haunting thought of;

and we had certainly an eye to past ages when lanterns were more common, and to certain story-books in which we had found them to figure very largely. But take it for all in all, the pleasure of the thing was substantive; and to be a boy with a bull's-eye under his top-coat was good enough for us.

"When two of these asses met, there would be an anxious 'Have you got your lantern?' and a gratified 'Yes!' That was the shibboleth, and very needful, too; for, as it was the rule to keep our glory contained, none could recognize a lantern-bearer unless (like the polecat) by the smell. Four or five would sometimes climb into the belly of a ten-man lugger, with nothing but the thwarts above them, — for the cabin was usually locked, — or chose out some hollow of the links where the wind might whistle overhead. Then the coats would be unbuttoned, and the bull's-eyes discovered; and in the chequering glimmer, under the huge, windy hall of the night, and cheered by a rich steam of toasting tinware, these fortunate young gentlemen would crouch together in the cold sand of the links, or on the scaly bilges of the fishing-boat, and delight them with inappropriate talk. Woe is me that I cannot give some specimens! . . . But the talk was but a condiment, and these gatherings themselves only accidents in the career of the lantern-bearer. The essence of this bliss was to walk by yourself in the black night, the slide shut, the top-coat buttoned, not a ray escaping, whether to conduct your footsteps or to make your glory public, — a mere pillar of darkness in the dark; and all the while, deep down in the privacy of your fool's heart, to know you had a bull's-eye at your belt, and to exult and sing over the knowledge.

"It is said that a poet has died young in the breast
of the most stolid. It may be contended rather that
a (somewhat minor) bard in almost every case survives, and is the spice of life to his possessor. Justice
is not done to the versatility and the unplumbed
childishness of man's imagination. His life from
without may seem but a rude mound of mud: there
will be some golden chamber at the heart of it, in
which he dwells delighted; and for as dark as his
pathway seems to the observer, he will have some kind
of bull's-eye at his belt.

. . . "There is one fable that touches very near the
quick of life, — the fable of the monk who passed into
the woods, heard a bird break into song, hearkened
for a trill or two, and found himself at his return a
stranger at his convent gates; for he had been absent
fifty years, and of all his comrades there survived but
one to recognize him. It is not only in the woods
that this enchanter carols, though perhaps he is native
there. He sings in the most doleful places. The
miser hears him and chuckles, and his days are moments. With no more apparatus than an evil-smelling
lantern, I have evoked him on the naked links. All
life that is not merely mechanical is spun out of two
strands, — seeking for that bird and hearing him.
And it is just this that makes life so hard to value,
and the delight of each so incommunicable. And it
is just a knowledge of this, and a remembrance of
those fortunate hours in which the bird *has* sung to
us, that fills us with such wonder when we turn to the
pages of the realist. There, to be sure, we find a picture of life in so far as it consists of mud and of old
iron, cheap desires and cheap fears, that which we are
ashamed to remember and that which we are careless

whether we forget; but of the note of that time-de-
vouring nightingale we hear no news.

. . . "Say that we came [in such a realistic ro-
mance] on some such business as that of my lantern-
bearers on the links, and described the boys as very
cold, spat upon by flurries of rain, and drearily surrounded, all of which they were; and their talk as silly
and indecent, which it certainly was. To the eye of
the observer they *are* wet and cold and drearily surrounded; but ask themselves, and they are in the
heaven of a recondite pleasure, the ground of which
is an ill-smelling lantern.

"For, to repeat, the ground of a man's joy is often
hard to hit. It may hinge at times upon a mere
accessory, like the lantern; it may reside in the mysterious inwards of psychology. . . . It has so little
bond with externals . . . that it may even touch them
not, and the man's true life, for which he consents to
live, lie together in the field of fancy. . . . In such
a case the poetry runs underground. The observer
(poor soul, with his documents!) is all abroad. For
to look at the man is but to court deception. We
shall see the trunk from which he draws his nourish-
ment; but he himself is above and abroad in the
green dome of foliage, hummed through by winds and
nested in by nightingales. And the true realism
were that of the poets, to climb after him like a squir-
rel, and catch some glimpse of the heaven in which
he lives. And the true realism, always and everywhere, is that of the poets: to find out where joy resides, and give it a voice far beyond singing.

"For to miss the joy is to miss all. In the joy of the
actors lies the sense of any action. That is the explanation, that the excuse. To one who has not the
secret of the lanterns the scene upon the links is mean-

ingless. And hence the haunting and truly spectral unreality of realistic books. . . . In each we miss the personal poetry, the enchanted atmosphere, that rainbow work of fancy that clothes what is naked and seems to ennoble what is base; in each, life falls dead like dough, instead of soaring away like a balloon into the colors of the sunset; each is true, each inconceivable; for no man lives in the external truth among salts and acids, but in the warm, phantasmagoric chamber of his brain, with the painted windows and the storied wall." *

These paragraphs are the best thing I know in all Stevenson. "To miss the joy is to miss all." Indeed, it is. Yet we are but finite, and each one of us has some single specialized vocation of his own. And it seems as if energy in the service of its particular duties might be got only by hardening the heart toward everything unlike them. Our deadness toward all but one particular kind of joy would thus be the price we inevitably have to pay for being practical creatures. Only in some pitiful dreamer, some philosopher, poet, or romancer, or when the common practical man becomes a lover, does the hard externality give way, and a gleam of insight into the ejective world, as Clifford called it, the vast world of inner life beyond us, so different from that of outer seeming, illuminate our mind. Then the whole scheme of our customary values gets confounded, then our self is riven and its narrow interests fly to pieces, then a new centre and a new perspective must be found.

The change is well described by my colleague, Josiah Royce:

* 'The Lantern-bearers,' in the volume entitled 'Across the Plains.' Abridged in the quotation.

"What, then, is our neighbor?   Thou hast regarded his thought, his feeling, as somehow different from thine.   Thou hast said, 'A pain in him is not like a pain in me, but something far easier to bear.'   He seems to thee a little less living than thou; his life is dim, it is cold, it is a pale fire beside thy own burning desires. . . . So, dimly and by instinct hast thou lived with thy neighbor, and hast known him not, being blind.   Thou hast made [of him] a thing, no Self at all.   Have done with this illusion, and simply try to learn the truth.   Pain is pain, joy is joy, everywhere, even as in thee.   In all the songs of the forest birds; in all the cries of the wounded and dying, struggling in the captor's power; in the boundless sea where the myriads of water-creatures strive and die; amid all the countless hordes of savage men; in all sickness and sorrow; in all exultation and hope, everywhere, from the lowest to the noblest, the same conscious, burning, wilful life is found, endlessly manifold as the forms of the living creatures, unquenchable as the fires of the sun, real as these impulses that even now throb in thine own little selfish heart.   Lift up thy eyes, behold that life, and then turn away, and forget it as thou canst; but, if thou hast *known* that, thou hast begun to know thy duty." *

This higher vision of an inner significance in what, until then, we had realized only in the dead external way, often comes over a person suddenly; and, when it does so, it makes an epoch in his history.   As Emerson says, there is a depth in those moments that constrains us to ascribe more reality to them than to all other experiences.   The passion of love will shake one like an explosion, or some act will awaken a remorse-

* The Religious Aspect of Philosophy, pp. 157-162 (abridged).

ful compunction that hangs like a cloud over all one's
later day.

This mystic sense of hidden meaning starts upon us
often from non-human natural things. I take this
passage from 'Obermann,' a French novel that had
some vogue in its day: "Paris, March 7. — It was dark
and rather cold. I was gloomy, and walked because
I had nothing to do. I passed by some flowers placed
breast-high upon a wall. A jonquil in bloom was
there. It is the strongest expression of desire: it was
the first perfume of the year. I felt all the happiness
destined for man. This unutterable harmony of souls,
the phantom of the ideal world, arose in me complete.
I never felt anything so great or so instantaneous. I
know not what shape, what analogy, what secret of
relation it was that made me see in this flower a limitless beauty. . . . I shall never enclose in a conception
this power, this immensity that nothing will express;
this form that nothing will contain; this ideal of a
better world which one feels, but which it would
seem that nature has not made." *

Wordsworth and Shelley are similarly full of this
sense of a limitless significance in natural things. In
Wordsworth it was a somewhat austere and moral significance, — a 'lonely cheer.'

"To every natural form, rock, fruit, or flower,
Even the loose stones that cover the highway,
I gave a moral life: I saw them feel
Or linked them to some feeling: the great mass
Lay bedded in some quickening soul, and all
That I beheld respired with inward meaning." †

* De Sénancour: Obermann, Lettre XXX.
† The Prelude, Book III.

"Authentic tidings of invisible things!"   Just what
this hidden presence in nature was, which Wordsworth
so rapturously felt, and in the light of which he lived,
tramping the hills for days together, the poet never
could explain logically or in articulate conceptions.
Yet to the reader who may himself have had gleaming
moments of a similar sort the verses in which Wordsworth simply proclaims the fact of them come with a
heart-satisfying authority:—

>   "Magnificent
> The morning rose, in memorable pomp,
> Glorious as ere I had beheld.   In front
> The sea lay laughing at a distance; near
> The solid mountains shone, bright as the clouds,
> Grain-tinctured, drenched in empyrean light;
> And in the meadows and the lower grounds
> Was all the sweetness of a common dawn, —
> Dews, vapors, and the melody of birds,
> And laborers going forth to till the fields.
>
> "Ah! need I say, dear Friend, that to the brim
> My heart was full; I made no vows, but vows
> Were then made for me; bond unknown to me
> Was given, that I should be, else sinning greatly,
> A dedicated Spirit.   On I walked,
> In thankless blessedness, which yet survives." *

As Wordsworth walked, filled with his strange inner
joy, responsive thus to the secret life of nature
round about him, his rural neighbors, tightly and
narrowly intent upon their own affairs, their crops
and lambs and fences, must have thought him a very
insignificant and foolish personage.   It surely never
occurred to any one of them to wonder what was
going on inside of *him* or what it might be worth.

* The Prelude, Book IV.

And yet that inner life of his carried the burden of a significance that has fed the souls of others, and fills them to this day with inner joy.

Richard Jeffries has written a remarkable autobiographic document entitled 'The Story of my Heart.' It tells, in many pages, of the rapture with which in youth the sense of the life of nature filled him. On a certain hill-top he says:—

"I was utterly alone with the sun and the earth. Lying down on the grass, I spoke in my soul to the earth, the sun, the air, and the distant sea, far beyond sight. . . . With all the intensity of feeling which exalted me, all the intense communion I held with the earth, the sun and sky, the stars hidden by the light, with the ocean, — in no manner can the thrilling depth of these feelings be written, — with these I prayed as if they were the keys of an instrument. . . . The great sun, burning with light, the strong earth, — dear earth, — the warm sky, the pure air, the thought of ocean, the inexpressible beauty of all filled me with a rapture, an ecstasy, an inflatus. With this inflatus, too, I prayed. . . . The prayer, this soul-emotion, was in itself, not for an object: it was a passion. I hid my face in the grass. I was wholly prostrated, I lost myself in the wrestle, I was rapt and carried away. . . . Had any shepherd accidentally seen me lying on the turf, he would only have thought I was resting a few minutes. I made no outward show. Who could have imagined the whirlwind of passion that was going on in me as I reclined there!" *

Surely, a worthless hour of life, when measured by the usual standards of commercial value. Yet in what other *kind* of value can the preciousness of any hour,

* *Op. cit.*, Boston, Roberts, 1883, pp. 5, 6.

made precious by any standard, consist, if it consist not in feelings of excited significance like these, engendered in some one, by what the hour contains?

Yet so blind and dead does the clamor of our own practical interests make us to all other things, that it seems almost as if it were necessary to become worthless as a practical being, if one is to hope to attain to any breadth of insight into the impersonal world of worths as such, to have any perception of life's meaning on a large objective scale. Only your mystic, your dreamer, or your insolvent tramp or loafer, can afford so sympathetic an occupation, an occupation which will change the usual standards of human value in the twinkling of an eye, giving to foolishness a place ahead of power, and laying low in a minute the distinctions which it takes a hard-working conventional man a lifetime to build up. You may be a prophet, at this rate; but you cannot be a worldly success.

Walt Whitman, for instance, is accounted by many of us a contemporary prophet. He abolishes the usual human distinctions, brings all conventionalisms into solution, and loves and celebrates hardly any human attributes save those elementary ones common to all members of the race. For this he becomes a sort of ideal tramp, a rider on omnibus-tops and ferry-boats, and, considered either practically or academically, a worthless, unproductive being. His verses are but ejaculations — things mostly without subject or verb, a succession of interjections on an immense scale. He felt the human crowd as rapturously as Wordsworth felt the mountains, felt it as an overpoweringly significant presence, simply to absorb one's mind in which should be business sufficient and worthy to fill the days of a serious man. As he crosses Brooklyn ferry, this is what he feels:

"Flood-tide below me!   I watch you, face to face;
Clouds of the west! sun there half an hour high!   I see
  you also face to face.
Crowds of men and women attired in the usual cos-
  tumes! how curious you are to me!
On the ferry-boats, the hundreds and hundreds that
  cross, returning home, are more curious to me
  than you suppose;
And you that shall cross from shore to shore years
  hence, are more to me, and more in my medita-
  tions, than you might suppose.
Others will enter the gates of the ferry, and cross from
  shore to shore;
Others will watch the run of the flood-tide;
Others will see the shipping of Manhattan north and
  west, and the heights of Brooklyn to the south
  and east;
Others will see the islands large and small;
Fifty years hence, others will see them as they cross,
  the sun half an hour high.
A hundred years hence, or ever so many hundred
  years hence, others will see them,
Will enjoy the sunset, the pouring in of the flood-tide,
  the falling back to the sea of the ebb-tide.
It avails not, neither time or place — distance avails
  not.
Just as you feel when you look on the river and sky,
  so I felt;
Just as any of you is one of a living crowd, I was one
  of a crowd;
Just as you are refresh'd by the gladness of the river
  and the bright flow, I was refresh'd;
Just as you stand and lean on the rail, yet hurry with
  the swift current, I stood, yet was hurried;
Just as you look on the numberless masts of ships, and
  the thick-stemmed pipes of steamboats, I looked.
I too many and many a time cross'd the river, the
  sun half an hour high;

I watched the Twelfth-month sea-gulls — I saw them
  high in the air, with motionless wings, oscillating
  their bodies,
I saw how the glistening yellow lit up parts of their
  bodies, and left the rest in strong shadow,
I saw the slow-wheeling circles, and the gradual edging
  toward the south.
Saw the white sails of schooners and sloops, saw the
  ships at anchor,
The sailors at work in the rigging, or out astride the
  spars;
The scalloped-edged waves in the twilight, the ladled
  cups, the frolicsome crests and glistening;
The stretch afar growing dimmer and dimmer, the
  gray walls of the granite store-houses by the docks;
On the neighboring shores, the fires from the foundry
  chimneys burning high . . . . into the night,
Casting their flicker of black . . . . into the clefts of
  streets.
These, and all else, were to me the same as they are
  to you." *

And so on, through the rest of a divinely beautiful
poem.   And, if you wish to see what this hoary loafer
considered the most worthy way of profiting by life's
heaven-sent opportunities, read the delicious volume
of his letters to a young car-conductor who had become
his friend:

                    "NEW YORK, Oct. 9, 1868.
  "*Dear Pete,* — It is splendid here this forenoon —
bright and cool.   I was out early taking a short walk
by the river only two squares from where I live. . . .
Shall I tell you about [my life] just to fill up?   I gen-

  * 'Crossing Brooklyn's Ferry' (abridged).

erally spend the forenoon in my room writing, etc.,
then take a bath fix up and go out about twelve and
loafe somewhere or call on someone down town or on
business, or perhaps if it is very pleasant and I feel
like it ride a trip with some driver friend on Broadway from 23rd Street to Bowling Green, three miles
each way. (Every day I find I have plenty to do,
every hour is occupied with something.) You know
it is a never ending amusement and study and recrea-
tion for me to ride a couple of hours on a pleasant
afternoon on a Broadway stage in this way. You see
everything as you pass, a sort of living, endless panorama — shops and splendid buildings and great windows: on the broad sidewalks crowds of women richly
dressed continually passing, altogether different, superior in style and looks from any to be seen anywhere
else — in fact a perfect stream of people — men too
dressed in high style, and plenty of foreigners — and
then in the streets the thick crowd of carriages, stages,
carts, hotel and private coaches, and in fact all sorts
of vehicles and many first class teams, mile after mile,
and the splendor of such a great street and so many
tall, ornamental, noble buildings many of them of
white marble, and the gayety and motion on every
side: you will not wonder how much attraction all this
is on a fine day, to a great loafer like me, who enjoys
so much seeing the busy world move by him, and
exhibiting itself for his amusement, while he takes it
easy and just looks on and observes." *

Truly a futile way of passing the time, some of you
may say, and not altogether creditable to a grown-up
man. And yet, from the deepest point of view, who
knows the more of truth, and who knows the less, —

* Calamus, Boston, 1897, pp. 41, 42.

Whitman on his omnibus-top, full of the inner joy
with which the spectacle inspires him, or you, full of
the disdain which the futility of his occupation excites?

When your ordinary Brooklynite or New Yorker,
leading a life replete with too much luxury, or tired and
careworn about his personal affairs, crosses the ferry or
goes up Broadway, *his* fancy does not thus 'soar away
into the colors of the sunset' as did Whitman's, nor
does he inwardly realize at all the indisputable fact
that this world never did anywhere or at any time
contain more of essential divinity, or of eternal meaning, than is embodied in the fields of vision over which
his eyes so carelessly pass. There is life; and there, a
step away, is death. There is the only kind of beauty
there ever was. There is the old human struggle and
its fruits together. There is the text and the sermon,
the real and the ideal in one. But to the jaded and
unquickened eye it is all dead and common, pure
vulgarism, flatness, and disgust. "Hech! it is a sad
sight!" says Carlyle, walking at night with some one
who appeals to him to note the splendor of the stars.
And that very repetition of the scene to new generations of men in *secula seculorum,* that eternal recur-
rence of the common order, which so fills a Whitman
with mystic satisfaction, is to a Schopenhauer, with
the emotional anæsthesia, the feeling of 'awful inner
emptiness' from out of which he views it all, the chief
ingredient of the tedium it instils. What is life on
the largest scale, he asks, but the same recurrent inanities, the same dog barking, the same fly buzzing,
forevermore? Yet of the kind of fibre of which such
inanities consist is the material woven of all the excitements, joys, and meanings that ever were, or ever
shall be, in this world.

To be rapt with satisfied attention, like Whitman, to the mere spectacle of the world's presence, is one way, and the most fundamental way, of confessing one's sense of its unfathomable significance and importance. But how can one attain to the feeling of the vital significance of an experience, if one have it not to begin with? There is no receipt which one can follow. Being a secret and a mystery, it often comes in mysteriously unexpected ways. It blossoms sometimes from out of the very grave wherein we imagined that our happiness was buried. Benvenuto Cellini, after a life all in the outer sunshine, made of adventures and artistic excitements, suddenly finds himself cast into a dungeon in the Castle of San Angelo. The place is horrible. Rats and wet and mould possess it. His leg is broken and his teeth fall out, apparently with scurvy. But his thoughts turn to God as they have never turned before. He gets a Bible, which he reads during the one hour in the twenty-four in which a wandering ray of daylight penetrates his cavern. He has religious visions. He sings psalms to himself, and composes hymns. And thinking, on the last day of July, of the festivities customary on the morrow in Rome, he says to himself: "All these past years I celebrated this holiday with the vanities of the world: from this year henceforward I will do it with the divinity of God. And then I said to myself, 'Oh, how much more happy I am for this present life of mine than for all those things remembered!'" *

But the great understander of these mysterious ebbs and flows is Tolstoï. They throb all through his novels. In his 'War and Peace,' the hero, Peter, is

* Vita, lib. 2, chap. iv.

supposed to be the richest man in the Russian empire. During the French invasion he is taken prisoner, and dragged through much of the retreat. Cold, vermin, hunger, and every form of misery assail him, the result being a revelation to him of the real scale of life's values. "Here only, and for the first time, he appreciated, because he was deprived of it, the happiness of eating when he was hungry, of drinking when he was thirsty, of sleeping when he was sleepy, and of talking when he felt the desire to exchange some words. . . . Later in life he always recurred with joy to this month of captivity, and never failed to speak with enthusiasm of the powerful and ineffaceable sensations, and especially of the moral calm which he had experienced at this epoch. When at daybreak, on the morrow of his imprisonment, he saw [I abridge here Tolstoï's description] the mountains with their wooded slopes disappearing in the grayish mist; when he felt the cool breeze caress him; when he saw the light drive away the vapors, and the sun rise majestically behind the clouds and cupolas, and the crosses, the dew, the distance, the river, sparkle in the splendid, cheerful rays, — his heart overflowed with emotion. This emotion kept continually with him, and increased a hundred-fold as the difficulties of his situation grew graver. . . . He learnt that man is meant for happiness, and that this happiness is in him, in the satisfaction of the daily needs of existence, and that unhappiness is the fatal result, not of our need, but of our abundance. . . . When calm reigned in the camp, and the embers paled, and little by little went out, the full moon had reached the zenith. The woods and the fields roundabout lay clearly visible; and, beyond the inundation of light which filled them, the view plunged into the limitless horizon. Then Peter cast his eyes upon the firmament, filled at that hour with myriads of stars. 'All that is mine,' he thought. 'All that is in me, is me! And that is what they think they have taken prisoner! That is what they have shut up in a cabin!' So he smiled, and turned in to sleep among his comrades." *

The occasion and the experience, then, are nothing. It all depends on the capacity of the soul to be grasped, to have its life-currents absorbed by what is given. "Crossing a bare common," says Emerson, "in snow puddles, at twilight, under a clouded sky, without having in my thoughts any occurrence of special good fortune, I have enjoyed a perfect exhilaration. I am glad to the brink of fear."

Life is always worth living, if one have such responsive sensibilities. But we of the highly educated classes (so called) have most of us got far, far away from Nature. We are trained to seek the choice, the rare, the exquisite exclusively, and to overlook the common. We are stuffed with abstract conceptions, and glib with verbalities and verbosities; and in the culture of these higher functions the peculiar sources of joy connected with our simpler functions often dry up, and we grow stone-blind and insensible to life's more elementary and general goods and joys.

The remedy under such conditions is to descend to a more profound and primitive level. To be imprisoned or shipwrecked or forced into the army would permanently show the good of life to many an over-educated pessimist. Living in the open air and on the ground, the lop-sided beam of the balance slowly rises to the level line; and the over-sensibilities

* La Guerre et la Paix, Paris, 1884, vol. iii. pp. 268, 275, 316.

and insensibilities even themselves out. The good of all the artificial schemes and fevers fades and pales; and that of seeing, smelling, tasting, sleeping, and daring and doing with one's body, grows and grows. The savages and children of nature, to whom we deem ourselves so much superior, certainly are alive where we are often dead, along these lines; and, could they write as glibly as we do, they would read us impressive lectures on our impatience for improvement and on our blindness to the fundamental static goods of life. "Ah! my brother," said a chieftain to his white guest, "thou wilt never know the happiness of both thinking of nothing and doing nothing. This, next to sleep, is the most enchanting of all things. Thus we were before our birth, and thus we shall be after death. Thy people, . . . when they have finished reaping one field, they begin to plough another; and, if the day were not enough, I have seen them plough by moonlight. What is their life to ours, — the life that is as naught to them? Blind that they are, they lose it all! But we live in the present." *

The intense interest that life can assume when brought down to the non-thinking level, the level of pure sensorial perception, has been beautifully described by a man who *can* write, — Mr. W. H. Hudson, in his volume, "Idle Days in Patagonia."

"I spent the greater part of one winter," says this admirable author, "at a point on the Rio Negro, seventy or eighty miles from the sea.

. . . "It was my custom to go out every morning on horseback with my gun, and, followed by one dog, to ride away from the valley; and no sooner would I

* Quoted by Lotze, Microcosmus, English translation, vol. ii, p. 240.

climb the terrace, and plunge into the gray, universal
thicket, than I would find myself as completely alone
as if five hundred instead of only five miles separated
me from the valley and river. So wild and solitary
and remote seemed that gray waste, stretching away
into infinitude, a waste untrodden by man, and where
the wild animals are so few that they have made no
discoverable path in the wilderness of thorns. . . . Not
once nor twice nor thrice, but day after day I returned
to this solitude, going to it in the morning as if to
attend a festival, and leaving it only when hunger
and thirst and the westering sun compelled me.   And
yet I had no object in going, — no motive which could
be put into words; for, although I carried a gun, there
was nothing to shoot, — the shooting was all left behind in the valley. . . . Sometimes I would pass a
whole day without seeing one mammal, and perhaps
not more than a dozen birds of any size. The weather
at that time was cheerless, generally with a gray film
of cloud spread over the sky, and a bleak wind, often
cold enough to make my bridle-hand quite numb. . . .
At a slow pace, which would have seemed intolerable
under other circumstances, I would ride about for
hours together at a stretch. On arriving at a hill, I
would slowly ride to its summit, and stand there to
survey the prospect. On every side it stretched away
in great undulations, wild and irregular. How gray
it all was! Hardly less so near at hand than on the
haze-wrapped horizon where the hills were dim and
the outline obscured by distance. Descending from
my outlook, I would take up my aimless wanderings
again, and visit other elevations to gaze on the same
landscape from another point; and so on for hours.
And at noon I would dismount, and sit or lie on my

folded poncho for an hour or longer. One day in these rambles I discovered a small grove composed of twenty or thirty trees, growing at a convenient distance apart, that had evidently been resorted to by a herd of deer or other wild animals. This grove was on a hill differing in shape from other hills in its neighborhood; and, after a time, I made a point of finding and using it as a resting-place every day at noon. I did not ask myself why I made choice of that one spot, sometimes going out of my way to sit there, instead of sitting down under any one of the millions of trees and bushes on any other hillside. I thought nothing about it, but acted unconsciously. Only afterward it seemed to me that, after having rested there once, each time I wished to rest again, the wish came associated with the image of that particular clump of trees, with polished stems and clean bed of sand beneath; and in a short time I formed a habit of returning, animal like, to repose at that same spot.

"It was, perhaps, a mistake to say that I would sit down and rest, since I was never tired; and yet, without being tired, that noon-day pause, during which I sat for an hour without moving, was strangely grateful. All day there would be no sound, not even the rustling of a leaf. One day, while *listening* to the silence, it occurred to my mind to wonder what the effect would be if I were to shout aloud. This seemed at the time a horrible suggestion, which almost made me shudder. But during those solitary days it was a rare thing for any thought to cross my mind. In the state of mind I was in, thought had become impossible. My state was one of *suspense* and *watchfulness;* yet I had no expectation of meeting an adventure, and felt as free from apprehension as I feel now while sitting in a room in London. The state seemed familiar rather than strange, and accompanied by a strong feeling of elation; and I did not know that something had come between me and my intellect until I returned to my former self, — to thinking, and the old insipid existence [again].

"I had undoubtedly *gone back;* and that state of intense watchfulness or alertness, rather, with suspension of the higher intellectual faculties, represented the mental state of the pure savage. He thinks little, reasons little, having a surer guide in his [mere sensory perceptions]. He is in perfect harmony with nature, and is nearly on a level, mentally, with the wild animals he preys on, and which in their turn sometimes prey on him." *

For the spectator, such hours as Mr. Hudson writes of form a mere tale of emptiness, in which nothing happens, nothing is gained, and there is nothing to describe. They are meaningless and vacant tracts of time. To him who feels their inner secret, they tingle with an importance that unutterably vouches for itself. I am sorry for the boy or girl, or man or woman, who has never been touched by the spell of this mysterious sensorial life, with its irrationality, if so you like to call it, but its vigilance and its supreme felicity. The holidays of life are its most vitally significant portions, because they are, or at least should be, covered with just this kind of magically irresponsible spell.

And now what is the result of all these considerations and quotations? It is negative in one sense, but positive in another. It absolutely forbids us to be forward in pronouncing on the meaninglessness of

* *Op. cit.,* pp. 210-222 (abridged).

forms of existence other than our own; and it commands us to tolerate, respect, and indulge those whom
we see harmlessly interested and happy in their own
ways, however unintelligible these may be to us.
Hands off: neither the whole of truth nor the whole
of good is revealed to any single observer, although
each observer gains a partial superiority of insight
from the peculiar position in which he stands.   Even
prisons and sick-rooms have their special revelations.
It is enough to ask of each of us that he should be
faithful to his own opportunities and make the most
of his own blessings, without presuming to regulate
the rest of the vast field.

WHAT MAKES A LIFE SIGNIFICANT?

I N MY previous talk, 'On a Certain Blindness,' I tried
to make you feel how soaked and shot-through life
is with values and meanings which we fail to realize
because of our external and insensible point of view.
The meanings are there for the others, but they are
not there for us. There lies more than a mere interest
of curious speculation in understanding this. It has
the most tremendous practical importance. I wish
that I could convince you of it as I feel it myself. It
is the basis of all our tolerance, social, religious, and
political. The forgetting of it lies at the root of every
stupid and sanguinary mistake that rulers over sub-
ject-peoples make. The first thing to learn in inter-
course with others is non-interference with their own
peculiar ways of being happy, provided those ways do
not assume to interfere by violence with ours. No
one has insight into all the ideals. No one should
presume to judge them off-hand. The pretension to
dogmatize about them in each other is the root of
most human injustices and cruelties, and the trait in
human character most likely to make the angels weep.

Every Jack sees in his own particular Jill charms
and perfections to the enchantment of which we stolid
onlookers are stone-cold. And which has the superior
view of the absolute truth, he or we? Which has the
more vital insight into the nature of Jill's existence, as
a fact? Is he in excess, being in this matter a maniac?

or are we in defect, being victims of a pathological anæsthesia as regards Jill's magical importance? Surely the latter; surely to Jack are the profounder truths revealed; surely poor Jill's palpitating little life-throbs *are* among the wonders of creation, *are* worthy of this sympathetic interest; and it is to our shame that the rest of us cannot feel like Jack. For Jack realizes Jill concretely, and we do not. He struggles toward a union with her inner life, divining her feelings, anticipating her desires, understanding her limits as manfully as he can, and yet inadequately, too; for he is also afflicted with some blindness, even here. Whilst we, dead clods that we are, do not even seek after these things, but are contented that that portion of eternal fact named Jill should be for us as if it were not. Jill, who knows her inner life, knows that Jack's way of taking it — so importantly — is the true and serious way; and she responds to the truth in him by taking him truly and seriously, too. May the ancient blindness never wrap its clouds about either of them again! Where would any of *us* be, were there no one willing to know us as we really are or ready to repay us for *our* insight by making recognizant return? We ought, all of us, to realize each other in this intense, pathetic, and important way.

If you say that this is absurd, and that we cannot be in love with everyone at once, I merely point out to you that, as a matter of fact, certain persons do exist with an enormous capacity for friendship and for taking delight in other people's lives; and that such persons know more of truth than if their hearts were not so big. The vice of ordinary Jack and Jill affection is not its intensity, but its exclusions and its jealousies. Leave those out, and you see that the ideal I am

holding up before you, however impracticable today,
yet contains nothing intrinsically absurd.

We have unquestionably a great cloud-bank of ancestral blindness weighing down upon us, only tran-
siently riven here and there by fitful revelations of the
truth.   It is vain to hope for this state of things to
alter much.   Our inner secrets must remain for the
most part impenetrable by others, for beings as essentially practical as we are are necessarily short of sight.
But, if we cannot gain much positive insight into one
another, cannot we at least use our sense of our
own blindness to make us more cautious in going
over the dark places?   Cannot we escape some of those
hideous ancestral intolerances and cruelties, and positive reversals of the truth?

For the remainder of this hour I invite you to seek
with me some principle to make our tolerance less
chaotic.   And, as I began my previous lecture by a
personal reminiscence, I am going to ask your indul-
gence for a similar bit of egotism now.

A few summers ago I spent a happy week at the
famous Assembly Grounds on the borders of Chautauqua Lake.   The moment one treads that sacred
enclosure, one feels one's self in an atmosphere of success.   Sobriety and industry, intelligence and goodness, orderliness and ideality, prosperity and cheerfulness, pervade the air.   It is a serious and studious
picnic on a gigantic scale.   Here you have a town of
many thousands of inhabitants, beautifully laid out
in the forest and drained, and equipped with means
for satisfying all the necessary lower and most of the
superfluous higher wants of man.   You have a first-
class college in full blast.   You have magnificent music
— a chorus of seven hundred voices, with possibly the

most perfect open-air auditorium in the world. You have every sort of athletic exercise from sailing, rowing, swimming, bicycling, to the ball-field and the more artificial doings which the gymnasium affords. You have kindergartens and model secondary schools. You have general religious services and special clubhouses for the several sects. You have perpetually running soda-water fountains, and daily popular lectures by distinguished men. You have the best of company, and yet no effort. You have no zymotic diseases, no poverty, no drunkenness, no crime, no police. You have culture, you have kindness, you have cheapness, you have equality, you have the best fruits of what mankind has fought and bled and striven for under the name of civilization for centuries. You have, in short, a foretaste of what human society might be, were it all in the light, with no suffering and no dark corners.

I went in curiosity for a day. I stayed for a week, held spell-bound by the charm and ease of everything, by the middle-class paradise, without a sin, without a victim, without a blot, without a tear.

And yet what was my own astonishment, on emerging into the dark and wicked world again, to catch myself quite unexpectedly and involuntarily saying: "Ouf! what a relief! Now for something primordial and savage, even though it were as bad as an Armenian massacre, to set the balance straight again. This order is too tame, this culture too second-rate, this goodness too uninspiring. This human drama without a villain or a pang; this community so refined that ice-cream and soda-water is the utmost offering it can make to the brute animal in man; this city simmering in the tepid lakeside sun; this atrocious harmlessness of all things, — I cannot abide with them.   Let me take my chances again in the big outside worldly wilderness with all its sins and sufferings.   There are the heights and depths, the precipices and the steep ideals, the gleams of the awful and the infinite; and there is more hope and help a thousand times than in this dead level and quintessence of every mediocrity."

Such was the sudden right-about-face performed for me by my lawless fancy!   There had been spread before me the realization — on a small, sample scale of course — of all the ideals for which our civilization has been striving: security, intelligence, humanity, and order; and here was the instinctive hostile reaction, not of the natural man, but of a so-called cultivated man upon such a Utopia.   There seemed thus to be a self-contradiction and paradox somewhere, which I, as a professor drawing a full salary, was in duty bound to unravel and explain, if I could.

So I meditated.   And, first of all, I asked myself what the thing was that was so lacking in this Sabbatical city, and the lack of which kept one forever falling short of the higher sort of contentment.   And I soon recognized that it was the element that gives to the wicked outer world all its moral style, expressiveness and picturesqueness, — the element of precipitousness, so to call it, of strength and strenuousness, intensity and danger.   What excites and interests the looker-on at life, what the romances and the statues celebrate and the grim civic monuments remind us of, is the everlasting battle of the powers of light with those of darkness; with heroism, reduced to its bare chance, yet ever and anon snatching victory from the jaws of death.   But in this unspeakable Chautauqua there was no potentiality of death in sight anywhere·

and no point of the compass visible from which danger might possibly appear. The ideal was so completely victorious already that no sign of any previous battle remained, the place just resting on its oars. But what our human emotions seem to require is the sight of the struggle going on. The moment the fruits are being merely eaten, things become ignoble. Sweat and effort, human nature strained to its uttermost and on the rack, yet getting through alive, and then turning its back on its success to pursue another more rare and arduous still — this is the sort of thing the presence of which inspires us, and the reality of which it seems to be the function of all the higher forms of literature and fine art to bring home to us and suggest. At Chautauqua there were no racks, even in the place's historical museum; and no sweat, except possibly the gentle moisture on the brow of some lecturer, or on the sides of some player in the ball-field.

Such absence of human nature *in extremis* anywhere seemed, then, a sufficient explanation for Chautauqua's flatness and lack of zest.

But was not this a paradox well calculated to fill one with dismay? It looks indeed, thought I, as if the romantic idealists with their pessimism about our civilization were, after all, quite right. An irremediable flatness is coming over the world. Bourgeoisie and mediocrity, church sociables and teachers' conventions, are taking the place of the old heights and depths and romantic chiaroscuro. And, to get human life in its wild intensity, we must in future turn more and more away from the actual, and forget it, if we can, in the romancer's or the poet's pages. The whole world, delightful and sinful as it may still appear for a moment to one just escaped from the Chautauquan enclosure, is nevertheless obeying more and more just those ideals that are sure to make of it in the end a mere Chautauqua Assembly on an enormous scale. *Was im Gesang soll leben muss im Leben untergehn.* Even now, in our own country, correctness, fairness, and compromise for every small advantage are crowding out all other qualities. The higher heroisms and the old rare flavors are passing out of life.*

With these thoughts in my mind, I was speeding with the train toward Buffalo, when, near that city, the sight of a workman doing something on the dizzy edge of a sky-scaling iron construction brought me to my senses very suddenly. And now I perceived, by a flash of insight, that I had been steeping myself in pure ancestral blindness, and looking at life with the eyes of a remote spectator. Wishing for heroism and the spectacle of human nature on the rack, I had never noticed the great fields of heroism lying around about me, I had failed to see it present and alive. I could only think of it as dead and embalmed, labelled and costumed, as it is in the pages of romance. And yet there it was before me in the daily lives of the laboring classes. Not in clanging fights and desperate marches only is heroism to be looked for, but on every railway bridge and fire-proof building that is going up today. On freight-trains, on the decks of vessels, in cattle-yards and mines, on lumber-rafts, among the firemen and the policemen, the demand for courage is incessant; and the supply never fails. There, every day of the year somewhere, is human nature *in ex-*

---

* This address was composed before the Cuban and Philippine wars. Such outbursts of the passion of mastery are, however, only episodes in social process which in the long run seems everywhere tending toward the Chautauquan ideals.

tremis for you.   And wherever a scythe, an axe, a pick, or a shovel is wielded, you have it sweating and aching and with its powers of patient endurance racked to the utmost under the length of hours of the strain.

As I awoke to all this unidealized heroic life around me, the scales seemed to fall from my eyes; and a wave of sympathy greater than anything I had ever before felt with the common life of common men began to fill my soul.   It began to seem as if virtue with horny hands and dirty skin were the only virtue genuine and vital enough to take account of.   Every other virtue poses; none is absolutely unconscious and simple, and unexpectant of decoration or recognition, like this.   These are our soldiers, thought I, these our sustainers, these the very parents of our life.

Many years ago, when in Vienna, I had had a similar feeling of awe and reverence in looking at the peasant-women, in from the country on their business at the market for the day.   Old hags many of them were, dried and brown and wrinkled, kerchiefed and short-petticoated, with thick wool stockings on their bony shanks, stumping through the glittering thoroughfares, looking neither to the right nor the left, bent on duty, envying nothing, humble-hearted, remote; — and yet at bottom, when you came to think of it, bearing the whole fabric of the splendors and corruptions of that city on their laborious backs.   For where would any of it have been without their unremitting, unrewarded labor in the fields?   And so with us: not to our generals and poets, I thought, but to the Italian and Hungarian laborers in the Subway, rather, ought the monuments of gratitude and reverence of a city like Boston to be reared.

If any of you have been readers of Tolstoï, you will
see that I passed into a vein of feeling similar to his,
with its abhorrence of all that conventionally passes
for distinguished, and its exclusive deification of the
bravery, patience, kindliness, and dumbness of the
unconscious natural man.

Where now is *our* Tolstoï, I said, to bring the truth
of all this home to our American bosoms, fill us with
a better insight, and wean us away from that spurious
literary romanticism on which our wretched culture
— as it calls itself — is fed? Divinity lies all about us,
and culture is too hide-bound to even suspect the fact.
Could a Howells or a Kipling be enlisted in this mission? or are they still too deep in the ancestral blindness, and not humane enough for the inner joy and
meaning of the laborer's existence to be really revealed? Must we wait for some one born and bred
and living as a laborer himself, but who, by grace of
Heaven, shall also find a literary voice?

And there I rested on that day, with a sense of
widening of vision, and with what it is surely fair to
call an increase of religious insight into life. In God's
eyes the differences of social position, of intellect, of
culture, of cleanliness, of dress, which different men
exhibit, and all the other rarities and exceptions on
which they so fantastically pin their pride, must be
so small as practically quite to vanish; and all that
should remain is the common fact that here we are,
a countless multitude of vessels of life, each of us pent
in to peculiar difficulties, with which we must severally
struggle by using whatever of fortitude and goodness
we can summon up. The exercise of the courage,
patience, and kindness, must be the significant portion
of the whole business; and the distinctions of position

can only be a manner of diversifying the phenomenal surface upon which these underground virtues may manifest their effects.   At this rate, the deepest human life is everywhere, is eternal.   And, if any human attributes exist only in particular individuals, they must belong to the mere trapping and decoration of the surface-show.

Thus are men's lives levelled up as well as levelled down, — levelled up in their common inner meaning, levelled down in their outer gloriousness and show. Yet always, we must confess, this levelling insight tends to be obscured again; and always the ancestral blindness returns and wraps us up, so that we end once more by thinking that creation can be for no other purpose than to develop remarkable situations and conventional distinctions and merits.   And then always some new leveller in the shape of a religious prophet has to arise — the Buddha, the Christ, or some Saint Francis, some Rousseau or Tolstoï — to redispel our blindness.   Yet, little by little, there comes some stable gain; for the world does get more humane, and the religion of democracy tends toward permanent increase.

This, as I said, became for a time my conviction, and gave me great content.   I have put the matter into the form of a personal reminiscence, so that I might lead you into it more directly and completely, and so save time.   But now I am going to discuss the rest of it with you in a more impersonal way.

Tolstoï's levelling philosophy began long before he had the crisis of melancholy commemorated in that wonderful document of his entitled 'My Confession,' which led the way to his more specifically religious works.   In his masterpiece 'War and Peace,' — assuredly the greatest of human novels, — the rôle of the spiritual hero is given to a poor little soldier named Karataïeff, so helpful, so cheerful, and so devout that, in spite of his ignorance and filthiness, the sight of him opens the heavens, which have been closed, to the mind of the principal character of the book; and his example evidently is meant by Tolstoï to let God into the world again for the reader. Poor little Karataïeff is taken prisoner by the French; and, when too exhausted by hardship and fever to march, is shot as other prisoners were in the famous retreat from Moscow. The last view one gets of him is his little figure leaning against a white birch-tree, and uncomplainingly awaiting the end.

"The more," writes Tolstoï in the work 'My Confession,' "the more I examined the life of these laboring folks, the more persuaded I became that they veritably have faith, and get from it alone the sense and the possibility of life. . . . Contrariwise to those of our own class, who protest against destiny and grow indignant at its rigor, these people receive maladies and misfortunes without revolt, without opposition, and with a firm and tranquil confidence that all had to be like that, could not be otherwise, and that it is all right so. . . . The more we live by our intellect, the less we understand the meaning of life. We see only a cruel jest in suffering and death, whereas these people live, suffer, and draw near to death with tranquillity, and oftener than not with joy. . . . There are enormous multitudes of them happy with the most perfect happiness, although deprived of what for us is the sole good of life. Those who understand life's meaning, and know how to live and die thus, are to be counted not by twos, threes, tens, but by hundreds,

thousands, millions.   They labor quietly, endure privations and pains, live and die, and throughout everything see the good without seeing the vanity.   I had
to love these people.   The more I entered into their
life, the more I loved them; and the more it became
possible for me to live, too.   It came about not only
that the life of our society, of the learned and of the
rich, disgusted me — more than that, it lost all sem-
blance of meaning in my eyes.   All our actions, our
deliberations, our sciences, our arts, all appeared to
me with a new significance.   I understood that these
things might be charming pastimes, but that one need
seek in them no depth, whereas the life of the hard-
working populace, of that multitude of human beings
who really contribute to existence, appeared to me in
its true light.   I understood that there veritably is life,
that the meaning which life there receives is the truth;
and I accepted it." *

In a similar way does Stevenson appeal to our piety
toward the elemental virtue of mankind.

"What a wonderful thing," he writes, † "is this
Man!   How surprising are his attributes!   Poor soul,
here for so little, cast among so many hardships,
savagely surrounded, savagely descended, irremediably
condemned to prey upon his fellow-lives, — who
should have blamed him, had he been of a piece
with his destiny and a being merely barbarous? . . .
[Yet] it matters not where we look, under what
climate we observe him, in what stage of society, in
what depth of ignorance, burdened with what erroneous morality; in ships at sea, a man inured to hardship and vile pleasures, his brightest hope a fiddle in

* My Confession, X. (condensed).
† Across the Plains: "Pulvis et Umbra" (abridged).

a tavern, and a bedizened trull who sells herself to
rob him, and he, for all that, simple, innocent, cheerful, kindly like a child, constant to toil, brave to
drown, for others; . . . in the slums of cities, moving
among indifferent millions to mechanical employ-
ments, without hope of change in the future, with
scarce a pleasure in the present, and yet true to his
virtues, honest up to his lights, kind to his neighbors,
tempted perhaps in vain by the bright gin-palace,
. . . often repaying the world's scorn with service,
often standing firm upon a scruple; . . . everywhere
some virtue cherished or affected, everywhere some
decency of thought and courage, everywhere the ensign
of man's ineffectual goodness, — ah! if I could show
you this! If I could show you these men and women
all the world over, in every stage of history, under
every abuse of error, under every circumstance of
failure, without hope, without help, without thanks,
still obscurely fighting the lost fight of virtue, still
clinging to some rag of honor, the poor jewel of their
souls."

All this is as true as it is splendid, and terribly do
we need our Tolstoïs and Stevensons to keep our sense
for it alive. Yet you remember the Irishman who,
when asked, "Is not one man as good as another?" replied, "Yes; and a great deal better, too!" Similarly
(it seems to me) does Tolstoï overcorrect our social
prejudices, when he makes his love of the peasant so
exclusive, and hardens his heart toward the educated
man as absolutely as he does. Grant that at Chautauqua there was little moral effort, little sweat or
muscular strain in view. Still, deep down in the souls
of the participants we may be sure that something of
the sort was hid, some inner stress, some vital virtue

not found wanting when required.   And, after all, the
question recurs, and forces itself upon us, Is it so
certain that the surroundings and circumstances of the
virtue do make so little difference in the importance
of the result?   Is the functional utility, the worth to
the universe of a certain definite amount of courage,
kindliness, and patience, no greater if the possessor of
these virtues is in an educated situation, working out
far-reaching tasks, than if he be an illiterate nobody,
hewing wood and drawing water, just to keep himself
alive?   Tolstoï's   philosophy,   deeply   enlightening
though it certainly is, remains a false abstraction.   It
savors too much of that Oriental pessimism and nihil-
ism of his, which declares the whole phenomenal
world and its facts and their distinctions to be a cunning fraud.

A mere bare fraud is just what our Western common
sense will never believe the phenomenal world to be.
It admits fully that the inner joys and virtues are the
essential part of life's business, but it is sure that *some*
positive part is also played by the adjuncts of the show.
If it is idiotic in romanticism to recognize the heroic
only when it sees it labelled and dressed-up in books,
it is really just as idiotic to see it only in the dirty
boots and sweaty shirt of some one in the fields.   It is
with us really under every disguise: at Chautauqua;
here in your college; in the stock-yards and on the
freight-trains; and in the czar of Russia's court.   But,
instinctively, we make a combination of two things in
judging the total significance of a human being.   We
feel it to be some sort of a product (if such a product
only could be calculated) of his inner virtue *and* his
outer place, — neither singly taken, but both con-

joined. If the outer differences had no meaning for
life, why indeed should all this immense variety of
them exist?   They *must* be significant elements of the
world as well.

Just test Tolstoï's deification of the mere manual
laborer by the facts. This is what Mr. Walter
Wyckoff, after working as an unskilled laborer in the
demolition of some buildings at West Point, writes
of the spiritual condition of the class of men to which
he temporarily chose to belong: —

"The salient features of our condition are plain
enough. We are grown men, and are without a trade.
In the labor-market we stand ready to sell to the
highest bidder our mere muscular strength for so
many hours each day. We are thus in the lowest
grade of labor. And, selling our muscular strength in
the open market for what it will bring, we sell it under
peculiar conditions. It is all the capital that we have.
We have no reserve means of subsistence, and cannot,
therefore, stand off for a 'reserve price.' We sell under the necessity of satisfying imminent hunger.
Broadly speaking, we must sell our labor or starve;
and, as hunger is a matter of a few hours, and we have
no other way of meeting this need, we must sell at
once for what the market offers for our labor.

"Our employer is buying labor in a dear market,
and he will certainly get from us as much work as he
can at the price. The gang-boss is secured for this
purpose, and thoroughly does he know his business.
He has sole command of us. He never saw us before,
and he will discharge us all when the débris is cleared
away. In the meantime he must get from us, if he
can, the utmost physical labor which we, individually
and collectively, are capable of. If he should drive

some of us to exhaustion, and we should not be able to continue at work, he would not be the loser; for the market would soon supply him with others to take our places.

"We are ignorant men, but so much we clearly see, — that we have sold our labor where we could sell it dearest, and our employer has bought it where he could buy it cheapest. He has paid high, and he must get all the labor that he can; and, by a strong instinct which possesses us, we shall part with as little as we can. From work like ours there seems to us to have been eliminated every element which constitutes the nobility of labor. We feel no personal pride in its progress, and no community of interest with our employer. There is none of the joy of responsibility, none of the sense of achievement, only the dull monotony of grinding toil, with the longing for the signal to quit work, and for our wages at the end.

"And being what we are, the dregs of the labor-market, and having no certainty of permanent employment, and no organization among ourselves, we must expect to work under the watchful eye of a gang-boss, and be driven, like the wage-slaves that we are, through our tasks.

"All this is to tell us, in effect, that our lives are hard, barren, hopeless lives."

And such hard, barren, hopeless lives, surely, are not lives in which one ought to be willing permanently to remain. And why is this so? Is it because they are so dirty? Well, Nansen grew a great deal dirtier on his polar expedition; and we think none the worse of his life for that. Is it the insensibility? Our soldiers have to grow vastly more insensible, and we extol them to the skies. Is it the poverty? Poverty has been reckoned the crowning beauty of many a heroic career. Is it the slavery to a task, the loss of finer pleasures? Such slavery and loss are of the very essence of the higher fortitude, and are always counted to its credit, — read the records of missionary devotion all over the world. It is not any one of these things, then, taken by itself, — no, nor all of them together, — that make such a life undesirable. A man might in truth live like an unskilled laborer, and do the work of one, and yet count as one of the noblest of God's creatures. Quite possibly there were some such persons in the gang that our author describes; but the current of their souls ran underground; and he was too steeped in the ancestral blindness to discern it.

If there *were* any such morally exceptional individuals, however, what made them different from the rest? It can only have been this, — that their souls worked and endured in obedience to some inner *ideal*, while their comrades were not actuated by anything worthy of that name. These ideals of other lives are among those secrets that we can almost never penetrate, although something about the man may often tell us when they are there. In Mr. Wyckoff's own case we know exactly what the self-imposed ideal was. Partly he had stumped himself, as the boys say, to carry through a strenuous achievement; but mainly he wished to enlarge his sympathetic insight into fellow-lives. For this his sweat and toil acquire a certain heroic significance, and make us accord to him exceptional esteem. But it is easy to imagine his fellows with various other ideals. To say nothing of wives and babies, one may have been a convert of the Salvation Army, and had a nightingale singing of expiation and forgiveness in his heart all the while he

labored. Or there might have been an apostle like
Tolstoï himself, or his compatriot Bondareff, in the
gang, voluntarily embracing labor as their religious
mission.   Class-loyalty was undoubtedly an ideal with
many.   And who knows how much of that higher
manliness of poverty, of which Phillips Brooks has
spoken so penetratingly, was or was not present in that
gang?

"A rugged, barren land," says Phillips Brooks, "is
poverty to live in, — a land where I am thankful very
often if I can get a berry or a root to eat.   But living
in it really, letting it bear witness to me of itself, not
dishonoring it all the time by judging it after the
standard of the other lands, gradually there come out
its qualities.   Behold! no land like this barren and
naked land of poverty could show the moral geology
of the world.   See how the hard ribs . . . stand out
strong and solid.   No life like poverty could so get
one to the heart of things and make men know their
meaning, could so let us feel life and the world with
all the soft cushions stripped off and thrown away.
. . . Poverty makes men come very near each other,
and recognize each other's human hearts; and poverty, highest and best of all, demands and cries out
for faith in God. . . . I know how superficial and
unfeeling, how like mere mockery, words in praise of
poverty may seem. . . . But I am sure that the poor
man's dignity and freedom, his self-respect and energy,
depend upon his cordial knowledge that his poverty
is a true region and kind of life, with its own chances
of character, its own springs of happiness and revelations of God.   Let him resist the characterlessness
which often goes with being poor.   Let him insist on
respecting the condition where he lives.   Let him

learn to love it, so that by and by, (if) he grows rich, he shall go out of the low door of the old familiar poverty with a true pang of regret, and with a true honor for the narrow home in which he has lived so long." *

The barrenness and ignobleness of the more usual laborer's life consist in the fact that it is moved by no such ideal inner springs. The backache, the long hours, the danger, are patiently endured — for what? To gain a quid of tobacco, a glass of beer, a cup of coffee, a meal, and a bed, and to begin again the next day and shirk as much as one can. This really is why we raise no monument to the laborers in the Subway, even though they be our conscripts, and even though after a fashion our city is indeed based upon their patient hearts and enduring backs and shoulders. And this is why we do raise monuments to our soldiers, whose outward conditions were even brutaller still. The soldiers are supposed to have followed an ideal, and the laborers are supposed to have followed none.

You see, my friends, how the plot now thickens; and how strangely the complexities of this wonderful human nature of ours begin to develop under our hands. We have seen the blindness and deadness to each other which are our natural inheritance; and, in spite of them, we have been led to acknowledge an inner meaning which passeth show, and which may be present in the lives of others where we least descry it. And now we are led to say that such inner meaning can be *complete* and *valid for us also*, only when the inner joy, courage, and endurance are joined with an ideal.

* Sermons, 5th Series, New York, 1893, pp. 166, 167.

But what, exactly, do we mean by an ideal? Can we give no definite account of such a word?

To a certain extent we can. An ideal, for instance, must be something intellectually conceived, something of which we are not unconscious, if we have it; and it must carry with it that sort of outlook, uplift, and brightness that go with all intellectual facts. Secondly, there must be *novelty* in an ideal, — novelty at least for him whom the ideal grasps. Sodden routine is incompatible with ideality, although what is sodden routine for one person may be ideal novelty for another. This shows that there is nothing absolutely ideal: ideals are relative to the lives that entertain them. To keep out of the gutter is for us here no part of consciousness at all, yet for many of our brethren it is the most legitimately engrossing of ideals.

Now, taken nakedly, abstractly, and immediately, you see that mere ideals are the cheapest things in life. Everybody has them in some shape or other, personal or general, sound or mistaken, low or high; and the most worthless sentimentalists and dreamers, drunkards, shirks and verse-makers, who never show a grain of effort, courage, or endurance, possibly have them on the most copious scale. Education, enlarging as it does our horizon and perspective, is a means of multiplying our ideals, of bringing new ones into view. And your college professor, with a starched shirt and spectacles, would, if a stock of ideals were all alone by itself enough to render a life significant, be the most absolutely and deeply significant of men. Tolstoï would be completely blind in despising him for a prig, a pedant and a parody; and all our new insight into the divinity of muscular labor would be altogether off the track of truth.

But such consequences as this, you instinctively feel, are erroneous. The more ideals a man has, the more contemptible, on the whole, do you continue to deem him, if the matter ends there for him, and if none of the laboring man's virtues are called into action on his part, — no courage shown, no privations undergone, no dirt or scars contracted in the attempt to get them realized. It is quite obvious that something more than the mere possession of ideals is required to make a life significant in any sense that claims the spectator's admiration. Inner joy, to be sure, it may *have*, with its ideals; but that is its own private sentimental matter. To extort from us, outsiders as we are, with our own ideals to look after, the tribute of our grudging recognition, it must back its ideal visions with what the laborers have, the sterner stuff of manly virtue; it must multiply their sentimental surface by the dimension of the active will, if we are to have *depth*, if we are to have anything cubical and solid in the way of character.

The significance of a human life for communicable and publicly recognizable purposes is thus the offspring of a marriage of two different parents, either of whom alone is barren. The ideals taken by themselves give no reality, the virtues by themselves no novelty. And let the orientalists and pessimists say what they will, the thing of deepest — or, at any rate, of comparatively deepest — significance in life does seem to be its character of *progress*, or that strange union of reality with ideal novelty which it continues from one moment to another to present. To recognize ideal novelty is the task of what we call intelligence. Not every one's intelligence can tell which novelties are ideal. For many the ideal thing will always seem to cling still to the older more familiar good. In this case character, though not significant totally, may be still significant pathetically. So, if we are to choose which is the more essential factor of human character, the fighting virtue or the intellectual breadth, we must side with Tolstoï and choose that simple faithfulness to his light or darkness which any common unintellectual man can show.

But, with all this beating and tacking on my part, I fear you take me to be reaching a confused result. I seem to be just taking things up and dropping them again. First I took up Chautauqua, and dropped that; then Tolstoï and the heroism of common toil, and dropped them; finally, I took up ideals, and seem now almost dropping those. But please observe in what sense it is that I drop them. It is when they pretend *singly* to redeem life from insignificance. Culture and refinement all alone are not enough to do so. Ideal aspirations are not enough, when uncombined with pluck and will. But neither are pluck and will, dogged endurance and insensibility to danger enough, when taken all alone. There must be some sort of fusion, some chemical combination among these principles, for a life objectively and thoroughly significant to result.

Of course, this is a somewhat vague conclusion. But in a question of significance, of worth, like this, conclusions can never be precise. The answer of appreciation, of sentiment, is always a more or a less, a balance struck by sympathy, insight, and good will. But it is an answer, all the same, a real conclusion. And, in the course of getting it, it seems to me that our eyes have been opened to many important things.

Some of you are, perhaps, more livingly aware than you were an hour ago of the depths of worth that lie around you, hid in alien lives. And, when you ask how much sympathy you ought to bestow, although the amount is, truly enough, a matter of ideal on your own part, yet in this notion of the combination of ideals with active virtues you have a rough standard for shaping your decision. In any case, your imagination is extended. You divine in the world about you matter for a little more humility on your own part, and tolerance, reverence, and love for others; and you gain a certain inner joyfulness at the increased importance of our common life. Such joyfulness is a religious inspiration and an element of spiritual health, and worth more than large amounts of that sort of technical and accurate information which we professors are supposed to be able to impart.

To show the sort of thing I mean by these words, I will just make one brief practical illustration, and then close.

We are suffering today in America from what is called the labor-question; and, when you go out into the world, you will each and all of you be caught up in its perplexities. I use the brief term labor-question to cover all sorts of anarchistic discontents and socialistic projects, and the conservative resistances which they provoke. So far as this conflict is unhealthy and regrettable, — and I think it is so only to a limited extent, — the unhealthiness consists solely in the fact that one-half of our fellow-countrymen remain entirely blind to the internal significance of the lives of the other half. They miss the joys and sorrows, they fail to feel the moral virtue, and they do

not guess the presence of the intellectual ideals. They
are at cross-purposes all along the line, regarding each
other as they might regard a set of dangerously ges-
ticulating automata, or, if they seek to get at the
inner motivation, making the most horrible mistakes.
Often all that the poor man can think of in the rich
man is a cowardly greediness for safety, luxury, and
effeminacy, and a boundless affectation. What he is,
is not a human being, but a pocket-book, a bank-ac-
count. And a similar greediness, turned by disappointment into envy, is all that many rich men can
see in the state of mind of the dissatisfied poor. And,
if the rich man begins to do the sentimental act over
the poor man, what senseless blunders does he make,
pitying him for just those very duties and those very
immunities which, rightly taken, are the condition
of his most abiding and characteristic joys! Each, in
short, ignores the fact that happiness and unhappiness
and significance are a vital mystery; each pins them
absolutely on some ridiculous feature of the external
situation; and everybody remains outside of everybody else's sight.

Society has, with all this, undoubtedly got to pass
toward some newer and better equilibrium, and the
distribution of wealth has doubtless slowly got to
change: such changes have always happened, and will
happen to the end of time. But if, after all that I
have said, any of you expect that they will make any
genuine vital difference on a large scale, to the lives
of our descendants, you will have missed the significance of my entire lecture. The solid meaning of
life is always the same eternal thing, — the marriage,
namely, of some unhabitual ideal, however special, with
some fidelity, courage, and endurance; with some

man's or woman's pains. — And, whatever or wherever life may be, there will always be the chance for that marriage to take place.

Fitz-James Stephen wrote many years ago words to this effect more eloquent than any I can speak: "The 'Great Eastern,' or some of her successors," he said, "will perhaps defy the roll of the Atlantic, and cross the seas without allowing their passengers to feel that they have left the firm land. The voyage from the cradle to the grave may come to be performed with similar facility. Progress and science may perhaps enable untold millions to live and die without a care, without a pang, without an anxiety. They will have a pleasant passage and plenty of brilliant conversation. They will wonder that men ever believed at all in clanging fights and blazing towns and sinking ships and praying hands; and, when they come to the end of their course, they will go their way, and the place thereof will know them no more. But it seems unlikely that they will have such a knowledge of the great ocean on which they sail, with its storms and wrecks, its currents and icebergs, its huge waves and mighty winds, as those who battled with it for years together in the little craft, which, if they had few other merits, brought those who navigated them full into the presence of time and eternity, their maker and themselves, and forced them to have some definite view of their relations to them and to each other." *

In this solid and tridimensional sense, so to call it, those philosophers are right who contend that the world is a standing thing, with no progress, no real history. The changing conditions of history touch only the surface of the show. The altered equilib-

* Essays by a Barrister, London, 1862, p. 318.

riums and redistributions only diversify our opportunities and open chances to us for new ideals. But,
with each new ideal that comes into life, the chance
for a life based on some old ideal will vanish; and he
would needs be a presumptuous calculator who should
with confidence say that the total sum of significances
is positively and absolutely greater at any one epoch
than at any other of the world.

I am speaking broadly, I know, and omitting to consider certain qualifications in which I myself believe.
But one can only make one point in one lecture,
and I shall be well content if I have brought my point
home to you this evening in even a slight degree.
There are compensations: and no outward changes of
condition in life can keep the nightingale of its
eternal meaning from singing in all sorts of different
men's hearts. That is the main fact to remember. If
we could not only admit it with our lips, but really
and truly believe it, how our convulsive insistencies,
how our antipathies and dreads of each other, would
soften down! If the poor and the rich could look at
each other in this way, *sub specie æternatis,* how
gentle would grow their disputes! what tolerance and
good humor, what willingness to live and let live,
would come into the world!

THE MORAL EQUIVALENT OF WAR*

THE war against war is going to be no holiday excursion or camping party. The military feelings are too deeply grounded to abdicate their place among our ideals until better substitutes are offered than the glory and shame that come to nations as well as to individuals from the ups and downs of politics and the vicissitudes of trade. There is something highly paradoxical in the modern man's relation to war. Ask all our millions, north and south, whether they would vote now (were such a thing possible) to have our war for the Union expunged from history, and the record of a peaceful transition to the present time substituted for that of its marches and battles, and probably hardly a handful of eccentrics would say yes. Those ancestors, those efforts, those memories and legends, are the most ideal part of what we now own together, a sacred spiritual possession worth more than all the blood poured out. Yet ask those same people whether they would be willing in cold blood to start another civil war now to gain another similar possession, and not one man or woman would vote for the proposition. In modern eyes,

* Written for and first published by the Association for International Conciliation (Leaflet No. 27) and also published in *McClure's Magazine*, August, 1910, and *The Popular Science Monthly*, October, 1910.

precious though wars may be, they must not be
waged solely for the sake of the ideal harvest. Only
when forced upon one, only when an enemy's injustice
leaves us no alternative, is a war now thought per-
missible.

It was not thus in ancient times. The earlier men
were hunting men, and to hunt a neighboring tribe,
kill the males, loot the village and possess the females,
was the most profitable, as well as the most exciting,
way of living. Thus were the more martial tribes
selected, and in chiefs and people a pure pugnacity
and love of glory came to mingle with the more
fundamental appetite for plunder.

Modern war is so expensive that we feel trade to
be a better avenue to plunder; but modern man
inherits all the innate pugnacity and all the love of
glory of his ancestors. Showing war's irrationality and
horror is of no effect upon him. The horrors make
the fascination. War is the *strong* life; it is life *in
extremis;* war-taxes are the only ones men never hesitate to pay, as the budgets of all nations show us.

History is a bath of blood. The Iliad is one long
recital of how Diomedes and Ajax, Sarpedon and
Hector *killed.* No detail of the wounds they made
is spared us, and the Greek mind fed upon the story.
Greek history is a panorama of jingoism and im-
perialism — war for war's sake, all the citizens being
warriors. It is horrible reading, because of the irrationality of it all — save for the purpose of making
'history' — and the history is that of the utter ruin of a
civilization in intellectual respects perhaps the highest
the earth has ever seen.

Those wars were purely piratical. Pride, gold,
women, slaves, excitement, were their only motives.

In the Peloponnesian war for example, the Athenians ask the inhabitants of Melos (the island where the 'Venus of Milo' was found), hitherto neutral, to own their lordship. The envoys meet, and hold a debate which Thucydides gives in full, and which, for sweet reasonableness of form, would have satisfied Matthew Arnold. "The powerful exact what they can," said the Athenians, "and the weak grant what they must." When the Meleans say that sooner than be slaves they will appeal to the gods, the Athenians reply: "Of the gods we believe and of men we know that, by a law of their nature, wherever they can rule they will. This law was not made by us, and we are not the first to have acted upon it; we did but inherit it, and we know that you and all mankind, if you were as strong as we are, would do as we do. So much for the gods; we have told you why we expect to stand as high in their good opinion as you." Well, the Meleans still refused, and their town was taken. "The Athenians," Thucydides quietly says, "thereupon put to death all who were of military age and made slaves of the women and children. They then colonized the island, sending thither five hundred settlers of their own."

Alexander's career was piracy pure and simple, nothing but an orgy of power and plunder, made romantic by the character of the hero. There was no rational principle in it, and the moment he died his generals and governors attacked one another. The cruelty of those times is incredible. When Rome finally conquered Greece, Paulus Aemilius was told by the Roman Senate to reward his soldiers for their toil by 'giving' them the old kingdom of Epirus. They sacked seventy cities and carried off a hundred and fifty thousand inhabitants as slaves. How many they killed I know not; but in Etolia they killed all the senators, five hundred and fifty in number. Brutus was "the noblest Roman of them all," but to reanimate his soldiers on the eve of Philippi he similarly promises to give them the cities of Sparta and Thessalonica to ravage, if they win the fight.

Such was the gory nurse that trained societies to cohesiveness. We inherit the warlike type; and for most of the capacities of heroism that the human race is full of we have to thank this cruel history. Dead men tell no tales, and if there were any tribes of other type than this they have left no survivors. Our ancestors have bred pugnacity into our bone and marrow, and thousands of years of peace won't breed it out of us. The popular imagination fairly fattens on the thought of wars. Let public opinion once reach a certain fighting pitch, and no ruler can withstand it. In the Boer war both governments began with bluff but couldn't stay there, the military tension was too much for them. In 1898 our people had read the word 'war' in letters three inches high for three months in every newspaper. The pliant politician McKinley was swept away by their eagerness, and our squalid war with Spain became a necessity.

At the present day, civilized opinion is a curious mental mixture. The military instincts and ideals are as strong as ever, but are confronted by reflective criticisms which sorely curb their ancient freedom. Innumerable writers are showing up the bestial side of military service. Pure loot and mastery seem no longer morally avowable motives, and pretexts must be found for attributing them solely to the enemy. England and we, our army and navy authorities repeat

without ceasing, arm solely for 'peace,' Germany and
Japan it is who are bent on loot and glory. 'Peace'
in military mouths today is a synonym for 'war expected.' The word has become a pure provocative,
and no government wishing peace sincerely should
allow it ever to be printed in a newspaper. Every
up-to-date dictionary should say that 'peace' and
'war' mean the same thing, now *in posse,* now *in actu.*
It may even reasonably be said that the intensely sharp
competitive *preparation* for war by the nations *is the
real war,* permanent, unceasing; and that the battles
are only a sort of public verification of the mastery
gained during the 'peace'-interval.

It is plain that on this subject civilized man has
developed a sort of double personality. If we take
European nations, no legitimate interest of any one
of them would seem to justify the tremendous de-
structions which a war to compass it would necessarily entail. It would seem as though common
sense and reason ought to find a way to reach agreement in every conflict of honest interests. I myself
think it our bounden duty to believe in such international rationality as possible. But, as things stand,
I see how desperately hard it is to bring the peace-
party and the war-party together, and I believe that the
difficulty is due to certain deficiencies in the program
of pacificism which set the militarist imagination
strongly, and to a certain extent justifiably, against it.
In the whole discussion both sides are on imaginative
and sentimental ground. It is but one utopia against
another, and everything one says must be abstract and
hypothetical. Subject to this criticism and caution,
I will try to characterize in abstract strokes the opposite imaginative forces, and point out what to my

own very fallible mind seems the best utopian hypothesis, the most promising line of conciliation.

In my remarks, pacificist though I am, I will refuse to speak of the bestial side of the war-*régime* (already done justice to by many writers) and consider only the higher aspects of militaristic sentiment. Patriotism no one thinks discreditable; nor does any one deny that war is the romance of history. But inordinate ambitions are the soul of every patriotism, and the possibility of violent death the soul of all romance. The militarily patriotic and romantic-minded everywhere, and especially the professional military class, refuse to admit for a moment that war may be a transitory phenomenon in social evolution. The notion of a sheep's paradise like that revolts, they say, our higher imagination. Where then would be the steeps of life? If war had ever stopped, we should have to re-invent it, on this view, to redeem life from flat degeneration.

Reflective apologists for war at the present day all take it religiously. It is a sort of sacrament. Its profits are to the vanquished as well as to the victor; and quite apart from any question of profit, it is an absolute good, we are told, for it is human nature at its highest dynamic. Its 'horrors' are a cheap price to pay for rescue from the only alternative supposed, of a world of clerks and teachers, of co-educational and zo-ophily, of 'consumer's leagues' and 'associated charities,' of industrialism unlimited, and femininism unabashed. No scorn, no hardness, no valor any more! Fie upon such a cattleyard of a planet!

So far as the central essence of this feeling goes, no healthy minded person, it seems to me, can help to some degree partaking of it. Militarism is the great

preserver of our ideals of hardihood, and human life
with no use for hardihood would be contemptible.
Without risks or prizes for the darer, history would
be insipid indeed; and there is a type of military
character which every one feels that the race should
never cease to breed, for every one is sensitive to its
superiority. The duty is incumbent on mankind, of
keeping military characters in stock — of keeping
them, if not for use, then as ends in themselves and
as pure pieces of perfection, — so that Roosevelt's
weaklings and mollycoddles may not end by making
everything else disappear from the face of nature.

This natural sort of feeling forms, I think, the innermost soul of army-writings. Without any exception
known to me, militarist authors take a highly mystical
view of their subject, and regard war as a biological
or sociological necessity, uncontrolled by ordinary
psychological checks and motives. When the time
of development is ripe the war must come, reason or
no reason, for the justifications pleaded are invariably
fictitious. War is, in short, a permanent human
obligation. General Homer Lea, in his recent book
'The Valor of Ignorance,' plants himself squarely on
this ground. Readiness for war is for him the essence
of nationality, and ability in it the supreme measure
of the health of nations.

Nations, General Lea says, are never stationary —
they must necessarily expand or shrink, according to
their vitality or decrepitude. Japan now is culminat-
ing; and by the fatal law in question it is impossible
that her statesmen should not long since have entered,
with extraordinary foresight, upon a vast policy of
conquest — the game in which the first moves were
her wars with China and Russia and her treaty with

England, and of which the final objective is the cap-
ture of the Philippines, the Hawaiian Islands, Alaska,
and the whole of our Coast west of the Sierra Passes.
This will give Japan what her ineluctable vocation
as a state absolute forces her to claim, the possession
of the entire Pacific Ocean; and to oppose these deep
designs we Americans have, according to our author,
nothing but our conceit, our ignorance, our commercialism, our corruption, and our feminism. General
Lea makes a minute technical comparison of the military strength which we at present could oppose to the
strength of Japan, and concludes that the islands,
Alaska, Oregon, and Southern California, would fall
almost without resistance, that San Francisco must
surrender in a fortnight to a Japanese investment,
that in three or four months the war would be over,
and our republic, unable to regain what it had heed-
lessly neglected to protect sufficiently, would then 'dis-
integrate,' until perhaps some Cæsar should arise to
weld us again into a nation.

A dismal forecast indeed! Yet not unplausible, if
the mentality of Japan's statesmen be of the Cæsarian
type of which history shows so many examples, and
which is all that General Lea seems able to imagine.
But there is no reason to think that women can no
longer be the mothers of Napoleonic or Alexandrian
characters; and if these come in Japan and find
their opportunity, just such surprises as 'The Valor
of Ignorance' paints may lurk in ambush for us. Ignorant as we still are of the innermost recesses of
Japanese mentality, we may be foolhardy to disregard
such possibilities.

Other militarists are more complex and more moral
in their considerations. The 'Philosophie des Krieges,'

by S. R. Steinmetz is a good example. War, according to this author, is an ordeal instituted by God, who weighs the nations in its balance. It is the essential form of the State, and the only function in which peoples can employ all their powers at once and convergently. No victory is possible save as the resultant of a totality of virtues, no defeat for which some vice or weakness is not responsible. Fidelity, cohesiveness, tenacity, heroism, conscience, education, inventiveness, economy, wealth, physical health and vigor — there isn't a moral or intellectual point of superiority that doesn't tell, when God holds his assizes and hurls the peoples upon one another. *Die Weltgeschichte ist das Weltgericht;* and Dr. Steinmetz does not believe that in the long run chance and luck play any part in apportioning the issues.

The virtues that prevail, it must be noted, are virtues anyhow, superiorities that count in peaceful as well as in military competition; but the strain on them, being infinitely intenser in the latter case, makes war infinitely more searching as a trial. No ordeal is comparable to its winnowings. Its dread hammer is the welder of men into cohesive states, and nowhere but in such states can human nature adequately develop its capacity. The only alternative is 'degeneration.'

Dr. Steinmetz is a conscientious thinker, and his book, short as it is, takes much into account. Its upshot can, it seems to me, be summed up in Simon Patten's word, that mankind was nursed in pain and fear, and that the transition to a 'pleasure-economy' may be fatal to a being wielding no powers of defence against its disintegrative influences. If we speak of the *fear of emancipation from the fear-régime,* we put the whole situation into a single phrase; fear regarding ourselves now taking the place of the ancient fear of the enemy.

Turn the fear over as I will in my mind, it all seems to lead back to two unwillingnesses of the imagination, one æsthetic, and the other moral; unwillingness, first to envisage a future in which army-life, with its many elements of charm, shall be forever impossible, and in which the destinies of peoples shall nevermore be decided quickly, thrillingly, and tragically, by force, but only gradually and insipidly by 'evolution'; and, secondly, unwillingness to see the supreme theatre of human strenuousness closed, and the splendid military aptitudes of men doomed to keep always in a state of latency and never show themselves in action. These insistent unwillingnesses, no less than other æsthetic and ethical insistencies, have, it seems to me, to be listened to and respected. One cannot meet them effectively by mere counter-insistency on war's expensiveness and horror. The horror makes the thrill; and when the question is of getting the extremest and supremest out of human nature, talk of expense sounds ignominious. The weakness of so much merely negative criticism is evident — pacificism makes no converts from the military party. The military party denies neither the bestiality nor the horror, nor the expense; it only says that these things tell but half the story. It only says that war is *worth* them; that, taking human nature as a whole, its wars are its best protection against its weaker and more cowardly self, and that mankind cannot *afford* to adopt a peace-economy.

Pacificists ought to enter more deeply into the æsthetical and ethical point of view of their opponents.

Do that first in any controversy, says J. J. Chapman, *then move the point,* and your opponent will follow. So long as anti-militarists propose no substitute for war's disciplinary function, no *moral equivalent* of war, analogous, as one might say, to the mechanical equivalent of heat, so long they fail to realize the full inwardness of the situation.   And as a rule they do fail.   The duties, penalties, and sanctions pictured in the utopias they paint are all too weak and tame to touch the military-minded.   Tolstoï's pacificism is the only exception to this rule, for it is profoundly pessimistic as regards all this world's values, and makes the fear of the Lord furnish the moral spur provided elsewhere by the fear of the enemy.   But our socialistic peace-advocates all believe absolutely in this world's values; and instead of the fear of the Lord and the fear of the enemy, the only fear they reckon with is the fear of poverty if one be lazy.   This weakness pervades all the socialistic literature with which I am acquainted.   Even in Lowes Dickinson's exquisite dialogue,* high wages and short hours are the only forces invoked for overcoming man's distaste for repulsive kinds of labor.   Meanwhile men at large still live as they always have lived, under a pain-and-fear economy — for those of us who live in an ease-economy are but an island in the stormy ocean — and the whole atmosphere of present-day utopian literature tastes mawkish and dishwatery to people who still keep a sense for life's more bitter flavors.   It suggests, in truth, ubiquitous inferiority.

Inferiority is always with us, and merciless scorn of it is the keynote of the military temper.   "Dogs, would you live forever?" shouted Frederick the Great.   "Yes,"

* "Justice and Liberty," N.Y., 1909.

say our utopians, "let us live forever, and raise our level gradually." The best thing about our 'inferiors' today is that they are as tough as nails, and physically and morally almost as insensitive. Utopianism would see them soft and squeamish, while militarism would keep their callousness, but transfigure it into a meritorious characteristic, needed by 'the service,' and redeemed by that from the suspicion of inferiority. All the qualities of a man acquire dignity when he knows that the service of the collectivity that owns him needs them. If proud of the collectivity, his own pride rises in proportion. No collectivity is like an army for nourishing such pride; but it has to be confessed that the only sentiment which the image of pacific cosmopolitan industrialism is capable of arousing in countless worthy breasts is shame at the idea of belonging to *such* a collectivity. It is obvious that the United States of America as they exist today impress a mind like General Lea's as so much human blubber. Where is the sharpness and precipitousness, the contempt for life, whether one's own, or another's? Where is the savage 'yes' and 'no,' the unconditional duty? Where is the conscription? Where is the blood-tax? Where is anything that one feels honored by belonging to?

Having said thus much in preparation, I will now confess my own utopia. I devoutly believe in the reign of peace and in the gradual advent of some sort of a socialistic equilibrium. The fatalistic view of the war-function is to me nonsense, for I know that war-making is due to definite motives and subject to prudential checks and reasonable criticisms, just like any other form of enterprise. And when whole nations are the armies, and the science of destruction vies in intellectual refinement with the sciences of production, I see that war becomes absurd and impossible from its own monstrosity. Extravagant ambitions will have to be replaced by reasonable claims, and nations must make common cause against them. I see no reason why all this should not apply to yellow as well as to white countries, and I look forward to a future when acts of war shall be formally outlawed as between civilized peoples.

All these beliefs of mine put me squarely into the anti-militarist party. But I do not believe that peace either ought to be or will be permanent on this globe, unless the states pacifically organized preserve some of the old elements of army-discipline. A permanently successful peace-economy cannot be a simple pleasure-economy. In the more or less socialistic future towards which mankind seems drifting we must still subject ourselves collectively to those severities which answer to our real position upon this only partly hospitable globe. We must make new energies and hardihoods continue the manliness to which the military mind so faithfully clings. Martial virtues must be the enduring cement; intrepidity, contempt of softness, surrender of private interest, obedience to command, must still remain the rock upon which states are built — unless, indeed, we wish for dangerous reactions against commonwealths fit only for contempt, and liable to invite attack whenever a centre of crystallization for military-minded enterprise gets formed anywhere in their neighborhood.

The war-party is assuredly right in affirming and reaffirming that the martial virtues, although originally gained by the race through war, are absolute and permanent human goods. Patriotic pride and

ambition in their military form are, after all, only
specifications of a more general competitive passion.
They are its first form, but that is no reason for supposing them to be its last form. Men now are proud of
belonging to a conquering nation, and without a murmur they lay down their persons and their wealth, if
by so doing they may fend off subjection. But who
can be sure that *other aspects of one's country* may
not, with time and education and suggestion enough,
come to be regarded with similarly effective feelings of
pride and shame? Why should men not some day
feel that it is worth a blood-tax to belong to a collectivity superior in *any* ideal respect? Why should
they not blush with indignant shame if the community
that owns them is vile in any way whatsoever? Individuals, daily more numerous, now feel this civic passion.
It is only a question of blowing on the spark till the
whole population gets incandescent, and on the ruins
of the old morals of military honor, a stable system
of morals of civic honor builds itself up. What the
whole community comes to believe in grasps the individual as in a vise. The war-function has grasped
us so far; but constructive interests may some day
seem no less imperative, and impose on the individual
a hardly lighter burden.

Let me illustrate my idea more concretely. There
is nothing to make one indignant in the mere fact that
life is hard, that men should toil and suffer pain.
The planetary conditions once for all are such, and
we can stand it. But that so many men, by mere
accidents of birth and opportunity, should have a life
of *nothing else* but toil and pain and hardness and
inferiority imposed upon them, should have *no* vaca-
tion, while others natively no more deserving never

get any taste of this campaigning life at all, — *this* is. capable of arousing indignation in reflective minds. It may end by seeming shameful to all of us that some of us have nothing but campaigning, and others nothing but unmanly ease. If now — and this is my idea — there were, instead of military conscription a conscription of the whole youthful population to form for a certain number of years a part of the army enlisted against *Nature,* the injustice would tend to be evened out, and numerous other goods to the commonwealth would follow. The military ideals of hardihood and discipline would be wrought into the growing fibre of the people; no one would remain blind as the luxurious classes now are blind, to man's relations to the globe he lives on, and to the permanently sour and hard foundations of his higher life. To coal and iron mines, to freight trains, to fishing fleets in December, to dishwashing, clothes-washing, and window-washing, to road-building and tunnel-making, to foundries and stoke-holes, and to the frames of skyscrapers, would our gilded youths be drafted off, according to their choice, to get the childishness knocked out of them, and to come back into society with healthier sympathies and soberer ideas. They would have paid their blood-tax, done their own part in the immemorial human warfare against nature; they would tread the earth more proudly, the women would value them more highly, they would be better fathers and teachers of the following generation.

Such a conscription, with the state of public opinion that would have required it, and the many moral fruits it would bear, would preserve in the midst of a pacific civilization the manly virtues which the mili-

tary party is so afraid of seeing disappear in peace.
We should get toughness without callousness, authority with as little criminal cruelty as possible, and painful work done cheerily because the duty is temporary,
and threatens not, as now, to degrade the whole remainder of one's life.   I spoke of the 'moral equivalent' of war.   So far, war has been the only force that
can discipline a whole community, and until an
equivalent discipline is organized, I believe that war
must have its way.   But I have no serious doubt that
the ordinary prides and shames of social man, once
developed to a certain intensity, are capable of organiz-
ing such a moral equivalent as I have sketched, or
some other just as effective for preserving manliness
of type.   It is but a question of time, of skilful propa-
gandism, and of opinion-making men seizing historic
opportunities.
The martial type of character can be bred without
war.   Strenuous honor and disinterestedness abound
elsewhere.   Priests and medical men are in a fashion
educated to it, and we should all feel some degree of
it imperative if we were conscious of our work as an
obligatory service to the state.   We should be *owned,*
as soldiers are by the army, and our pride would rise
accordingly.   We could be poor, then, without hu-
miliation, as army officers now are.   The only thing
needed henceforward is to inflame the civic temper as
past history has inflamed the military temper.   H. G.
Wells, as usual, sees the centre of the situation.   "In
many ways, he says, "military organization is the most
peaceful of activities.   When the contemporary man
steps from the street, of clamorous insincere adver-
tisement, push, adulteration, underselling and inter-
mittent employment into the barrack-yard, he steps on

to a higher social plane, into an atmosphere of service
and coöperation and of infinitely more honorable
emulations. Here at least men are not flung out of
employment to degenerate because there is no immediate work for them to do. They are fed and drilled
and trained for better services. Here at least a man is
supposed to win promotion by self-forgetfulness and
not by self-seeking. And beside the feeble and irregular endowment of research by commercialism, its
little short-sighted snatches at profit by innovation
and scientific economy, see how remarkable is the
steady and rapid development of method and appli-
ances in naval and military affairs! Nothing is more
striking than to compare the progress of civil con-
veniences which has been left almost entirely to the
trader, to the progress in military apparatus during
the last few decades. The house-appliances of today,
for example, are little better than they were fifty years
ago. A house of today is still almost as ill-ventilated,
badly heated by wasteful fires, clumsily arranged and
furnished as the house of 1858. Houses a couple of
hundred years old are still satisfactory places of resi-
dence, so little have our standards risen. But the
rifle or battleship of fifty years ago was beyond all
comparison inferior to those we possess; in power, in
speed, in convenience alike. No one has a use now
for such superannuated things." *

Wells adds† that he thinks that the conceptions of
order and discipline, the tradition of service and devotion, of physical fitness, unstinted exertion, and universal responsibility, which universal military duty is
now teaching European nations, will remain a per-

* "First and Last Things," 1908, p. 215.
† "First and Last Things," 1908, p. 226.

manent acquisition, when the last ammunition has been used in the fireworks that celebrate the final peace. I believe as he does. It would be simply preposterous if the only force that could work ideals of honor and standards of efficiency into English or American natures should be the fear of being killed by the Germans or Japanese. Great indeed is Fear; but it is not, as our military enthusiasts believe and try to make us believe, the only stimulus known for awakening the higher ranges of men's spiritual energy. The amount of alteration in public opinion which my utopia postulates is vastly less than the difference between the mentality of those black warriors who pursued Stanley's party on the Congo with their cannibal war-cry of "Meat! Meat!" and that of the 'general staff' of any civilized nation. History has seen the latter interval bridged over: the former one can be bridged over much more easily.

APPENDIX

AT most of our American Colleges there are Clubs
formed by the students devoted to particular
branches of learning; and these clubs have the laud-
able custom of inviting once or twice a year some
maturer scholar to address them, the occasion often
being made a public one. I have from time to time
accepted such invitations, and afterwards had my discourse printed in one or other of the Reviews. It
has seemed to me that these addresses might now be
worthy of collection in a volume, as they shed explanatory light upon each other, and taken together express a tolerably definite philosophic attitude in a
very untechnical way.

Were I obliged to give a short name to the attitude
in question, I should call it that of *radical empiricism,* in spite of the fact that such brief nicknames
are nowhere more misleading than in philosophy.
I say ' empiricism,' because it is contented to regard its
most assured conclusions concerning matters of fact
as hypotheses liable to modification in the course of
future experience; and I say ' radical,' because it treats
the doctrine of monism itself as an hypothesis, and,
unlike so much of the half-way empiricism that is
current under the name of positivism or agnosticism
or scientific naturalism, it does not dogmatically affirm monism as something with which all experience
has got to square. The difference between monism

and pluralism is perhaps the most pregnant of all the differences in philosophy. *Primâ facie* the world is a pluralism; as we find it, its unity seems to be that of any collection; and our higher thinking consists chiefly of an effort to redeem it from that first crude form. Postulating more unity than the first experiences yield, we also discover more. But absolute unity, in spite of brilliant dashes in its direction, still remains undiscovered, still remains a *Grenzbegriff*. " Ever not quite " must be the rationalistic philosopher's last confession concerning it. After all that reason can do has been done, there still remains the opacity of the finite facts as merely given, with most of their peculiarities mutually unmediated and unexplained. To the very last, there are the various ' points of view ' which the philosopher must distinguish in discussing the world; and what is inwardly clear from one point remains a bare externality and datum to the other. The negative, the alogical, is never wholly banished. Something — " call it fate, chance, freedom, spontaneity, the devil, what you will " — is still wrong and other and outside and unincluded, from *your* point of view, even though you be the greatest of philosophers. Something is always mere fact and *givenness;* and there may be in the whole universe no one point of view extant from which this would not be found to be the case. " Reason," as a gifted writer says, " is but one item in the mystery; and behind the proudest consciousness that ever reigned, reason and wonder blushed face to face. The inevitable stales, while doubt and hope are sisters. Not unfortunately the universe is wild, — game-flavored as a hawk's wing. Nature is miracle all; the same returns not save to bring the different. The slow round of the engraver's lathe gains but the breadth of a hair, but the difference is distributed back over the whole curve, never an instant true, — ever not quite." *

This is pluralism, somewhat rhapsodically expressed. He who takes for his hypothesis the notion that it is the permanent form of the world is what I call a radical empiricist. For him the crudity of experience remains an eternal element thereof. There is no possible point of view from which the world can appear an absolutely single fact. Real possibilities, real indeterminations, real beginnings, real ends, real evil, real crises, catastrophes, and escapes, a real God, and a real moral life, just as common-sense conceives these things, may remain in empiricism as conceptions which that philosophy gives up the attempt either to 'overcome' or to reinterpret in monistic form.

Many of my professionally trained *confrères* will smile at the irrationalism of this view, and at the artlessness of my essays in point of technical form. But they should be taken as illustrations of the radically empiricist attitude rather than as argumentations for its validity. That admits meanwhile of being argued in as technical a shape as any one can desire, and possibly I may be spared to do later a share of that work. Meanwhile these essays seem to light up with a certain dramatic reality the attitude itself, and make it visible alongside of the higher and lower dogmatisms between which in the pages of philosophic history it has generally remained eclipsed from sight.

The first four essays are largely concerned with

* B. P. Blood: The Flaw in Supremacy: Published by the Author, Amsterdam, N. Y., 1893.

defending the legitimacy of religious faith. To some rationalizing readers such advocacy will seem a sad misuse of one's professional position. Mankind, they will say, is only too prone to follow faith unreasoningly, and needs no preaching nor encouragement in that direction. I quite agree that what mankind at large most lacks is criticism and caution, not faith. Its cardinal weakness is to let belief follow recklessly upon lively conception, especially when the conception has instinctive liking at its back. I admit, then, that were I addressing the Salvation Army or a miscellaneous popular crowd it would be a misuse of opportunity to preach the liberty of believing as I have in these pages preached it. What such audiences most need is that their faiths should be broken up and ventilated, that the northwest wind of science should get into them and blow their sickliness and barbarism away. But academic audiences, fed already on science, have a very different need. Paralysis of their native capacity for faith and timorous *abulia* in the religious field are their special forms of mental weakness, brought about by the notion, carefully instilled, that there is something called scientific evidence by waiting upon which they shall escape all danger of shipwreck in regard to truth. But there is really no scientific or other method by which men can steer safely between the opposite dangers of believing too little or of believing too much. To face such dangers is apparently our duty, and to hit the right channel between them is the measure of our wisdom as men. It does not follow, because recklessness may be a vice in soldiers, that courage ought never to be preached to them. What *should* be preached is courage weighted with responsibility, — such courage

as the Nelsons and Washingtons never failed to show
after they had taken everything into account that
might tell against their success, and made every provision to minimize disaster in case they met defeat.
I do not think that any one can accuse me of preaching reckless faith. I have preached the right of the
individual to indulge his personal faith at his personal
risk. I have discussed the kinds of risk; I have contended that none of us escape all of them; and I
have only pleaded that it is better to face them open-
eyed than to act as if we did not know them to be
there.

After all, though, you will say, Why such an ado
about a matter concerning which, however we may
theoretically differ, we all practically agree? In this
age of toleration, no scientist will ever try actively to
interfere with our religious faith, provided we enjoy
it quietly with our friends and do not make a public nuisance of it in the market-place. But it is just
on this matter of the market-place that I think the
utility of such essays as mine may turn. If religious hypotheses about the universe be in order at
all, then the active faiths of individuals in them,
freely expressing themselves in life, are the experimental tests by which they are verified, and the only
means by which their truth or falsehood can be
wrought out. The truest scientific hypothesis is that
which, as we say, 'works' best; and it can be no
otherwise with religious hypotheses. Religious history proves that one hypothesis after another has
worked ill, has crumbled at contact with a widening
knowledge of the world, and has lapsed from the
minds of men. Some articles of faith, however,
have maintained themselves through every vicissi-

tude, and possess even more vitality to-day than ever before: it is for the 'science of religions' to tell us just which hypotheses these are. Meanwhile the freeest competition of the various faiths with one another, and their openest application to life by their several champions, are the most favorable conditions under which the survival of the fittest can proceed. They ought therefore not to lie hid each under its bushel, indulged-in quietly with friends. They ought to live in publicity, vying with each other; and it seems to me that (the régime of tolerance once granted, and a fair field shown) the scientist has nothing to fear for his own interests from the liveliest possible state of fermentation in the religious world of his time. Those faiths will best stand the test which adopt also his hypotheses, and make them integral elements of their own. He should welcome therefore every species of religious agitation and discussion, so long as he is willing to allow that some religious hypothesis *may* be true. Of course there are plenty of scientists who would deny that dogmatically, maintaining that science has already ruled all possible religious hypotheses out of court. Such scientists ought, I agree, to aim at imposing privacy on religious faiths, the public manifestation of which could only be a nuisance in their eyes. With all such scientists, as well as with their allies outside of science, my quarrel openly lies; and I hope that my book may do something to persuade the reader of their crudity, and range him on my side. Religious fermentation is always a symptom of the intellectual vigor of a society; and it is only when they forget that they are hypotheses and put on rationalistic and authoritative pretensions, that our faiths do harm. The most interesting and valuable things about a man are his ideals and over-beliefs. The same is true of nations and historic epochs; and the excesses of which the particular individuals and epochs are guilty are compensated in the total, and become profitable to mankind in the long run.

The Crillon-quotation on page 31 is due to Mr. W. M. Salter (who employed it in a similar manner in the 'Index' for August 24, 1882), and the dream-metaphor on page 174 is a reminiscence from some novel of George Sand's — I forget which — read by me thirty years ago.

Finally, the revision of the essays has consisted almost entirely in excisions. Probably less than a page and a half in all of new matter has been added.

HARVARD UNIVERSITY
   CAMBRIDGE, MASSACHUSETTS
      December, 1896

INDEX

337

338 Index